Downstream

Downstream

A History and Celebration of
Swimming the River Thames

Caitlin Davies

Aurum
Press

First published in Great Britain
2015 by Aurum Press Ltd
74–77 White Lion Street
Islington
London N1 9PF
www.aurumpress.co.uk

© Anne Jessel: 64; Courtesy of Andy Nation: 370; Courtesy of Barbara Allen: 149, 153; Courtesy
of Brian Gautier: 237; Courtesy of Charlie Wittmack: 25; Courtesy of Ian Gordon: 3, 66, 113,
117, 121, 139, 141, 164-7, 194, 234, 246, 248, 250, 275, 277, 285, 306, 308, 355; Courtesy of Ian
McAllister: 180, 182; Courtesy of Jack Taylor: 144, 145; Courtesy of John Weedy: 359; Courtesy
of Keith Myerscough: 5; Courtesy of the Otter Swimming Club: 82; Courtesy of Peter Rae: 349;
Courtesy of Richard Walsh: 22; Courtesy of River & Rowing Museum: 92; Courtesy of Sue
Newell: 188; © Emma Craggs: 97; © Getty Images: 42, 163, 183, 204, 225, 252, 290, 323; © Gillian
Clark: 75; © Great Swim: 314; © Ross George Photography: 374; © www.jeffhopkins.net: 104; ©
Katia Vastiau: 58; © Mary Evans: 78; © Matt Alexander / Human Race Events: 101, 124; © Port
of London Authority: 211, 215; © RBKC Libraries: 222; © Southend Museum Service: 340, 346;
© Studio Octopi / Picture Plane: 266; © Thames Valley Police Museum: 72; © TopFoto: 328

A catalogue record for this book is available from the British Library.

ISBN 978 1 78131 119 6
ebook ISBN 978 1 7813 488 3

1 3 5 7 9 10 8 6 4 2
2015 2017 2019 2018 2016

Typeset in Minion Pro by SX Composing DTP, Rayleigh, Essex
Printed and bound by CPI Group (UK) Ltd, Croydon, CR0 4YY

To all Thames swimmers, past, present and future…

Contents

Introduction

'For they were young and the Thames was old,
And this is the tale that the River told'
Rudyard Kipling, 'The River's Tale', 1911

I'm standing at the edge of a marshy meadow in Gloucestershire, cold water seeping into my wellington boots. In front of me, under an ancient ash tree, is a squat monument that looks like a tombstone, inscribed with the words: THE CONSERVATORS OF THE RIVER THAMES 1857–1974. THIS STONE WAS PLACED HERE TO MARK THE SOURCE OF THE RIVER THAMES. A wooden sign shows the direction of the Thames Path, which follows the river for most of its length, while the sign below reads 'Thames Barrier London 184 miles'. It's early February and there have been flood warnings all along the path, following heavy snow, a thaw and general downpours. Normally this spot is bone dry, but today I could almost swim in it.

Beneath my boots is a clear pool of water, with blades of grass and smooth pale stones. A handful of bubbles rise to the surface and for a moment I wonder if there are fish in here, but this is water straight out of the Cotswolds earth, where a spring becomes a pool and then a stream. This is where, in theory, it all begins, this trickle of water that forms the longest river that is entirely in England, covering 215 miles from the heart of the countryside through its capital and out to the North Sea.

The River Thames has existed in one form or another for millions of years. It has been written and sung about, painted and mapped, portrayed as a place both majestic and dangerous, refreshing and polluted. It is father – or grandfather – Thames when noble or particularly chilly; it is mother Thames when tranquil and offering a watery embrace. People have drunk from it, washed and fished in it, and used it to dispose of every sort of waste. It has been a highway, a boundary and a food store, home to porpoises, whales, otters and sharks. An important trade and transport route since prehistoric times, it has carried passengers and goods from and to all over the world in boats of all shapes and sizes. We have rowed, sailed, canoed and punted along it; we've held regattas and aquatic carnivals, played water polo and skated over its frozen surface. But what of its swimmers? What of all those who have been drawn to its waters for enjoyment and to show off their skills, swims daring and reckless, theatrical and highly symbolic?

Before I started researching this book I'd only ever swum once in the River Thames, some forty years ago on a warm summer's evening near Taplow in Berkshire. I was ten years old and staying with a schoolfriend and I remember laughing as we tried to swim against the current. I'd never considered its history as a place to swim, or stopped to wonder if my childhood splash made me part of a tradition. But it did, because this has been our bathing spot for centuries.

This is the story of Thames swimming as I travel from source to sea, visiting places with long traditions of river swimming, delving into town and city archives, interviewing modern-day swimmers, and looking for evidence, whether written, photographic or oral, of how we used to swim. I want to explore the character of the Thames and discover what it has meant, and still means, to the people who live by it and swim in it, to celebrate all those who have meandered along it and raced down it, who have submerged themselves for pleasure or for charity, who have performed spectacular dives

Victorian 'swimming professors' taught people how to swim as well as giving public displays at indoor baths and in the Thames.

from boats and bridges. What remains of how we once swam, what happened to the individuals and the clubs? Who has been documented and who has been forgotten?

The Romans, who built the first bridge over the Thames, enjoyed military training swims, and for hundreds of years the river was the playground of royalty. Edward II swam as both Prince and King in the twelfth century; King Charles II was nearly assassinated while swimming near Battersea in the seventeenth century when the Thames was so 'clear and pure' that 'noblemen' swam in it all the time. Jonathan Swift took regular dips in the early 1700s; Lord Byron boasted of having swum three miles from Lambeth to London Bridge in 1807.

Soon the Thames was a major trading route for ships and, as a result, the river became the haunt of pirates and thieves. Yet even as London became industrialised, as docks were built and warehouses lined its banks, people still swam. While history tells us that princes, kings, earls and poets swam in the Thames, as did the privileged public school boys of Westminster and Eton, the students and dons of Oxford University, what of the average person? This has always been our summer bathing spot. Seventeenth-century poet Robert Herrick sent his 'supremest kiss/ To thee, my silver-footed Thamesis' where in the 'summer sweeter evenings' thousands 'bathe in thee'.

But it was the fact people bathed naked that led to the first regulation of Thames swimming. In the mid-1800s 'indecency' was seen as such a problem that male bathers were issued fines by local magistrates. 'What are the poor people to do?' asked one letter writer to *The Times*, but to use the 'great highway of the Thames', when there were no baths in which to swim. But then the 1846 Baths and Washhouses Act allowed the building of indoor pools, swimming became popularised and it wasn't long before societies and clubs were formed. Soon the pupils of the National Swimming Society were racing in the Thames, despite the fact that sewage pollution was so severe it would result in cholera outbreaks.

Originally races were held for a bet and a dare. In 1791 three men apparently swam from Westminster Bridge to London Bridge for an eight-guinea wager. The winner was carried to a pub to celebrate, where he drank so much gin he 'expired'. Then races for men became far more organised; in 1840 the 'aquatic jockeys' raced twice across the Thames near Battersea, naked. The one-mile amateur championships began in 1869, from Putney to Hammersmith, while in 1877 the Lords and Commons race, the long-distance amateur championships of Great Britain, went from Putney to Westminster. Endurance swimmers also used it as their training ground, including Captain Matthew Webb, the first man to swim across the Channel successfully and unaided in 1875 and whose feat would transform the world of swimming.

Girls and women often swam in the Thames in Victorian times, where they won numerous medals and trophies.

Yet, while some of these swimmers' exploits have gone down in history, for others their adventures have been wiped out, especially the women. It's a common belief that in Victorian times women rarely swam, at least competitively. But they did, and their venue of choice was often the Thames, where men proved their 'manliness' and women proved not only that they could swim but that they could successfully compete in a male arena.

Thousands gathered on banks and bridges to watch teenage champions such as Agnes Beckwith, 'the youthful water sprite', Emily Parker, the 'heroine of the Thames', and famed diver Marie Finney.

By the 1890s there were men-only swimming clubs all along the Thames – in Oxford, Reading, Henley, Windsor, Kingston and Southend – with seventeen swimming clubs holding their captaincy races in the Thames in London. Soon swimmers were flocking from all over the world to compete, although there remains confusion about some of the distances swum, their starting and ending points. It can be difficult tracing the history of the various swimming societies, groups and clubs, and establishing who won what at a time when swimmers frequently called themselves 'champion of London' or 'champion of the world'.

As swimming became a leisure activity for the masses, floating baths were opened near Hungerford Bridge in London with filtered water 'clear and green'. All along the Thames places were created for swimmers: at Tumbling Bay in Oxford, King's Meadow in Reading, Solomon's Hatch in Henley and Cuckoo Weir in Eton there were bathing islands, open-air baths, floating platforms and pontoons, and temporary lidos.

Londoners flocked to the upper Thames on houseboats and steam launches, attending regattas and Venetian-style fêtes, river picnics and carnivals. Jerome K. Jerome immortalised the boating trip in his 1889 book *Three Men in a Boat* in which his narrator sets off with two friends and a dog to journey upriver from Kingston. The river is an escape, a landscape and way of life 'free from that fretful haste, that vehement striving', and bathing would form a big part of the trip; 'we all talked as if we were going to have a long swim every morning'. But at once things begin to go wrong: the river is full of inept city boaters, parties of provincial 'Arrys and 'Arriets, just like themselves. While the plan is to get up early and 'fling off our rugs and shawls' and 'spring into the river with a joyous shout, and revel in a long delicious swim', once morning dawns the notion is less tempting. Still, their intention is to head upstream to Oxford 'on a fortnight's enjoyment on the river, if it killed us'.

By now the Thames was seen as 'quite respectable' compared with a hundred years earlier. It had 'come to be largely used as a place of public recreation and resort' according to the 1885 Thames Preservation Act, although men still swam naked. A Thames Conservancy by-law of 1887 warned that 'no person shall bathe without proper bathing dress or drawers, bathe or prepare to bathe between the hours of eight in the morning and nine in the evening during the months of June, July and August or during the remaining months between the hours of eight in the morning and eight in the evening, except in bathing places authorized by the Conservators'. In 1889 this was amended so that no one should bathe without proper dress or drawers 'unless properly screened from view', which would have a significant impact on many Thames bathing places.

But the river could also be dangerous, the scene of fatal collisions, drownings, murder and tragedy. 'Few things are pleasanter on a hot day than a plunge into one of the deep, quiet, shady pools in which the Thames abounds,' commented *Dickens's Dictionary of the Thames* in 1887. 'But it should always be remembered that any sudden flood . . . may transform the usually safe bathing place into what is practically nothing more nor less than a death trap.' The dangers of the Thames were ever-present, many died because they didn't know how to swim, while around 500 Londoners killed themselves each year by jumping into the river.

At the beginning of the twentieth century, with the success of the British team at the 1908 Olympic Games in London, swimming gained even more favour. Women began to form their own clubs, at Kingston, Reading and Windsor, holding regular races in the often icy Thames. Australian Annette Kellerman – the most famous woman swimmer of the last century – swam thirteen miles from Putney to Blackwell in her debut British swim in 1905. Others included Elsie Aykroyd, the American 'girl fish', Lily Smith, the only woman to compete in the first Richmond to Blackfriars race in 1907, and Eileen Lee, who beat the world record for women after swimming thirty-six miles from Teddington in 1916. Women didn't have the vote, they were still seen as the weaker sex – physically and mentally – and yet here they were swimming for hours over long distances in the Thames.

Annette Kellerman, the champion Australian swimmer, made her British debut in the River Thames in 1905. Here an illustration from her 1919 book *How to Swim* shows her demonstrating a dive.

River racing was put on hold during the First World War, and then the growth of municipal baths drew people away from rivers and into purpose-built pools. Yet still in the 1920s championships and endurance swims continued, and river swimming was a popular family activity until at least the 1940s. The Thames became a seaside resort for Londoners, with beaches at Putney, Tower Bridge, Greenwich and Grays. When the children's beach at the Tower of London opened in 1934 King George V declared that children would 'have this tidal playground as their own for ever'.

In 1957 the river was declared biologically dead, bombing during the Second World War had damaged infrastructure, sewage was heading straight into the Thames again and in some stretches there was no oxygen and no life form at all. Organised racing was now largely over, and by the 1970s swimming in the Thames was considered dangerous. Local boroughs began to ban swimming, citing pollution, warning signs were erected, access became harder. Traditional swimming spots were closed down, and although by now Thames water quality was improving, this was a trend that continued into the 1990s.

Yet in the past decade or so we have returned to the Thames, with thousands of swimmers, many of them triathletes in wetsuits, taking part in mass events at Windsor, Eton, Hampton Court and the London Docks. River swimming may be nowhere near the scale it used to be, but it is back: from the Bridge to Bridge swim between Henley and Marlow, to the Great River Swim from Chiswick Pier, and the Crowstone Crawl in the Thames Estuary. Wild swimming is more popular than it has been for decades, and the River Thames is what Kate Rew, founder of the Outdoor Swimming Society, calls 'a swimming super highway'.

Despite the modern cult of Health & Safety, and signs specifically banning swimming, people continue to enjoy the Thames. For many it's the memory of a childhood pleasure that takes them back, as if returning to the world of *The Wind in the Willows* in which the river – a 'sleek, sinuous, full-bodied animal, chasing and chuckling, gripping things with a gurgle and leaving them with a laugh' – is as much a character as Mole, Ratty, Badger and Mr Toad. It is Ratty's world and he wouldn't want any other, from the 'shock of the early plunge' in the morning to the bathing of an afternoon, radiant by day yet full of mystery and even terror at night. It is the place of his 'song-dream', striking awe into everyone who beholds it.

Today the Thames is, after the sea, our second favourite open-water place to swim in, according to the charity Swimathon, and the most common things we do while we swim are: relax, think about the day and sing. The river has a magnetic draw over anyone who likes to bathe, although there has always been conflict between its various users, and now, at least officially, we can't swim downstream from Putney any more. In 2012 a by-law was introduced preventing people from swimming between Putney Bridge and Crossness, just below the Thames Barrier, without prior permission from the Port of London Authority (PLA). It argues that 'this is a dangerous stretch of the river, with strong tides and eddies that can drag a person underwater without warning. It is also the busiest inland waterway in the UK.' There are passenger vessels 'which carry over six million people a year and 1,000-tonne barges carrying freight. In this environment, swimming in the Thames is akin to rambling on the M25. A hazardous undertaking.' But others question if swimming in the Thames should be a criminal offence when it has always been a natural pastime. And why, when the river is now generally seen as one of the world's cleanest metropolitan waterways, are we so worried about pollution?

In recent years Thames swims are more likely to be for stunts and protests, from John Prescott's 1983 swim against dumping nuclear waste in the sea, to Trenton Oldfield's disruption of the Oxford vs Cambridge boat race in 2012. When, in 2006, Lewis Pugh became the first person to swim the entire length of the Thames it was to bring attention to the issue of climate change.

Raising money for charity is another major motivation. It is one of the reasons Alison Streeter swam upstream from Gravesend to Richmond in 1986 and why Andy Nation became the first person to swim the length of the non-tidal Thames in 2005. It is why brothers Richard and Mark Walsh swam from Lechlade to Teddington in 2009, American Charlie Wittmack swam along the Thames and across the English Channel in 2010, and why David Walliams completed a 140-mile swim in 2011. While David wasn't the first modern swimmer to undertake a long-distance swim in the

Thames, the fact that he is a celebrity and the enormous publicity that surrounded his swim for Sport Relief raised its profile. And because he fell sick, it also put a lot of people off, convinced they too would get ill.

The biggest fear among non-river swimmers is contracting Weil's disease, a severe form of leptospirosis, a bacterial infection spread by animals. Swimmers can potentially catch the disease from water contaminated with the urine of infected rats, but leptospirosis is rare in the UK; forty-four cases were reported in England and Wales in 2011, of which fifteen originated overseas, and none was fatal.

Others swim for different reasons. Matthew Parris made a midnight excursion across the Thames in 2010, just to see if it could be done, while artist Amy Sharrocks is planning a mass swim across the Thames from Tower Bridge. 'It's our river,' she says. 'It is the whole reason we are here in London, it's the reason for the metropolis.' Others still swim the Thames to win a bet or for a dare, just as in Victorian times, individuals such as Peter Rae who in 2003 swam across the estuary from Southend to Kent – and back.

This book is a trip downstream, from a marshy meadow in Gloucestershire all the way to Southend Pier, an exploration of how we once used the river, why we stopped, and the reasons behind the current revival. This is a history of our relationship with the Thames from a swimmer's perspective.

1

Trewsbury Mead–Lechlade–Grafton Lock

'There's a little cup in the Cotswold hills
Which a spring in a meadow bubbles and fills'
Bret Harte, 'The Birds of Cirencester', 1898

My journey begins at Thames Head, at Trewsbury Mead, near the village of Kemble. This has been known since Victorian times as the 'lovely birth-place' of the River Thames, but it can be a difficult place to find. 'The exact spot is quested for with difficulty,' noted Charles G. Harper in his 1910 book *Thames Valley Villages*, 'and when the traveler has found it, he is, after all, not sure of his find . . . and even the road-men and the infrequent wayfarers . . . appear uncertain. That it is "over there, somewhere" is the most exact information the enquirer is likely, at a venture, to obtain.' While picturesque old histories of the Thames had painted 'dainty vignettes' of Thames Head 'with a little country-girl in homely pinafore dipping a foot in the water as it gushes forth', Harper found a buried well under 'fallen masses of the dull, ochre-coloured earth'. Nearby pumping stations had 'greedily sucked up all the water in summer' when the place was parched, although in winter the spring could still burst out three feet high and the meadow was a water-logged morass and often a lake.

Today Thames Head remains the river's official source, according to the Environment Agency and Ordnance Survey, and it's still not easy to find. After a three-hour drive from London I park at the Thames Head Inn, around half a mile away, where the barman responds to my request for directions by telling me I can't miss it. So I rush recklessly down a busy section of the A433, with no footpath for pedestrians, and turn on to a path, then it's over a stile and across the railway line, looking nervously right and left for trains.

I stand on a small hill looking down at a patchwork of fields, green and burnished brown, the undulating line of a drystone wall, two cows in the far distance. I can't see any signposts; which way is the source? I head down the hill and wade in shin-high water through a gate, the beige clay giving way beneath me like quicksand. By the time I see the Thames Head stone in the distance my legs are sodden from the knees down and my partner is muttering 'this is the most stupid thing you've ever asked me to do'.

In front of me the grass is a luminous green, the landscape laid with stretches of water like stepping stones; a clump of shiny white snowdrops are tucked away behind a fence. The mud around the stone is pitted with boot marks; I'm not the first person here this morning.

Until a few years ago this was also home to a statue of Father Thames, but it was removed downstream to St John's Lock after visitors started chipping pieces off as mementos. Retracing my steps I meet a woman and a man walking a dog. They live seven miles away but it's their first time here. 'It's just one of those things I've always wanted to see,' says the woman. The man is clutching a map and asks, 'Where is it then?' I tell him they are just opposite the stone that marks the source; it's a few hundred metres away. 'What?' he asks, 'that lake? That's it?' he laughs. 'No gift shop?'

Back at the Thames Head Inn the source of the Thames is said to be the most common topic of conversation around the bar. While the pub is around 250 years old, it only adopted its new name a couple of decades ago. 'People come in and ask where the source is on a daily basis,' says Nichola King, who has run the pub for the past eight years. 'And they come from all over the world. Last year we had two Japanese TV crews filming here. This is the source, I'm not going to argue with that, it brings me trade! And you can see how it becomes a river, it looks like a river. But for years there can be no water and, yes, people can be disappointed; they say, "is that it?"'

Thames Head also featured in the opening ceremony of the 2012 Olympics, filmed by Danny Boyle. 'It was supposed to be Thames Head, but it was too dry so they built a "replica" and then used some real footage,' explains Nichola. 'Four days after the crew left, there was water! But the place hasn't really been wet for years. People don't swim here, they cheat a bit and start at other places.' However, during a freezing cold winter a few years ago the pub's chefs decided to go for a splash: 'there was some significant water so they went in in their clothes, they're a hardy bunch, then they walked back. They haven't had the opportunity since then.'

The pub boldly declares its link with the Thames, with a frieze of Father Thames on the outside wall, photos and maps in the entranceway, a 50p postcard of the source on 1 January 2000, and inside a stone bust of Father Thames on top of an old sewing machine. But Thames Head's claim to fame as the source has been under dispute for at least 200 years. 'Like the source of the Nile, the position of the original fountain of the Thames has been variously assigned, and its birth place has been almost as much contested as that of Homer,' wrote the Scottish poet and author Tobias Smollett in 1801. In Victorian times some attributed the head of the Thames to a 'clear fountain' in the vicinity of Cricklade; others preferred the 'rivulets which advance from Swindon and Highworth in Wiltshire', or Seven Springs, a hamlet near Cheltenham and the source of the River Churn. 'What is the source of a river?' asked Smollett. 'There is no obvious one, right answer. In the end we are not dealing with a scientific issue but in the broadest sense a spiritual issue.' In 1937 there was a lively discussion in the House of Commons when Mr Perkins, MP for Stroud, which included Seven Springs, objected to the Ordnance Survey Map showing the source of the Thames as Thames Head. The Minister for Agriculture, Mr W.S. Morrison, who also happened to be MP for Cirencester and thus Thames Head, insisted this was correct. When a peeved Mr Perkins asked if the Minister was 'aware that the source known as "Thames Head" periodically dries up', an Honourable Member interjected to ask, 'Why don't you?' Today, however, there are plaques on the walls above the springs at Seven Springs with the inscription: 'HIC TUUS O TAMESINE PATER SEPTEMGEMINUS FONS' – 'Here, O Father Thames, is your sevenfold source'.

Whether or not Thames Head is the source, it's near impossible to swim from here. Instead it is downstream near the town of Lechlade where the Thames meets the Severn Canal and the River Coln that it becomes a navigable river. 'Where Lechlade sees thy current strong,/ First waft the unlaboring bark along,' wrote Thomas Love Peacock in 1810. Five years later he accompanied Percy Bysshe Shelley on a journey to Lechlade by boat, having set out from Old Windsor with Mary Wollstonecraft Godwin and her stepbrother Charles Clairmont. The plan was to travel to the river's source, but they failed to 'draw our boat up to the very spring of the Thames,' wrote Clairmont, and by the time they got three miles above Lechlade 'the weeds became so enormously thick & high, that all three of us tugging could not stir the empty boat an inch'.

The shallow water didn't even cover the hoofs of cows standing in the middle to drink, while at Inglesham Weir, remembered Peacock, 'a solitary sluice was hanging by a chain, swinging in the wind and creaking dismally'. So the boating party turned around and spent two nights at Lechlade, where Shelley wrote the poem 'A Summer Evening Churchyard' in St Lawrence's churchyard, where 'Silence and Twilight, unbeloved of men,/ Creep hand in hand from yon obscurest glen'. The path through the graveyard today bears his name – Shelley's Walk. Perhaps it was this Thames trip that inspired him to write, 'rivers are not like roads, the work of the hands of man; they imitate mind, which wanders at will over pathless deserts, and flows through nature's loveliest recesses'.

In the sixteenth century Lechlade had been a flourishing port, shipping goods to London, and it continued as an important inland trade route with the introduction of the Thames and Severn Canal in 1789. Docks were built and Lechlade became a loading place for cargo. But by the mid-1860s barges were now 'almost unknown' noted the press, part of a general 'decay and desuetude of the river'. In London the Thames was filthy; at Lechlade there were navigation problems.

In the coming decade leisure traffic replaced the barges, and rowing and punting became popular. Victorian Lechlade was a pretty little town, where boats could be hired and the river ran in 'a goodly stream' under the bridge. Yet I can find very few reports of any swimming in the period. In 1855 a man named Samuel Hope, who was 'in the service of the Vicar of Lechlade', drowned while bathing with some friends. He got 'put out of his depth into a large hole in the river, although cautioned by his companions not to do so'. Like most people, neither Hope nor his friends could swim.

Then, in 1905, the town launched an annual water carnival on the Thames on August bank holiday, and the following year the Lechlade Swimming Club took control of events. It's not clear when the club was formed, but like other Thames clubs they organised river races and fêtes. In 1909 the press reported fine weather, good attendance and a programme which started at two o'clock and 'kept the majority interested until well after dark'. There were boat races, including a 'mirth-provoking' tub race, and a 300 yards team swimming handicap in which five teams competed, four from Swindon and one from Bristol.

The Lechlade Swimming Club was still running the carnival in 1920, with gold medals now on offer, and it had a bathing hut near the Round House, a late eighteenth-century building that had probably once been a canal and lock keeper's house. In 1907 a Diving Championship was also launched at Lechlade, and although this created 'very little interest' the press accurately predicted the sport would become popular, for 'as a spectacular display there is nothing to equal diving'. In 1913 the Western Counties Diving Championships were held at Lechlade where now 'a large crowd' witnessed the Thames swimming and diving events, including a '50 Yards Ladies' race. The town continued to host diving galas until at least 1935. That year Cecily Cousens, a seventeen-year-old from Swindon who had recently won the women's high diving championship of England and a bronze medal at the Commonwealth Games, 'received injuries at Lechlade while practising from a temporary platform erected for a gala at which she was to give an exhibition. During her dive she struck a boulder and she was in a dazed condition when assisted out.' However, she recovered sufficiently to resume swimming.

Others weren't so lucky. In 1929 a student in Cirencester and a 'lady friend' had hired a rowing boat and when they reached the Round House they changed into bathing clothes. They then walked along the bank in the direction of Inglesham where the man dived in, immediately got into difficulties and drowned. The inquest found that although it looked like the bank shelved gradually, in fact there was a sudden drop. The student couldn't swim, and when his friend tried to help him, believing the water was shallow enough to stand up in, she ran down the bank, got stuck in the mud and couldn't move.

In the early twentieth century, with the closure of the canal, trade through the town dried up and Lechlade soon became a popular place for retirement. The broadcaster Piers Plowright used to come here in the 1940s, after the war, for family holidays: 'It was where I played and imagined and began to write.' In a recent radio programme Piers retraced the course of his beloved river along with the different stages of his life. In the process he wrote his own Thames-side stomp:

> From the Head of the River
> To Lechlade Town
> Nothing goes up and nothing goes down
> Till the water gathers from out of the hills
> Where childhood ends and history spills.

London children were also taken here for countryside holidays in the 1960s. One remembers, 'we were sent on holiday by the Country Holiday Fund. We were inner-city kids. The place was so beautiful and everyone so kind. I remember swimming in the Thames and there being a bridge. It was a world apart from our life in London. I have never forgotten it.'

While early records of swimming at Lechlade may be scarce, it's clear that people have bathed here since at least Victorian times, and while it could be a dangerous pastime by the early 1900s it had evolved into more organised displays of entertainment and sporting prowess, particularly diving. This then gave way to a more leisurely use of the Thames as an escape into the country for city dwellers who were free to enjoy the river.

Today Lechlade's website describes the place as 'a small attractive riverside town', with 'a healthy tourist trade, particularly in the summer when the Thames is busy with cruisers, narrowboats and small boats'. However, it warns: 'Swimmers beware; the depth of water is variable with many undertows along the reach above Halfpenny Bridge.' But this is a favourite place for modern river swimmers. 'Swims of up to two miles are possible if you plan your entry and exit points,' advises Wildswim.com, while Michael Worthington in his swimming logbook *I Love the Thames* promises 'proper swimming, a current that whisks you along and amazingly little human presence to spoil things'.

So loved is this stretch of the river that in 2003 the newly formed adventure company SwimTrek started a four-day swimming holiday from Lechlade. The following year veteran river swimmer Frank Chalmers signed up, swimming during the day and sleeping on the accompanying barge at night. 'Rivers define their people,' he says, 'every river has a character, with different industries and cultures, and I thought the River Thames was great. It's quite narrow going down from Lechlade and there are lots of swans. The adult swans are really protective of their cygnets, and when you see their wings raised in anger six feet above you, you think: "Oh my God, this is dangerous." But the support canoe would block you in so the swans didn't feel threatened. A swimmer's view is completely different from a walker's view. Early on in the Thames, the river is cocooned and you don't see the horizon – it's like a flume that you swim down. When you're walking, the river seems to punctuate the countryside. When you are *in* the river you might see nothing except the water and the bank, and then suddenly you are jolted upright by the blue of a kingfisher flashing across your vision.'

In 2005 property developer Andy Nation, the first person to swim the length of the non-tidal Thames, started his journey about a mile upstream from Lechlade at the Round House, 'because that's the first place you don't scrape your knuckles on the ground when you try to swim'. Born in Ilford, Essex, in 1949, his first charity swim was in 1970 when he completed 240 lengths of Barkingside swimming pool to raise £400 for a cancer charity, with his sponsors offering 1d per length. He went on to raise money in a variety of ways, such as flying on the wings of a Tiger Moth biplane, and when it came to the Thames, he says, 'I did it because no one had done it before. People's reactions were, "you're mad, it's never been done and it's too long".' But Andy covered over seventeen miles on his first day, and in the end swam 147 miles in twelve days to Teddington, where the Port of London Authority told him to stop, despite his initial aim of going all the way to Southend. In the process he raised £20,000 for the Anthony Nolan Trust.

Andy says the non-tidal Thames is very clean; the only problem was boat discharge and at one point 'there was a boat coming towards me and I got a slap in the face, I went high but not high enough and got two mouthfuls, luckily it went to my stomach not my lungs. It didn't taste very nice. I burped and spluttered and carried on. Then I went to that night's accommodation, ran a hot bath, and threw up in it. I was ill the rest of that day, it was suggested I take a day's rest.'

And what did he think about while swimming?

'Absolutely everything, the mind wanders. When I trained I counted the lengths but when doing a continuous swim I thought about my overnight accommodation, whether I'm pacing myself too fast or too slow, whether the escort boat is doing what it should be doing. You think and you swim, that's all you're doing, though you can come under a bridge and think, I wonder which bridge this is?

'You don't hear much in the water except for propellers and you don't know if it's a boat coming towards you or if it's behind you. There are signs. As a boat gets close you wait for a bow wave. The first little wave will tell you where the boat is coming from; if it rolls over your shoulder you don't worry because although the next one will be bigger, if it's from behind you, you will float, so you can maintain your normal breathing pattern. If the boat is coming from in front of you then you will get a slap on the forehead with the first little bow wave and then you have to raise yourself up or you will breathe in a mouthful of Thames from the next wave!' For sustenance on his trip, Andy ate Mars Bars, sandwiches, and 'a supplement in a squeezy sachet, it was like strawberry jam, it was so thick that I had to rinse my mouth out in the Thames it was so horrible. I was eating about 10,000 calories a day and still losing weight.'

The year after Andy's swim Lewis Pugh also started near Lechlade, in order to swim the length of the river, without a wetsuit. Then thirty-six, Lewis was already a noted endurance and cold-water swimmer. Born in Plymouth, his family emigrated to South Africa when he was ten. He returned to England in his mid-twenties, and after reading International Law at Cambridge worked as a maritime lawyer in the City of London, at the same time serving as a Reservist in the British Special Air Service. He then gave up his job to campaign for the protection of the environment. The year of his Thames swim Lewis had already completed an expedition to Antarctica, and the year before he'd been to Spitsbergen in the Arctic. Returning to England he was shocked that the threat to the wildlife environment he'd seen on his travels wasn't being taken more seriously, so in conjunction with the World Wide Fund for Nature he came up with the idea of swimming the Thames.

England was then in the middle of a major drought, water rationing had started in London, and Lewis hoped his swim would draw attention to climate change and show that people didn't have to travel far to see what was happening in their own environment. 'It was the toughest swim I'd ever done,' he says today. 'I was hugely unprepared. A couple of months before I did a recce looking at the flow with Nic Marshall [a friend from South Africa who was to accompany him on his swim]. We threw sticks into the water near Lechlade, Nic ran a hundred metres and we timed how long it took for the sticks to get to him.'

They calculated the river flow was three kilometres an hour and 'estimated it would take around a week for me to swim the Thames, possibly ten days. So my entire team took fourteen days' leave and we hired a barge. I was working in London at the time, I could only train for forty-five minutes three times a week, but because it was flowing nicely I thought, go for it! Then, on 7 July, I got to the source and saw it was dry and thought, this will be a slog.'

The Thames Head stone was surrounded with parched grass, so along with another friend, Alex Wales, he ran for twenty-five miles until they found the river deep enough to swim. Finally, Lewis entered the water near Buscot Lock, a couple of miles downstream from the Round House, and what struck him was the stillness of the river: after weeks without rain it was 'like a millpond'. There was no chance of being carried along; instead, a week's swim turned into a twenty-one-day odyssey.

Andy and Lewis are not the only long-distance swimmers to set their sights on the Thames, for a waterway that stretches over 200 miles is ideal for anyone who either wants a challenge or simply to experience what it's like to swim in the same river day after day.

In 2009 brothers Richard and Mark Walsh similarly started near Lechlade when they decided to swim the non-tidal Thames to

The Walsh brothers (Mark on the left and Richard on the right) share a laugh at Boveney Lock in the summer of 2009, after four days swimming along the Thames.

raise money for leukaemia research, following the death of one of Mark's teaching colleagues. Two years earlier the pair had swum the length of all the lakes in the Lake District – fifty miles in forty-eight hours to raise money for Guide Dogs for the Blind. 'We were looking for something bigger and better,' says Richard, 'we both grew up in and around Windsor so we had swum in the Thames, it had always been there as a backdrop and I knew of Lewis Pugh's swim and thought we could give it a go. It was just me and my brother swimming next to each other in the Thames, and Dad in a canoe.'

The idea was to begin at Cricklade Bridge, upstream from Lechlade, but 'there was just enough water to cover the top of our feet, I could see the river meandering off, but we didn't want to walk the whole of the first day dragging a canoe'. Even when they started swimming from St John's Lock on 24 August 'there was no flow at all. But we knew it was relatively clean, in some parts it was crystal clear, in others there was dead tree matter but it's all organic. I didn't get sick, my brother did afterwards but I kept my mouth shut. The Thames is a safe environment to do long distance, rather than swimming forty miles out to sea; if you get into trouble you can put your feet down and find a place to get out. It's a unique environment.'

The brothers' equipment was minimal. 'I later saw David Walliams on the TV, he had four people drying his wetsuit with hairdryers while he ate his lunch, whereas we camped by the river and put on the same cold wetsuit that we'd taken off six hours before. Every morning at four o'clock was difficult, especially the second day, but by the third day your body gets conditioned to it.' Richard found himself mentally drifting off while swimming and humming songs to himself: 'an hour would pass and I couldn't remember what I'd been thinking about.' While they succeeded in their challenge and finished the swim after five days, they only raised around half of their intended £2,500, but he would like to try it again: 'swimming is such a tonic, isn't it? It makes you full of life, especially in open water.'

The following year it was the turn of American Charlie Wittmack. His plan was to undertake an eleven-month 10,000-mile world triathlon, swimming the Thames and the Channel, cycling from France to Nepal and then climbing Mount Everest. 'Originally my idea was to connect Captain Webb's Channel swim and Edmund Hillary's ascent of Everest,' he explains, 'then I decided to make it a world triathlon.' Charlie tested things out by climbing Everest in 2003, where he learned about mother and child mortality in Nepal, and decided to raise money to improve basic health care by supporting community health workers. Charlie and his wife Cate withdrew their life savings, sold their house and car and took out a hefty loan, and Charlie also insured himself for $2.5 million – in case the journey killed him. 'I had read a lot about Pugh's swim, and as I researched further I got even more excited when I realised the environmental success story that the Thames presented. It was a dead river, now there were 320 types of aquatic life. I even heard on the BBC there were little seahorses swimming around London.'

Charlie was then thirty-three and working as an attorney and college professor, and, while he'd been to London a few times, he'd never swum in the Thames. He was aware of the Channel Association people who trained in the river, as well as SwimTrek, and he'd followed the progress of the Walsh brothers, 'but most people in the US don't know much about the Thames, people are not that intelligent about geography around the world and certainly not Britain or the Thames, so I would tell them its history, where it starts and goes'.

The reaction to his intended swim 'wasn't that great, it was more than people could imagine. A 250-mile swim is not something most Americans would ever think about, marathon swimming is not a very popular sport in the US, we don't have that rich history that you all have with the Channel Swimming Association. In the

A triumphant Charlie Wittmack on the escort boat just off the coast of Cap Griz Nez, having swum the Thames and then the Channel as part of his 2010 world triathlon.

US people don't really understand exploration and adventurers, the public are more interested in traditional sports, like American football and basketball. If you want to go climb a mountain that's even offensive to a lot of people, they see it as sort of selfish and egomaniacal and grandiose. So as an adventurer it's always fun being in the UK because you really understand why it is that people want to go out and push the limits of human endurance.' And that's why he chose the Thames, a testing ground for human endeavour for hundreds of years and where his hero Captain Webb once trained.

Like others before him, Charlie initially wanted to swim through London, but he couldn't get permission from the PLA. American press reports say he 'started at the source'; swimming 275 miles 'up' river, but in fact, like Lewis Pugh, he too began around Buscot

Lock. 'The first day was really tough, it was eight to ten miles and every few strokes I would get stuck on something and have to stand up and walk again, about twenty per cent of the first day was spent walking and a lot of it was just spent floating and doing breaststroke and trying to get through shallow water.'

Charlie was pleasantly surprised by the quality of the water: 'in the upper Thames it tasted great, it was very clear, and most of the time I could see the bottom.' However, like other long-distance Thames swimmers, he did get sick. 'I went to hospital twice, the doctors weren't really willing to say what exactly was wrong, some people thought it was some sort of amoebic dysentery, but your medical system is different from the US and folks in the UK don't worry about that sort of thing too much. In the US I would have gone through days and days of medical tests and evaluations at great expense. In the UK I was just told I was foolish for swimming in the Thames and I should go home and not do that any more.' Charlie also lost 'about four toenails' during his swim, cut his feet on wire and glass and one day, because he was so tired, accidentally dropped the kayak he was carrying on his foot.

'There was no real euphoric time, it's just hard, you're in water up to sixteen hours a day, you just take half an hour at a time. I knew I had ten months left of the rest of the expedition, swimming the Thames was only a small part. I tried to enter a meditative state because if you allow yourself the indulgence of thinking about things aside from the swim it really becomes such a distraction that it makes it hard to complete the challenge you have in front of you.'

Getting started each day was the most difficult thing and he 'ate everything I could find, sandwiches, bread, fruit', as well as consuming a litre of high-carbohydrate drink every half-hour. He had one person paddling in a canoe next to him, whereas for the Channel part of his swim he had a support crew of twelve.

Charlie says it's hard to say how much money he raised, but

'at the end of the day the programme in Nepal was fully funded through Save the Children. You need to be careful that the money goes to the charity and not to fund the expedition.' As for the future, 'I would absolutely love to swim the Thames again, without all the pressure of a world triathlon on the other end and the financial pressure of funding it. The Thames is such an extraordinary place, it's absolutely beautiful and the swim was so serene, but oftentimes I didn't have the opportunity to really appreciate it. I really regret that. It's difficult on a year-long expedition to stay in the moment and I struggled with that. My advice to others is absolutely do it, particularly the upper portion, wherever you can get in.'

In 2011, when David Walliams started his Thames swim he began upstream from Buscot Lock at Riverside Park near Halfpenny Bridge, striding into the water at 8.22 a.m. and 'walking into a bath of ice'. He'd assumed the river might be warm in September, but it was 15 degrees, colder than when he'd swum the Channel five years before. It was when 'a blue tinge' began creeping up his back, one of the first signs of hypothermia, that he was advised to put on a wetsuit.

David, already well known as a TV comedian and for his Channel swim that had raised a million pounds for Sport Relief, has a family tradition of Thames swimming. 'My mum swam in the Thames, she was a keen swimmer and in a swimming club and she did races in south London,' he explains. 'She always liked open water and lidos. Most people don't like swimming outdoors, they like swimming pools, they're clean and they like the temperature.' But his only experience in the Thames had been a dip on a summer's day in his twenties near Henley. 'When I told people that I was going to do it their eyes lit up because it was for Sport Relief and they were pleased and excited because it was something dramatic. For us, the thing was working out how to do it and make it interesting and make it work as entertainment on TV. That was the challenge, otherwise it might be boring.

'When I began my swim it was unseasonably cold after a bad summer, and it's tough. The cold really tires you out, you expend so much energy fighting the cold, just being in it is tough, you need to keep moving. My mind was focused but in the Thames there is so much to look at, the banks were lined with hundreds of people, you go through villages and towns, people come out to have a look. There's a lot to see and react to. But you don't hear so well in the water and it all gets a bit dreamy. You get glimpses, as you lift your head out to breathe, you get snaps and snatches, it doesn't feel like reality. Swimming the Thames is just very iconic, there are so many landmarks on the banks and it gives you a new perspective doing it at water level, it feels very special.'

While the Lechlade area is today known as a starting point for long-distance swims, and in David's case marked the point when watching someone swim the Thames became mass entertainment, others like to bathe here, too. Roger Deakin of *Waterlog* fame swam at Buscot Pool, where he found the river a 'modest affair', the water clear enough to see tench weaving among the lily stalks, but he decried the 'big, ugly notices proclaiming the danger of deep water'.

Grafton Lock, a couple of miles downstream, is another favourite spot for modern swimmers, such as Phil Tibenham. He first came to swimming after a back injury. 'I always wanted to try outdoor swimming and I had always swum in the sea, but I started swimming in the Thames around six years ago whenever I could.' He has taken part in a number of organised events, but also swims on his own. 'It feels like I've done it for ever, swimming in the Thames. First I tried a little paddle and it escalated from there. It's the most interesting way to swim. A couple of times I've swum at Grafton Lock alone, people are not happy about that, particularly Mum. Once I swam just before Christmas, it was chilly and I wore a wetsuit. Dusk was falling and the moon was just coming up, and I swam about half a kilometre. To be in water under a moon alone . . .!' When his daughter was seven he took her for a dip at

Grafton: 'it was cold and there were a couple of grumpy swans nearby, but swimming in the Thames is definitely something that one can pass on to one's children. It's a gift for life. I've never got ill. Higher up in the Cotswolds it's really clean. You get out and your hair feels like it's got conditioner in it and your skin feels like silk, it's like a mud treatment. I've swum other rivers and the Thames is cleaner. It's a sanctuary for me. I did a two-day swim near Grafton Lock, we got out there at night and the lock keeper made us tea and we became friends.' Phil usually straps a knife to his calf if he's swimming alone, not to fend off anything but in case he gets caught in something. But the worst thing that's ever happened is losing an earplug. He is a Shaw Method swimming instructor, a method that focuses on body awareness and a swimmer's relationship with water. To him, swimming is 'science crossed over with art and, for want of a better word, the spiritual side'.

It's because of this rich recent heritage of Thames swimming around Lechlade that I've signed up for a one-day swim with SwimTrek, covering five miles from Buscot Lock to Radcot Bridge in Oxfordshire. SwimTrek has been running Thames swims since its inception in 2003 and founder Simon Murie says he enjoys 'things that are iconic. I need something classical like the Greek islands, the Hellespont in Turkey, and the Thames; it's a famous river.' He has vivid memories of spending childhood summer holidays in Ham in south-west London in the late seventies. 'My mother was a keen river swimmer and I remember sitting on the side of the Thames with my thermos flask, her listening to the radio and me with my comics. I was a young boy and conscious of what others would think and I sort of dreaded it. But my mum liked getting away from things, the stresses of everyday life, and we spent a lot of summer days swimming against the current and crossing over to the canoe club. In the evenings there were pleasure boats with disco lights flashing and there was me, a thirteen-year-old, and people looking out of the windows thinking, "what the hell is he doing?" As I grew older, I got more into it. When I was young I would think, "who's looking at me?" By the time I was fifteen or sixteen it didn't worry me. It was very important for my mum to be able to get away from it all, and when she died we scattered her ashes on the place she liked most.'

So perhaps it's not surprising that he chose the Thames for SwimTrek's first swimming holiday. 'The reaction from people is different now, we used to be asked, "are you allowed to do it?" and "are you doing this for charity?" They couldn't think why else we'd be doing it; we had to explain we were doing it for pleasure.' With the first group of Thames swimmers many lived in London and wanted to immerse themselves in a river that flowed past their backyard. The company has continued to run Thames swims every year: 'we get a lot of Germans. After the British, they're into open-water swimming; it's the Saxon heritage. But ten years ago open-water swimming was not nearly as popular or fashionable as it is now.'

As I set off for Lechlade I'm wondering what my experience will be like swimming in the upper Thames. Will it be as clean as people say, or will I get ill? Can I enjoy a proper swim, whisked along by the current, or will I only be wading in freezing cold water?

2

Cotswolds Swim

'Of exercises, swimming's best,
Strengthens the muscles and the chest'
Dr E. Baynard, *Health*, 1764

It's a Monday lunchtime in early August and when I look out of the window of the train from London there are low black clouds most of the way to Swindon. I'm anxious about a few things: mainly if I will be able to cover the whole five miles. I'm a fair-weather swimmer; for me it's a solitary activity done for pleasure. I've always swum outdoors, starting as a toddler at the unheated lido on Hampstead Heath in north London and then as a teenager in the Heath's bathing ponds. But cold water has become more of a challenge as I've grown older and I only venture to the lido or ponds on warm days. While I don't mind swimming with weeds and fish, I've never been competitive and I've never swum any set distance.

In February, shortly after I visited Thames Head and the source, I started my 'training', aiming first to swim twice a week at an indoor pool. I knew I'd have to be able to swim for at least an hour at a time for this trip, and it was a couple of weeks before I managed a mile, with quite a bit of stopping and starting and a growing sense of lane rage. Then I decided, for the first time in my life, to wear a wetsuit, optional for SwimTrek but providing protection against the cold. The label on mine said it was inspired by the killer whale and when I tried it on I immediately felt encased; it was like wearing a thick rubbery inner tube. I tried it out at the Gospel Oak lido; the water was just 15 degrees, which would normally be too chilly for me, but with the wetsuit on I was able to swim straight away. I was oddly bouncy as I started doing front crawl, travelling on the surface of the water as if held up by some invisible force. Then I tried breaststroke. My feet popped up out of the water as if they were made of cork; I couldn't kick; I had no power in my legs at all. I did two lengths and gave up. As the weeks went by I managed to swim further, then I moved to the Heath's mixed bathing pond, deciding this would more resemble the experience I would have in the River Thames, but I still didn't know if I could do five miles.

As the train reaches Reading I see the river from the window again: it looks very wide, empty and cold. I have other worries apart from the distance, especially swans. I've heard many tales of having to escape hissing swans, or what it feels like to be at water level faced with a 6-foot wingspan. I was scared enough of swans to begin with; now I'm just praying I won't see any.

For weeks I've been telling everyone I meet that I'm going to swim in the Thames, partly because I can't believe I'm going to but also because I enjoy their reaction, which seems to be a mixture of admiration and disgust. But I soon find that swimming in the Thames seems perfectly normal in the Cotswolds. At the bus stop in Swindon a woman says 'fair play' when I tell her about my upcoming swimming holiday.

I get off the bus at Lechlade and walk down Thames Street to Halfpenny Bridge where David Walliams began his swim from Riverside Park. I pass low stone cottages and the Cotswold Canal Trust, then the road leads up to the small hump of a bridge – Halfpenny Bridge – named after the toll pedestrians were required to pay until 1839 and where there is still a small, square toll house. To the right the view is all but obscured by a huge weeping willow, beyond which I can see swans and moored canal boats. To my left the land looks as if it's been cut with dressmaker's scissors, leaving the banks a little frayed around the edges. Andy Nation began his 2005 swim around a mile upstream from here, while the Walsh brothers started just downstream at St John's Lock. I'm trying to imagine what it would have been like to set off, knowing there are some 147 miles to go, when there's a roll of thunder and so I rush back to the town centre, reaching the porch of the Lechlade library just as it begins to rain. I shelter from the downpour; behind me is the spire of St Lawrence church and the paved path amid the gravestones named after Shelley. Eventually the rain stops, a rainbow appears in the sky over Thames Street and the pavements shimmer.

'It's not a competition,' advises Clive the local cab man as he drives me to Kelmscott and I tell him about my swim; 'go with the flow, get your stroke right and get the right rhythm and you'll be fine.' I arrive at the seventeenth-century Plough Inn where I'm staying for two nights. A man at the bar says they get a lot of SwimTrek people in here and I ask if they are super-serious swimmers. 'No!' he laughs, as if this is the funniest thing he's ever heard, 'they only do fifty yards.' I walk through Kelmscott and past the manor, the old summer home of the Pre-Raphaelite artist William Morris who called this part of the river 'the Baby Thames' and whose 'Willow Boughs' wallpaper was inspired by the trees surrounding Buscot Pool. There are doves in the air; the emerald fields shine in the sun. I head down a lane and see a sign for the Thames Path, a small landing stage and the river. It's utterly silent, the river a milky white. It would be easy enough to jump in, I think, but where do you get out? I throw in a stick and watch for evidence of a current, just as Lewis Pugh did in 2006. The stick moves, ever so slightly, downstream.

The next morning it's a cloudy 13 degrees when Josie Arnold from the Plough drives me to Buscot Lock, close to where Lewis Pugh and Charlie Wittmack began their record-breaking swims.

During the recent heatwave Josie jumped in the Thames one night to cool off, as many people do, but she says she'd only ever do it with a friend, never alone. The first thing I see at Buscot Lock is a big sign reading: 'Welcome to the lock. Please stay safe during your visit. Warning deep water. No swimming'.

There's a boat moored on the side of the river, and a tarpaulin spread on the grass where a woman is sitting massaging her legs. Dawn Howard is an Associate Fellow at Sussex University; this is her second day swimming and she's not wearing a wetsuit. Others arrive and there is a general feeling of anticipation. Our swim guides are Yolande Joubert, an Australian, and former beach lifeguard Eleanor Selby who has been a competitive pool swimmer. They offer us tea, coffee, juice, biscuits and nuts, and ask, 'you have all eaten, haven't you?' Then our pre-tour briefing begins and we go round and introduce ourselves. Sandra Simpson says her swimming style is steady, not strong. She did a short triathlon five years ago and was afraid of the swimming part so she did a SwimTrek swim in Majorca to get tips. She's annoyed that, as she's over sixty, she had to provide a letter from her doctor, who basically said 'she seems fine to me'.

I've been told I must have insurance for this Thames trip and have to produce evidence of it at the start or I won't be able to swim. So a few months ago I'd contacted the Post Office who said they couldn't provide cover if it was for a professional, tournament or competition swim. They also said I'd need a minimum of two nights' pre-booked accommodation – which is why I'm staying at the Plough Inn. But the Post Office doesn't seem sure about wild swimming and they ring their underwriters before calling back. The final answer is that, as long as the Thames trip is 'professionally organised, supervised and supported', I have cover. But now we're here at the Thames, and I'm told insurance isn't necessary after all.

Aside from Sandra and me, there are ten others in the group. Ian Rees, the only man, is going to do a triathlon and he wants to try the whole way using front crawl. Many have done organised swims and races, often raising money for charity, and I'm getting a bit worried until two women, Kate Beevers and Lisa Romanczuk, announce that this will be the first time they've ever swum in a river. When Kate adds that the maximum she can do in a pool is a mile, I want to hug her. We're then all given a laminated card explaining Weil's disease: 'This card is for your protection. Whenever you go to your doctor or to a hospital on account of illness show this card and make sure they know you have been river swimming'. The other side of the card explains that diagnosis is based on lab investigations and in the early stages it may resemble influenza. We're also encouraged to use antibacterial wash after removing our wetsuits and before eating. A final suggestion is to drink Coca-Cola, as there is a theory that it kills Thames bugs. But boats are the main concern and we are to 'stay river right'. We are also not

A group photo at Buscot Lock, Oxfordshire, where a sign reads, 'No Swimming'. I'm second from left and nervous about whether I can cover the full five miles.

to upset the locals, and this includes swans. We're then told the various communication signals: stop, go left, come to the boat and 'are you OK?', which means putting your fingers on top of your head as Mo Farah does after he has won a race. The next topic is chafing and Yolande offers to apply Vaseline to our necks. Chafing has never occurred to me: we're not exactly going to be swimming the Channel, are we?

'It's fun,' says Eleanor, 'pace yourself and you can always get out.' Four of us then go to the toilet and I'm so revved up about the fact I'm about to swim five miles in the River Thames that, instead of pulling the toilet chain, I pull the emergency cord and the alarm goes off.

It's after 11 a.m. when we cross over the lock to wait for the boat. We're split into two groups – breaststroke and front crawl – and I choose the former. How anyone is going to swim the whole way breaststroke in a wetsuit I have no idea, but I assume they will be slower. I walk backwards down a short, thin ladder. The water is 20 degrees and feels amazingly clean; there is no smell at all. We're told not to stretch before getting in, but to do so for a few minutes once we are in the water. Then off we go. The river is lush and lined with trees and foxgloves; a bright blue dragonfly hovers over my head. I float on my back, hearing nothing but the plop of a fish from a nearby clump of water lilies. I'm in a world of green, from the vivid grassy banks to the water itself. The great thing about a river is that you don't know what you will see next, but as I turn a corner I am face to face with my worst nightmare: two big swans with a group of cygnets. We're told to keep to the left now and my heart is pounding. I feel so vulnerable down at water level, but we swim past the swans without any problem and carry on. The front-crawl people have caught up now and soon they overtake us. I relax again, enjoying the scenery and the blueness of the sky, even the thick, sticky reeds that wrap themselves around me in big fluttery wads. Then Ian calls out in surprise: he's standing up in the middle of the river. I put down my feet and feel silt squeezing between my toes. Cautiously I stand up as well and the water doesn't even reach my waist.

The front-crawlers are way ahead now and even though this is supposed to be fun I feel pressure to keep up with them. Someone is beside me and I don't recognise her because everyone is wearing hats and goggles. There is something odd about her face, as if her skin has been spattered with mud, and it takes me a while to realise that, if she looks like this, then I must, too. It's tricky keeping to where I'm supposed to be – to stay right and follow the curve of the river – and I frequently find myself in the middle. Ahead of me a woman is doing backstroke straight into a bunch of reeds. Then along comes another swan, the small support boat is in front of me and I can't remember what hand signal to use. I try a full wave, then I shout, 'help! Swan!' The boat turns and comes back but the swan has decided it's in charge and so it leads us majestically, carrying twelve swimmers and two boats in its wake until eventually it glides off to the right. Now we're at a bridge and a mooring point. I approach the smaller support boat and ask for some water, only to be told there are just 500 metres to go. I'm ecstatic. I can't think how long this will take but, incredibly, our first and longest swim of the day is nearly over.

We get out near the Kelmscott landing stage and as we walk to the inn for lunch I ask the others what they most feared. 'I was worried about death,' says Kate May, 'and drowning. But it was an amazing experience, it was so relaxing. The river carries you and the scenery is lovely.' Kate Beevers, who has never swum in a river before, says she had a moment of panic: she didn't want to put her head in the water, so she did side stroke for a while until she managed to overcome her fear. We talk about our families and our jobs: our group includes a civil servant, a local authority public heath official, a clinical psychologist and an adult education tutor. We chat about what other people think of our swim and one woman explains that her friends generally say, 'you're doing what? The Thames? Ugh!'

Our Australian guide says the English like organised adventure holidays – stressing the word 'organised' – and that we like rules and we're obsessed with Health & Safety. I ask about the training programme and everyone says they did no training at all; you just need to be someone who swims regularly. As we walk back to the landing stage two women drive past. 'Are you going to William Morris' manor?' asks the driver. 'No!' I say, 'we're going to swim.' 'Well, the manor is closed,' says the driver, not reacting to what I've said at all.

Swim number two starts well. I've had lunch and I'm warmed up, but I also feel a little lazy and that quickly turns to feeling very tired. I trail at the back, my shoulders seem to be made of metal and urgently need oiling. In the first swim I was somewhere in the middle, now I'm second from last. 'Try some side stroke,'

Travelling down the Thames with SwimTrek, where the river is lush and the water is clean.

says Kate Beevers kindly. Then I see another group of swans and cygnets almost hidden from sight, nestled on the bank. Our guide thinks she recognises one of the swans from the day before and she instructs us all to group together and swim to one side of the boat. This doesn't deter the swans; they are both in the river now, and they're following us round the boat. At this point I put my head down and swim as fast as I can.

But soon I'm exhausted again, my arms and shoulders ache and I can't swim breaststroke because of my wetsuit. The river seems to just go on and on. Unlike in a pond or a pool, there is no end point, no markers to swim towards, and I don't know where we're heading because every view is new.

I feel cocooned in the water, but at the same time oddly exposed. There is a huge gap between me and the swimmer in front and, behind, just a wide expanse of river. I try to swim on my back, then on my front; I feel as if I'm on a long plane journey and I can't get comfortable and I can't get out. I want to relax and enjoy where I am, to remember this journey down the upper Thames. I think of Charlie Wittmack explaining how he tried to enter a meditative state and spent much of the first day of his world triathlon just floating. But, more importantly, I remember how he said he regretted he didn't have time to appreciate where he was.

So I tell myself: this is the Thames, this beautiful, clear, empty river, lined with weeping willows. I'm part of a tradition; I'm swimming in a place where for more than a hundred years women and men have bathed and paddled and raced. Then I see the nose of a crocodile peeping just above the water, disguised as a log. I tell myself I'm in the Thames, I must be going mad.

I come to a white house on the right bank; we've been told this means we're about three-quarters of the way. Yet still our swim goes on and on. I can hear a boat behind me but when I turn round there is nothing; instead it's a helicopter in the sky. The few times a boat does pass, it is carrying day trippers, meandering downriver, just as in Victorian times. I call out, 'which way is London?' and a woman on board gives a tight smile.

Then we arrive at Grafton Lock, a working lock since 1896, and I'm looking forward to having a rest; with two swims down there is just a kilometre and a half to go. This time when I'm offered tea I take it, with lots of sugar, then I accept a piece of chocolate, too. To make it worse I then drink some Coke. Now I'm not only tired but also feeling a bit sick. And I'm so dazed and disorientated that I've washed my hands with antibacterial gel, removed the top of my wetsuit, eaten the chocolate and then used the hand gel again.

We walk to an iron jetty on the other side of the lock to wait for the boat. I look at the woman next to me: she seems a bit jittery. 'Why am I doing this?' she asks. At lunch she was one of several women who said they had young children and wanted the chance to do something for themselves, to have a challenge. I say I feel sick, and the guides ask if I want to get on the boat. I say no, because I'm expecting us all to have a nice lie-down. But several of the group are laughing and taking off their wetsuits for the final swim. That was my intention, to swim in the Thames as naturally as possible, but I think the wetsuit is the only thing that will keep me going. A man on the bank comes up to the fence and asks, 'are you doing this for charity?' 'No!' we shout in unison.

Someone suggests I wear flippers but I haven't worn flippers since I was a little kid and I'm feeling hysterical as I step backwards down a ladder and put on the fins, which takes me a long while. And then surprise! I'm as speedy as anything. I whip through the water. For one glorious moment I'm even leading the pack, a family of pink-hatted otters down the River Thames. I turn on my back and realise that with flippers on I can fold my arms over my stomach, lift my head up out of the water and just comfortably speed along. I see a pillbox left over from the Second World War, a concrete lookout post on the bank of the river, built to halt an anticipated German advance through the English countryside. As we approach

Radcot Bridge, often said to be the oldest on the Thames and built in the thirteenth century, we're told to swim together because there are lots of boats. I swim underneath the stone arch and then look up; there is a hotel to my left and people having a drink outside look at us as if we're crazy.

I don't want to get out now. I peel off half my wetsuit, take off my hat and flippers, and have one final splash. Then Cliff, the boat driver, puts a long ladder into the water and one by one we haul ourselves up as he watches us, expressionless, not even a flicker of a smile. Sandra looks at her watch: 'the total we've swum is less than four hours. Think how many days Walliams did.'

I'm feeling triumphant, but there is no way I would do a two-day swimming trip, although two of the group will be swimming all day tomorrow and others are already saying that's exactly what they're going to do next year.

The following morning during breakfast at the inn a couple ask, 'were you one of the swimmers in the Thames? We saw you, people were talking about you. Were you doing it for charity?' I say we were doing it just for pleasure, and expect them to look surprised and ask if I feel ill. But instead the man says thoughtfully, 'I've got a wetsuit in the attic; I haven't put it on for years. I used to love open-water swimming when I was younger. I wonder why I don't do it any more.'

I wonder this as well; perhaps somewhere along the line I lost my love of open-water swimming, too, influenced by fears of dirty, dangerous rivers and having grown far too used to indoor pools. If I hadn't spent months talking to other Thames swimmers and researching archive swims I would never have set myself this challenge. But the fact I succeeded is nothing compared to the beauty of the experience. I'm beginning to look at the Thames in a new way; why has it never occurred to me to swim here, ever since that dip when I was ten years old, when this morning I feel more refreshed and exhilarated than I have for years?

3

Oxford

'The best time to bathe in the open air is early morning, for then the
robust and healthy body has been strengthened by the night's repose'
Charles Steedman, *Manual of Swimming*, 1867

Members of Oxford University's 1936 water polo team dive in at Parson's
Pleasure on the River Cherwell, one of Oxford's most famous swimming spots.

If ever there was a city famous for its enjoyment of river swimming it's Oxford, from skinny dipping dons on the River Cherwell (a major tributary of the Thames), Victorian endurance swimmers on the Isis (as the Thames is locally known above Iffley Lock), to riverside family picnics and bathing in the 1960s. Yet while there were once several official swimming areas along the city's waterways, most have been closed down since the 1990s, leaving only remnants behind.

The most famous, Parson's Pleasure in the University Parks, was a male-only nude bathing spot on the Cherwell dating back to the seventeenth century. Women in passing punts were expected to get out at Parson's Pleasure and walk, a tradition that continued into the 1970s. 'I remember having to sink low in a punt, hat over face,' recalls Heather Armitage, Tourism Officer at Visit Oxfordshire. 'The men used to stand up at the riverside, gazing out, bits a-dangle. Ladies were supposed to get out of the punt and walk round the other side but no one did. You can still see the concrete blocks that formed the bases for diving boards.' In 1934 women and children were given their own area on the Cherwell, with the opening of Dames' Delight. But bathers had to wear costumes and pay an entrance fee, and after it was swept away in gales and floods in 1970 it was never repaired.

On the Thames there was Port Meadow, an area of ancient grazing land still used by swimmers, and Long Bridges, near Donnington Bridge, once the university bathing place. 'A lady told me the elderly lifeguard was a friend at Long Bridges and he used to pour a kettle of hot water into the river to warm it up for her!' says Heather. 'It was a large bathing area, with walled banks, changing rooms and toilets. You can still see the shape of a pool in concrete.' Tumbling Bay was another favoured spot, a pool between two weirs on a backwater of the Thames, which traces its history back to the nineteenth century.

It's no wonder then that many adults in Oxford spent their

childhoods immersed in local rivers. 'Our mum used to take us for picnics by the Thames, and we swam from what seemed to us to be miniature beaches. As far as I was concerned, that was what rivers were there for!' says Jenny Rogers, who was born in Oxford in 1952. 'I mourn the passing of the River Bathing Places that gave us such simple pleasures for so many years, and helped us to grow up strong and fit.'

Oxford also has a long tradition of competitive river racing. The earliest recorded race appears to have been in the summer of 1840 when the National Swimming Society, formed three years earlier, offered silver medals as prizes for 'swimming matches at Oxford'. The races were divided into five heats of four competitors, and the banks and towpath were thronged with up to 3,000 people. At 4 p.m. the starting gun was fired and the first men plunged in from a houseboat stationed at a bridge just beyond Iffley. The distance was 400 yards.

While the inhabitants of Oxford appear to have been far earlier participants in organised river racing than those at Lechlade, the impetus for learning to swim, at least among university students, was rowing, and early rowing almanacs suggest bathing was part of their training. The poet Robert Southey was said to have 'learned two things only at Oxford, to row and to swim'. But as was the case upstream, many people died in the much-loved rivers; some drowned while bathing, others were carried over a sluice in a boat and some perished after recklessly leaping from a skiff at a weir. In 1859, after four undergraduates had died 'in rapid succession', Dr Acland, Regius Professor of Medicine, called a meeting of 'boating men and others'. 'Of course a great deal of nonsense was talked,' reported one attendee, but it was agreed Oxford needed 'a tepid swimming-bath' and a rule that no one who 'did not possess a swimming certificate should row in any University race'.

In 1870 the press reported on the 'first' Oxford swimming races, which took place on the 'Isis between Harvey's Barge and Iffley', but spectators were 'scanty' and the race 'seemed little known to the Undergraduate world'.

However, the following year the *Penny Illustrated Paper* was 'glad to note that the Oxford University Boat Club has at last followed the example of Cambridge, and started some swimming races'. They took place between 'the Gut' (a bend or narrow passage in the river) and Iffley and included a half-mile race open to all university members, a distance diving race, a hurdle race and a 50-yard race open only to the 'pupils of Harvey, the University water bailiff, an old and valued servant of the University'. In 1890 the Oxford University Boat Club agreed members had to have a certificate from the Merton Street Baths proving that they had swum 'twice the length fully dressed', the Oxford University Swimming Club was formed, and by the early 1920s there would be a women's club as well.

An Oxford Regatta held during the First World War also included swimming. A Pathé News clip of the period opens with a row of boys diving off a long floating raft, then using an impressively fluid front crawl. Yet despite this tradition of river swimming there is very little in the way of documentation in any of the city's museums or archives. Why is the history of Thames swimming so hard to find and why are documents so scarce? Why aren't local museums full of evidence of how bathers once used the river? Perhaps, as local historian Mark Davies believes, 'it was too commonplace to mention'.

But there *is* a rare Victorian book at the Old Bodleian Library, a manual of swimming written by Charles Steedman in 1867. A Londoner by birth, Steedman learned to swim at thirteen and six years later became a champion swimmer. He then emigrated to Australia in 1854, during the gold rush, where he continued his swimming career as champion of the state of Victoria. Steedman's book is not the first of its kind; back in 1587 Everard Digby had written a treatise on swimming for Tudor gentlemen in Latin, *De arte natandi*, with woodcut illustrations. He argued that 'man swimmeth by nature' and set out when, where and how to swim, even including tips on cutting toenails while in the river. This was then translated into English by Christopher Middleton and a shortened version published in 1595, which now resides in the British Library. But Steedman's manual is said to be the first text on competitive swimming and its emphasis is on what would today be called wild swimming. It was initially published in Melbourne but a later London edition gave it international renown and it's often described as marking the beginning of swimming's modern era.

It's a dull spring day when I reach Oxford and I can barely move for people offering tours – walking tours, bus tours, ghost tours – the pavements before the grand sandstone buildings of the university packed with tourists. I head for the Bodleian Library on Broad Street, where I'm directed to the admissions building, closed today for a degree ceremony. Suddenly down the street comes a pack of graduates, black gowns and white scarves flapping in the breeze. I'm told to ask 'one of the men in bowler hats' to let me in, which he duly does, opening a pair of heavy black gates. Inside the office I watch a Canadian submit his forms, have his photograph taken and read out the Bodleian promise. He vows that he will not remove, mark, deface or injure any of the documents, he won't 'bring into the Library, or kindle therein, any fire or flame' and neither will he smoke. The words are a translation of a traditional Latin oath, from the days when libraries weren't heated because fires were so hazardous.

'It's bonkers today,' says Sara Langdon, assistant admissions officer, as I'm finally shown to her desk. She goes through my forms, her face serious as she reads the section where I have to justify why I need to use the Bodleian and where I've explained I'm writing a book about Thames swimming. 'How wonderful!' she says, looking up from my form. 'Swimming the Thames. It takes me back to my childhood.' River swimming was something Sara took for granted while growing up in Oxford, and she has fond memories of swinging from trees and ropes and launching herself into the Isis. Why, she asks, hasn't anyone written about this before?

'I live in Wolvercote and last year I was crossing Port Meadow when I saw some young people, in their early teens, jumping off the bridge by the marina. It was a jolly hot day and I didn't tell them off but I was quite concerned. I asked what they'd do if something went wrong and they said, "we do it all the time". You can't stop children, can you? But when I think of our mothers and how they let us swim in the Thames!'

I get my ID card and head back to the Bodleian, crossing the flagged courtyard as if about to enter a castle, heading for the lower reading room reserve on the first floor. There, at last, I get my hands on Steedman's *Manual of Swimming*. After all this, it's a disappointingly small book, just 270 pages. I was expecting a huge manual. I sit down at one of the reading desks; above the bookcases the white stone walls are hung with ancient portraits. The silence is broken only by the squeaking of shoes as someone walks past and the sound of my neighbour tapping away on her laptop.

I start leafing through the manual, looking at sections on bathing, plunging, diving, floating, scientific swimming, training, drowning and rescuing. Bathing has several subheadings including 'Necessity of Cleansing the Skin, Pores, Perspiration, Virtue of cleanliness, Gouty persons'. The English, it seems, weren't known for their cleanliness in Steedman's day: 'without exaggeration it may be safely asserted that the bodies of thousands have never been thoroughly washed.'

Swimming, he explains in capital letters, is THAT SPECIAL MODE OF PROGRESSION WHICH ENABLES A PERSON TO DERIVE ENTIRE SUPPORT FROM THE LIQUID IN WHICH HE IS IMMERSED. How complex this seems today, evidence that in Victorian times swimming was a new science, and a new art. It needed to be properly defined and would-be swimmers required

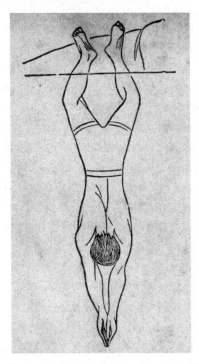

An illustration of the 'vertical header', part of a pack of swimming cards produced by a Professor H. Bocock in 1888. In Victorian times, swimming was a new science and a new art.

plenty of advice. The best time to bathe in the open air was the early morning, for then the 'robust and healthy body' had been 'strengthened by the night's repose' and benefited most from the shock of immersion. But it was 'injurious' to bathe on an empty stomach and Steedman advised, 'take a cup of warm milk or coffee with a biscuit or a slice of stale bread before going into the water'. However, it also wasn't a good idea to bathe on a full stomach.

Steedman devotes much of his book to the subjects of drowning and rescuing, at a time when 'more people have lost their lives' because they couldn't swim than from 'any other one cause of accidental death'. In England and Wales 'more than six persons' drowned on a daily basis. While swimming was not as popular with the English as it was with the Prussians and French, Steedman assures his readers that this was not due to any physical inferiority, but because there were few good teachers and too many 'amateur and defective ones'. This is presumably why he goes into great detail concerning proper leg and arm strokes, with accompanying diagrams. Cramp was a common affliction, but generally a minor one, and as far as Steedman is concerned made into more of a drama than necessary and unfairly blamed for several deaths.

Digestion and sweating are major concerns, however, and he gives plenty more tips on diet. Beef is most nutritious, but mutton is best thoroughly digested; underdone meat is better than overdone, and some swimmers, he notes, are partial to raw meat when training. It is all right to drink water, but no more than three pints a day; home-brewed ale is also acceptable as long as it is draught rather than bottled, and no more than a pint should be drunk. When training for a swim the ideal meal was an underdone steak or chop without fat, stale bread, a couple of mealy potatoes and greens.

Feeling hungry myself now, I leave the Bodleian in search of food as I make my way to the scene of a once famous endurance swim – undertaken by a man who may well have read Steedman's manual. Fifteen minutes later I'm standing in the middle of Folly Bridge, looking down over the river. The water is green, spotted

Professor Bocock explains how to swim fully clothed. Only 'really advanced swimmers (could) swim in women's garments on account of them wrapping around the feet'.

with silver glimmers of sunlight. Salter's Steamers Boatyard, established in 1858, juts out into the river; a boat full of rowers appears in the distance. It was here that Lewis Carroll set out for Godstow (a hamlet on the Thames) with Alice Liddell and her sisters and, while journeying upriver, first came up with the story that would become *Alice's Adventures in Wonderland*. His 1865 book includes Alice's swim with Mouse in the Pool of Tears, and illustrations variously show her doing a basic breaststroke or front crawl; but it's unlikely the real Alice knew how to swim.

It was also here at Folly Bridge that in 1890 the honorary secretary of the 'Professional Swimming Association' (otherwise known as the National Swimming Association), Mr. T.C. Easton, attempted a six-day swim to Teddington. On 22 September he 'commenced one of the most genuinely sportsmanlike performances ever attempted,' reported the *Morning Post* admiringly. He would swim ninety-one miles to Teddington, covering eight hours a day, 'and though the journey is a very favourite one for boating parties, the idea of accomplishing it by swimming does not seem to have previously occurred to any one'.

The American novelist Nathaniel Hawthorne joined one such boating party near Oxford when he toured England in the 1860s, finding the river narrow, shallow and bordered with bulrushes and water-weeds, the shores flat and meadow-like and the water 'clean and pure'. Boat trips from Folly Bridge to London were 'very much the thing to do,' explains Oxford historian Simon Wenham, 'it was known as "the Thames trip". Today the Boat House Tavern houses the drags for recovering bodies and the resuscitation apparatus. I've always wondered what the latter would have been in Victorian times.'

By then, Easton was already a well-known swimmer (in 1898 he came up with the idea of launching a professional long-distance championship from Kew to Putney) and he'd already made several attempts to swim from Richmond Bridge to London Bridge. In 1888, 'owing to a very sluggish tide', he'd only managed to get to Putney, but the following year he got as far as Westminster Bridge where he 'seemed to become weak' and left the water after completing fourteen miles in just over four hours. But he was back in the river again a few weeks later, this time covering twenty miles from London Bridge to Purfleet, and in 1890 he'd swum twenty miles from Blackwall to Gravesend. Now he'd turned his sights on Oxford and the press expected he would be 'fully qualified to wrestle with his arduous task', noting that he was thirty-seven, stood 5 feet 11 inches and weighed 16 stone.

At eight in the morning Easton entered the water at Folly Bridge and an hour later had reached Iffley Lock, a mile and a quarter downriver. 'The weather was beautifully fine, although there was a strong adverse wind' as, seven hours later, he reached Abingdon Lock and then stopped at Culham Lock after nine miles and five furlongs. Press coverage was substantial, with headlines such as EASTON'S LONG SWIM IN THE THAMES, though reports of the distances he covered each day varied. The *Star* reported a large assembly witnessed the start, and that Easton left the water 'in a good condition'. Oxford already had a basic sewage system in place by the early nineteenth century, with the drains emptying into the Thames or its tributaries, but there were several serious cholera epidemics in the first half of the 1800s. A more efficient sewage system was put in place in the 1870s, though how clean the water was during Easton's swim isn't mentioned in the newspapers.

The following day he resumed swimming and 'by means of a steady breaststroke' continued until 10 a.m. 'when a severe storm passed over'. However, he 'persevered gallantly with his task', according to the *Daily News*, and again stayed in the water for about eight hours. When he reached Shillingford Bridge, 'Easton was in capital condition . . . and intends resuming his swim at eight o'clock this morning'. But at some point things went wrong, and after several attacks of cramp, and 'a strained leg', he was compelled to abandon the attempt on the fourth day having managed twenty-seven miles. 'Folly Bridge may to some sound like an appropriate starting point for such an enterprise,' remarked one journalist, but Easton had 'plenty of pluck . . . He is, I believe, a milkman by trade – this perhaps explains his partiality for water!'

Although today no one seems to have heard of Easton's four-day feat, it's a clear precursor of modern-day endurance swims, and proof that since Victorian times we've seen the Thames as the ultimate challenge. Easton tried out different courses on the river and when he attempted a six-day swim no one, apparently, had ever thought of doing it before. It would be more than a hundred years before anyone did manage to swim between Oxford and Teddington, and that was Andy Nation as part of his non-tidal Thames swim in 2005. He had the same motivation as Easton – no one had done it before – although on this occasion he was also aiming to raise money for charity.

I find it strange that an event so widely reported at the time has now been forgotten; it's as if each time someone in the twenty-first century attempts to set a record in the Thames they're unaware that it has been tried before. I'm beginning to think that the history of Thames swimming has so many stops and starts that it will never be a straightforward, linear story; rather, we repeatedly need to flash back to the past in order to make sense of the way we use and view the river today.

I leave Folly Bridge and head to a very different river spot, a place for enjoyment rather than 'sportsmanlike' challenge. Tumbling Bay lies behind Oxford's railway station, through Botley Park. It's not clear when it first opened but in 1893 the town clerk put a notice in a local paper announcing that as from 5 May 'this Bathing Place will be OPEN, Free of Charge, for FEMALE BATHERS ONLY, on each FRIDAY during the Season, between the hours of 6am and 8.30pm. Bathing Dresses will be supplied, Free of Charge, and must be used.' In addition, a bathing attendant was engaged who would supply towels for a penny.

I walk past a community centre and across a field and I can hear the place before I see it, with a loud rushing sound coming from behind the trees. It's not as big as I'd expected, a rectangle of water between two weirs rather like a concrete-lined lido. Two teenage boys emerge from bushes on the opposite side and as they cross the bridge towards me I ask if they ever swim here. 'Yes,' one says, 'if it's a sunny day. My eighty-six-year-old grandma swam here. It's really packed in the summer. Some people say we shouldn't because of that rat thing, but I don't know anyone who ever got it.' And is the current fast? 'You can stand under the bridge if you need to,' he says, then he points to the far end. 'That part is weedy, but you can dive near the steps.' There is gravel on the ground, and quite a few pike and perch, which he's fished for in the past.

As the boys leave I walk around the pool; the bottom looks shallow and sandy and there are plenty of weeds and mud. On a hot day it must be a perfect place to cool off, and in the 1940s it was here that schoolchildren were taught to swim. 'We didn't have a bathroom at home, so the nearest I usually got to water was a quick rub round with a wet flannel,' Bob Hounslow told the *Oxford Mail*. 'The thought of immersing my whole body in cold water wasn't one I relished.' But at Tumbling Bay the instructor would order the scrawny boys to stand in a line in the water, then dive forwards, arms outstretched, 'and glide along until we bumped into the weir'. The process was then repeated, using the swimming strokes they had learned lying on straw mats in the school playground. Eventually they managed the width and then the length of the pool and gained swimming certificates. Today the old changing rooms have gone except for their concrete bases, but the ladders remain – apparently to ensure the council can't be sued if someone gets into trouble.

By far the most lethal place in the Oxford area is further downstream at Sandford Lock. 'The pools of Sandford Lasher, in the backwater by the lock, are dangerous for bathing in, and have acquired an ill name from the many fatal accidents which have happened there,' explained the 1893 *Oarsman's and Angler's Map of the River Thames from Its Source to London Bridge*. 'The pool under Sandford Lasher . . . is a very good place to drown yourself in,' comments the narrator of *Three Men in a Boat*, while *Dickens's Dictionary of the Thames* notes, 'It is notorious to all rowing men and *habitués* of the river.' The Pool of Tears in *Alice in Wonderland* was a result of Carroll's visit to Sandford, while Michael Llewelyn Davies, one of the inspirations for Peter Pan, drowned here in 1921. The lasher is described on modern maps as a treacherous weir pool with a very strong undercurrent, while the lock has the deepest drop on the non-tidal Thames.

While people still swim at Tumbling Bay and Port Meadow today, bathing in the Thames around Oxford is the subject of repeated warnings in the local press. It may once have been normal for schoolchildren to be taken to the river to learn to swim, a basic skill that everyone needed to know, but according to the media today it's a dangerous pursuit. 'The deadly lure of deep water during sunny spells has once again proved fatal,' reported the *Oxford Times* in 2000, following 'a long list of tragedies'. Youngsters are told 'not to indulge in the dangerous "sport" of jumping into the water from river bridges', and the Environment Agency (EA) estimates that 'between 50 and 100 children a day can be found playing unaccompanied along the Thames' as a whole. Swimming, it cautions, should always take place under adult supervision and 'preferably in a swimming pool'.

The EA, established in 1996, is the navigational authority on the Thames, operating under legislation that goes back to Magna Carta, and owns the forty-one locks on the upper Thames, where swimming is banned, as it is in weirs. It is responsible for registering craft and generally managing any river activity. But Russell Robson, Waterways Team Leader, stresses that there is a free right to use the Thames: 'we are not the owner of the river or of the water. The riparian landowners have rights to the banks and bed where their land adjoins the river, so if a house has a garden leading down to the riverbank then they own that bank. If you want to dive in we have no powers to stop anyone, but a landowner can restrict access and if there is damage then it's trespass.'

While he says that in general people have become 'softer' with the introduction of indoor pools, there has also been a growth in mass-participation events on the Thames. 'People see it as a fantastic backdrop for their event. You get the choice between an idyllic, tree-lined, sun-warmed river, or a twenty-five-metre-long municipal pool with hair floating in it. People have always paddled from the banks, fished, bathed, cleansed and played in it. The perception is it's getting cleaner, which it is. I grew up in south-east London in the 1970s and the Thames was a floating rubbish dump. Today it's an ever-improving environment for wildlife, but it's not bathing water.' The three main risks are the cold, flooding and possible infection, but 'if people take precautions there is no reason why they shouldn't swim'.

Yet while the EA monitors ecological and biological quality, there are no official bathing waters on the Thames, so it doesn't test for E. coli or strep. 'To be brutally honest, it wouldn't pass bathing water standards,' says Russell; 'there is land drainage, water for agriculture and drinking water, power industries and wastewater discharge. Climate change means we have warmer summers and people are attracted to riverbanks. It's a free activity and it's more popular now, but that doesn't mean it's safe. People still go and swim at Tumbling Bay, although it's not open any more, and there is a drowning there every few years.'

Perhaps the most dangerous activity on the Thames is jumping from bridges, which Russell says goes on all over the place with at least one incident every year. The annual May Day tradition of jumping off Magdalen Bridge into the Cherwell has led to numerous injuries. Recently the coroner at Oxford ruled on a case where a fourteen-year-old boy jumped into the Thames with his girlfriend, and hadn't told her he couldn't swim. 'I've jumped from bridges myself and it's great fun,' says Russell, 'but it's also hazardous and I never considered that people just chuck stuff in.' He cites stolen laptops and builders dumping debris: 'we had twenty bags of rubble at Godstow and the diver was standing on it and the water only came to his knees.' In the summer of 2012, the EA invited the public to Pangbourne, about twenty miles from Oxford, to watch Thames Valley Police Search and Recover divers remove hazardous materials by Whitchurch Bridge. In previous years divers had pulled out shopping trolleys, motorbikes, fridges, TVs, scooters, scaffolding and traffic cones, some firmly stuck in the riverbed. One year only a small sample of objects was recovered, partly because the diver was becoming entangled in a discarded fishing line.

The EA cites numerous possible risks associated with swimming and diving in the Thames, including falling on metal spikes, being struck by a boat or caught in a propeller, being swept along in a strong current, encountering cold water which can lead to cramp and breathing difficulties, and unstable slippery banks which can collapse suddenly. With warnings like these, no wonder people are put off and some Oxford residents, like Christopher Gray, think the idea of river swimming is crazy. 'Though a tributary of the Thames flows at the bottom of my garden, I would never dream of swimming in it,' he wrote in the *Oxford Times*, annoyed that the *Daily Telegraph* had just run a three-page feature on river swimming, recommending the Thames at Port Meadow and Clifton Hampden. To him this was 'Barking mad . . . River swimming is a new faddish activity. Like motorcycling and Morris dancing, it numbers many zealots among its supporters.'

Several well-known endurance swimmers have fallen sick around Oxford, including Lewis Pugh during his 2006 trip. 'The upper Thames was beautiful, clean and gorgeous,' he remembers. 'Oxford was really grotty. I ended up in hospital there, although we didn't mention it to the press at the time. I had started vomiting late one night; I was rushed in and given antibiotics. The next morning I was totally exhausted, I only managed 400 metres that day.'

David Walliams fell sick at the end of day two as he passed Oxford and reached Abingdon. 'I had Giardia, which people in the third world get from dirty water, and it makes you very ill with diarrhoea. It lays eggs in the lower intestine. I had antibiotics before I started, and during, and I can't say for certain how I got it.' Long-distance swimmer Frank Chalmers also got sick with 'the dreaded Thames lurgy' as he approached Oxford on his four-day swim, but despite being taken to hospital he says 'people swim here all the time and they are fine'.

Indeed they are, and despite warnings from the EA and in the press, swimming in the Thames at Oxford is seeing something of a revival. 'As the pound sinks and more of us stay at home instead of going abroad, such simple pleasures are being rediscovered,' says Chris Koenig from the *Oxford Times*. 'After all, the weather is getting hotter and the rivers cleaner.' Swimming teacher Dee Keane has lived in Oxford for thirty years yet didn't swim in the Thames until she took part in a full-moon swim with the Outdoor Swimming Society (OSS) downstream near South Stoke. 'There was thunder and lightning and we were all a bit hyped up. We assembled in a field and changed and then walked through the village and a mile up the towpath, just wearing costumes and goggles, and then swam back. It was dusk, around 7 or 8 p.m., and people were coming out of the pub to look at us. You could see them thinking, "Dear God, I've got to stop drinking."'

The dozen or so people swam with the current and, Dee continues, 'I remember thinking, well, I'm quite glad it's dark and I can't see what's in the water, what's down there in the murky depths. But it was quite silky, with an occasional leaf brushing past.' As for health risks, she says statistically you're as likely to pick up a bug or a verruca from a pool. However, she swam the Thames with her face out of the water, 'although I spend my professional life telling people not to do that because it places more stress on the back and neck. But in the Thames I was really careful not to swallow water.'

Esther Browning is another long-time Oxford resident, having arrived as an eighteen-year-old to study Human Sciences. One of the attractions was the river; she rowed for her college and was a member of the Wallingford Rowing Club, racing on the Thames as far as Putney. But then she had three children and rowing is 'a massive time commitment'. However, she managed to complete some triathlons that included swimming in an indoor pool, and then one day she saw an advertisement for a triathlon that involved an open-water swim. 'My big block was open water, but I felt like a bit of a fraud doing it in a pool.' Esther lives near Newbridge, south-west of Oxford, and that's where she first went into the Thames to swim, along with a friend – 'I squealed in barefoot from a little mud beach, swam upstream and then back. It was a perfect summer's day, and the water was gentle.' She then took part in an OSS swim

'People are put off by the cold of the Thames, but it's so beautiful': Katia Vastiau who regularly swims near Oxford with companions Esther Browning and Kate Bradley.

at Dorchester-on-Thames followed by swims at Port Meadow, Abingdon, Buckland and Wallingford. 'All the stretches are different. North of Wolvercote is Amazonian with long branches hanging down, whereas at Newbridge it's flat farmers' fields.' Then in the summer of 2012 she 'hooked up with faster, more serious swimmers' and now she and two other women – Kate and Katia – swim all year round. 'Men say, "ah, it's too cold to swim in the Thames", but women are hardier, or women are every bit as hardy as men.'

The three women try to swim every week, usually a 750-metre course through Abingdon. 'As the days get darker we go there because the light from the town means you can see where you are. I'm terrified of cold water, it's almost like I have to prove myself, but afterwards I'm always pleased. I get a kick out of making myself do it, there's a real rush of endorphins. Before a rowing race I would feel nervous, my heart would be racing, and that's what it's like before swimming in the Thames. And it's fun, we have a laugh, we wetsuit up and scamper through town. And we really laugh when we get out of the water and try to get out of our wetsuits, it's very difficult when you're cold. I'm surprised we haven't been arrested for indecent exposure; you're always baring more flesh than you intend. Kate and Katia really encouraged me, they're really fast, and you need a group, you need companions.'

Esther says it can be quite scary in the dark with a strong current and sometimes it's touch and go whether they will do it. The women can't see each other, so they call out as they swim along, and while they tried wearing head torches these didn't work well while doing front crawl. The Oxford trio post their swims on the OSS site and others join in. 'A lot of people swim in the Thames. It's going on all the time but the last couple of years Facebook has made it easier to hook up.'

Esther's companion Kate Bradley first swam in the Thames in 2010 downstream at Clifton Hampden. 'It was November, but it was incredibly warm for the time of year, about fifteen degrees.

The second time there was frost on the ground and mist in the air and there were some shocked looks from the locals as we headed down to the river. There are still people who won't go in the Thames and think it's dirty; you could say David Walliams' swim was bad publicity. But personally, after three years of swimming every week in the Thames, I've never been ill. There have been recent sewage leaks, but mainly it's scare-mongering.' As for other river users, 'most rowers are friendly and fine but there's the odd one . . . Once I nearly bumped into some and they thought we should be swimming under the trees and that we didn't have the right to be in the river. But mostly people just say "you're mad". I try to be pleasant to everyone.'

Katia Vastiau, the third member of the group, first swam in the Thames two years ago. Originally from Brussels, she was a competitive indoor pool swimmer until the age of nineteen; she semi-retired from swimming, studied and had children and found there was no time for it. Then she met someone from a triathlon club who told her she should just do the swimming part. 'People are put off by the cold of the Thames, but it's so beautiful, we see herons and ducks and you see the edge of the river and the villages from a different angle. If you're in a camper van you see one perspective, in the river there's another. It's pretty and mellow. By now we know where to get in and we know the currents, we're not mad, we don't just jump in, we know what we're doing. We go on the left where there are no boats, but change if there's a weir on the left.

'Rowers are a problem; they don't look where they're going because they're going backwards. We have bright hats and flash-lights, but when we reach a corner we shout, "swimmers in the water!" There are lots of boats around Oxford. Rowers and their coaches usually say, "oh my God, you're really brave" and are very nice. Sometimes someone might be a bit grumpy, having to reduce their stroke for five seconds. You have to keep sighting and to look at the rest of the group. We've never had a near miss. We have lots of chats with fishermen and people walking their kids, it's very social.' The women also pick up discarded packaging and plastic bottles and put them in their wetsuits because 'we use the river; we want to help clear it up. We want to show people the Thames is there, but respect it.'

Swimming around Abingdon isn't a new idea, and although they may not know it, the three women's regular swims are building on a long tradition. In 1881 an official bathing place opened 'at the back of the Island near Abingdon Lock Pool' with floating screens moored across the back stream. Four days a week were 'set apart for the ladies to have the exclusive right of bathing there,' explained one newspaper. 'We hear that a club has been formed by some ladies of the town for the purpose of learning the art of swimming.'

Abingdon was still a place for family dips in the 1960s and 1970s – as was Wallingford where, at the turn of the century, children had been taught to swim wearing safety devices attached to a rope and a stick. Tami Bowers, who was born and brought up in Abingdon, remembers swimming in the Thames when she was three or four. 'My mum took us; she enjoyed swimming, though she wasn't competitive. There was not a massive amount of people doing it, there was an open-air pool nearby that people went to and originally it had Thames water. There was a slight current, depending on the time of year, it seems stronger now but maybe I'm more aware. The Thames was always on my doorstep; it was a luxury I had, and a natural thing for me to swim there. At Abingdon you're spoilt for choice.' Tami has brought up her children, now fourteen and seventeen, to swim in the Thames, and the only experience of any illness was when her eleven-year-old Border Collie, Rebel, got Weil's disease: 'he spent nearly nine weeks at the vets and we didn't think he would come out the other side. But as soon as he was well again he went back to swimming and he swam in the Thames until the day he died aged seventeen.

He would run and jump in anywhere he could. He swam twice a day around Abingdon.'

Tami has taken part in mass events such as the Great London Swim, 'but I prefer to paddle on my own, it's me time'. However, she says anglers often don't like open-water swimmers. 'I've been catapulted with pellets and they've screamed at me to get out of the way. Boats don't mind, the rowers aren't a problem, and the fish like me, I know because I have pike nibble marks on my wetsuit which I wear in the winter.'

As I leave Oxford and take the train back to London I wonder what Charles Steedman, the Victorian author, would have made of modern-day swimmers around here. I think he would have loved it all; to know how far we've come, that while children may now be urged to swim indoors and many of the old bathing places have gone, the art of river swimming continues in the form of three women who swim every week in the darkness through Abingdon. We have tried out different ways to swim the Thames at Oxford, from one-off races in 1840 to four-day endurance swims fifty years later. In Victorian times 'ladies' were keen to learn the new art; now we plunge into cold water in wetsuits. Here we are again, returning to the Thames, and as the river winds its way south into Berkshire I'm keen to know what stories the town of Reading has to tell.

4

Reading

'It [is] as necessary that a boy should learn to swim as it [is] that he should learn to write'

Reading Swimming Club, 1897

Reading has two long, straight stretches of water, one above Caversham Bridge and the other below Caversham Lock, which may well explain why the town has one of the longest continuous traditions of Thames swimming. Regattas were held here in Victorian times, although this area of the Thames was famous then for another reason: it was where 'baby farmer' Amelia Dyer, eventually hanged in 1896, threw the bodies of the children she had murdered into the water. As for swimming, when the narrator of *Three Men in a Boat* arrived in Reading he declared 'the river is dirty and dismal here'. But that didn't stop bathers, although the fact they were naked, as elsewhere on the Thames, was a 'public nuisance', according to the press. In the summer of 1888 'Disgusted of Wargrave' complained that 'a dozen or more men and boys lark about the banks in a state of nudity' at Reading and Caversham.

As in Oxford, there would be several official swimming areas at Reading, but this time there would also be a pool especially for women. The oldest and best-known bathing spot is King's Meadow beside Caversham Lock, also called the Corporation Baths. In the early 1800s local brewer Jonathan Tanner occupied

Bathers enjoy the King's Meadow men's pool in 1876. It was opened in 1834, situated in an inland cut and filled directly from the river. Following improvements in 1893 it became 'one of the finest open air swimming baths in the country'.

the land and in the summer he and his two sons rode down the towpath on horseback where bathers were 'a great nuisance' during hay-making time, running through the hay and throwing it at each other. When the boys were chased, they 'pitched into the Thames and mixed with those who had not trespassed,' explained W.S. Darter in his *Reminiscences of Reading 1888*. So Tanner decided to have 'several cartloads of broken bottles' thrown into deep water 'where the older boys bathed at the foot of the lock. This did not wholly prevent bathing but many persons were injured by having their feet cut and ever after [he was] dubbed Mr Bottle Tanner.'

In 1834 the King's Meadow swimming baths were officially opened, situated in an inland cut and filled directly from the river, for men only with single, monthly or season tickets. Such was their popularity that they were improved more than once over the years, with a new bathing house built 'near the pound-keeper's lodge' in 1843 and a further renovation fifty years later.

There were also three local swimming clubs that used the Thames in Victorian and Edwardian times: Reading Swimming Club, the Island Bohemian Club and the Winter Bathers.

The Reading Swimming and Lifesaving Club was founded in 1885, and would eventually have its headquarters at the King's Meadow pool. A founding member was Harry John Isaacs who received a bronze medal from the Royal Humane Society, established by two doctors in London in 1774, for rescuing a man from the Thames, and he also played in the club's water polo team that held its matches near Caversham Bridge.

The Reading Swimming Club organised annual entertainments, just like its counterpart in Lechlade, with its 1892 event held at its headquarters at 'Simonds's Baths, in South-street', where the press reported 'many of the races were keenly contested, particularly that for the championship of Reading'. The programme included a life-saving exhibition and drill, with various methods of rescue first being explained by a Mr W. Henry, and then demonstrated by club members. Spectators were 'very numerous, the building crowded to excess'.

William Henry was none other than one of the founders of the Swimmers' Life Saving Society, which started in 1891 and later became the Royal Life Saving Society. He was an English Salt Water and Thames champion, winning the long-distance championships from Putney to Charing Cross Railway Bridge in 1887. He also played water polo for England, wrote prolifically on the art of swimming and was an expert in 'scientific swimming', the forerunner of modern synchronised swimming. Henry lived in London and organised massive swimming and life-saving galas at various places such as the Highgate Men's Pond on Hampstead Heath. He also kept in close contact with the Reading club. In 1893, when members turned their attention to life saving, he 'did what he could to start a class', as well as giving public demonstrations, and in 1897 he was the club's vice-chair.

The Reading Swimming and Lifesaving Club was founded in 1885, with its headquarters eventually at the King's Meadow men's pool.

By the end of 1893 the King's Meadow pool had undergone 'extensive alterations and enlargement'. The bath was now 230 feet long and 60 feet wide, with a 'water area of 1,400 square yards', 6 inches of concrete at the bottom and a springboard. The south end of the bath, at 3 feet deep, was reserved for learners with a lifeguard rail fixed just above the waterline. There were covered seats, with hat and coat hooks, nine large dressing boxes, a ticket office and toilets. Thames swimming at Reading was now becoming more sophisticated, for both spectators and participants. Sluice doors allowed water in and out of the pool; 'this arrangement was deemed necessary, as lowering the sluice door it will allow all leaves, etc., floating on the top of the water to run off'. An iron fence was erected around the bath, high enough at the south end to 'prevent the interior from being seen from the Railway', presumably to shield train passengers from the sight of naked bathers.

It may seem amazing now that a riverside town was actively encouraging its inhabitants to swim in the River Thames, providing not only a pool but a springboard, an area for learners and other amenities. But back in the 1890s this was seen as a civic responsibility, to meet the needs of swimmers by creating official bathing spots, and the Thames was the obvious place to do this. Reading, boasted the local press, 'may now congratulate itself on having one of the finest open air swimming baths in the country'.

During the opening ceremony at the King's Meadow pool a 100 yards scratch race was held, when swimmers set off together with the objective of being the first to finish, within a radius of three miles. There were just four competitors, the water was 'very cold' and they were watched by 150 spectators. By spring 1894 the Reading Swimming Club was said to be 'flourishing'. It now had a new clubhouse on 'Moss's Island' – an area of Fry's Island leased by local boat builder and water bailiff Bill Moss – 'for the use of the members' carrying out a life-saving class. The club had seventy-three paying members and twenty honorary members. Henry Creed, club president for many years, told that year's annual meeting that 'he had always felt a keen interest in swimming matters, looking upon natation as an art which the town ought to foster in every possible way'. He was also calling for 'the provision of swimming baths, with qualified instructors in life saving, for ladies'.

When the club held its eleventh costume entertainment in the new baths the following summer 'the weather was delightfully fine and the programme most attractive', but as with other Thames swimming clubs its fortunes were mixed and 'the attendance was decidedly meagre'. There was a Boys' Race, a 100 Yards Championship of Reading, a Plato Diving Competition – 'an exceedingly interesting event' – and a Two Widths' Blindfold Handicap for club members which 'produced much merriment, the swimmers taking nearly every direction but the right one'.

At the club's entertainment in 1897 swimming was 'not so popular as a spectacle it ought to be, and there was no very large crowd at the Corporation Baths', despite an 'excellent programme of events, ranging from grave to gay, and intermingling with the serious sport such items as greasy-pole climbing, blindfold race, etc.'.

At the club's annual dinner in 1897 Mr C.T. Murdoch stressed the 'great importance in a town like Reading, situated, as it was, on the banks of the principal river in the country, that there should be a good swimming club'. 'Hear, hear' came the response. The club was now affiliated with the Amateur Swimming Association (ASA), which meant it was 'one of the first institutions of its kind in the country'. The ASA had been formed in 1886 (although its history is complex and it's often said to have been founded much earlier) and by 1892 it had 404 affiliated clubs.

The Reading club had also established the Albert Palmer Challenge Cup for 'competition amongst boys of the Reading Board Schools' and teachers were urged to 'take the boys down to the baths and get them to practise swimming' because 'it was as necessary that a boy should learn to swim as it was that he should learn to write'. Club members competed outside Reading, winning prizes in Luton, Southampton, Basingstoke, Swindon and London, as well as Life Saving Society's awards and Royal Humane Society medallions.

In 1901 the club was still holding a water polo match and races at the King's Meadow pool in the presence of 'many spectators', but the following year was 'a variable one, successful in some ways and disappointing in others'. While the club had assisted the town's Mayor 'in the carrying out of the aquatic programme at the Coronation festivities, which were a great success', this meant its annual sports day held the next month 'financially and numerically was a fiasco'. However, the winner of the championship of Reading now received a 'new and handsome challenge vase' and the 'minor items were full of fun and amusement, especially the blindfold and bandbox race'. The polo team, meanwhile, had for the first time beaten Oxford University, by two goals to one.

In 1903 the women of Reading finally got their own bathing place, with the opening of a Ladies' Swimming Bath at King's Meadow. Women may have been allowed to swim at Abingdon's bathing place for four days a week in 1881, and one day a week at Oxford's Tumbling Bay in 1893, but in Reading they got a whole pool to themselves, in what appears to be the first women-only bathing spot on the River Thames.

The Ladies' Bath was a brick and tile building surrounding an open-air pool, smaller than the men's at 120 feet by 45 feet, with a depth of 6 feet at the deep end and 3 feet at the shallow, and a filter stopped fish getting into the pool. The press called it 'a handsome structure, replete with every convenience', completed after 'considerable engineering difficulties' and 'second to none in the country'. A women's section of the Reading Swimming Club was founded the following year, and by 1914 there was a separate Ladies' Swimming Club.

Both the men's and women's bathing places at King's Meadow had long opening hours, in the summer from 6 a.m. until 10 p.m., with free swimming on some afternoons. Schoolchildren were offered instruction in swimming and life saving, with an annual gala held at the Ladies' Bath.

The Reading Swimming Club also swam with the Island Bohemian Club, which had begun in 1908, with some overlap in membership. Bill Moss, who had the lease on Fry's Island, with a bowling green, tennis courts and chalets, was a founding member. Each April, swimmers who used the King's Meadow pool tended to 'migrate upstream' to the backwater side of Fry's Island. In 1909 the Reading Swimming Club and the Island Bohemian Club held a gala on the island, with a one-mile open race, comic costume competition, fancy diving, a mop tournament, duck hunt, greasy pole and water polo as well as school races. People were no longer simply racing in the Thames; as in Lechlade it was now a place for some serious entertainment, involving everyone from established athletes to schoolchildren.

A third group of local swimmers were the Winter Bathers, a mix of business people and members of the Reading Swimming Club, who swam year round, including on Christmas Day. The Thames has always been loved by cold-water bathers and the inhabitants of Victorian Reading were no exception. 'We must mention the unique Association of Winter Bathers who daily have their matutinal "dip" in the open river no matter how severe the weather,' reported *The Reading Illustrated* in 1899. 'They number twenty-six, ranging in age from the "Commodor" Mr Samuel Hood, who celebrated his ninety-second birthday last February, and Master Fred Russell aged thirteen!' Hood was said to have 'bathed almost from his earliest youth up to the present time'. Despite regulations against nude swimming, meanwhile, many still bathed naked. One member of the Winter Bathers reportedly went in with his drawers on his head, saying, 'they said we had to wear them, but they didn't say where!'

In 1902, the Winter Bathers had their customary New Year's morning swim and then a celebratory breakfast where toasts were honoured and a telegram sent 'To His Majesty the King, Sandringham, — The winter outdoor bathers of Reading assembled at their annual breakfast wish to you and her Majesty the Queen Happy New Year'. The reply they received read 'Am commanded by the King and Queen to thank you for your kind message of good wishes for the New Year'. In 1908, ten veterans were entered for the Winter Bathers' handicap race, and by 1911 there were two women in the group, including a Miss Cusden who was said to be a keen winter bather.

Then, in 1936, Reading residents were promised a new place to swim on the Thames when the town corporation bought View Island, four acres of land near Caversham Weir. 'It will not be possible to do more this season than make temporary arrangements for bathers,' explained the press, 'but eventually an elaborate lido is to be designed there. Facilities will be provided for bathing and sun-bathing, fishing and tennis. There will also be a tea pavilion.' Lidos were all the rage in the 1930s, with at least 180 being built in Britain between 1930 and 1939. This was part of a government drive to improve the nation's health, but lidos were also places where people could enjoy some leisure time, with sunbathing terraces, cafés and spectator areas. While the one on View Island doesn't seem to have materialised, another one was 'nearing completion on the south side of the river at Scours Lane', with accommodation for sixty-two men and sixty women. There were two other Thames lidos in the area as well, Freebody's lido on the Caversham bank and Cawston's on Piper's Island, both close to Caversham Bridge. The former was known for its high diving board and, alongside it, an iconic silhouette of a figure diving which featured in government propaganda after the Second World War to show Britain was 'back to its old self again'.

During the 1940s the King's Meadow pools were still used for school swimming lessons, just as children were taught at Tumbling Bay in Oxford. Local historian Gillian Clark, who was born in Caversham and grew up in a boat-building family in Reading, remembers, 'I was taken to the women's pool when I was at junior school, terrifying it was. It had thick green water, you couldn't see the bottom, and the tiles were slippery with algae. I can feel the terror now. I certainly didn't learn to swim there! There was a woman called Miss Francis with a long pole with a loop on it and she put the loop around you and walked around the bath and you'd be dragged along. Every one of my generation in Reading remembers Miss Francis. I suppose the school had a duty to teach us, as we were a riverside town. All the local children were marched down there in the late 1940s, it was run down even then, with wooden cubicles and no showers, but it was the only pool I knew. The King's Meadow bathing place was the council pool and we were at council

THE CHIEF CONSTABLE of Reading (Mr. J. Lawrence) presenting the cup
Barrett, winner for half-mile swim.

River racing in Reading continued into the 1970s, with the local police holding a one-mile race in July. Here PC Barrett receives the winner's cup from Chief Constable Jesse Lawrence.

schools.' Gillian's husband Tim, who had learned to swim 'in a clean sea-water pool in the West Country', got a shock when he had his first school lesson in Reading in 1948 at the King's Meadow men's pool: 'the water was cold, green and dirty, the surfaces slimy, the surroundings falling to pieces.'

Gillian, meanwhile, wasn't allowed to take a boat out on her own until she could swim across the river to Fry's Island and back, so her uncle taught her in the Thames when she was around eleven. 'We went in from our own landing stage outside what had once been Bill Moss's boathouse and continued to swim from there every summer. For others who wanted to swim it was about finding a place where there was a beach on public land and you could get in and out. Depth was the big issue; one step and you could be out of your depth, but we knew our own strip.'

But in the mid-1950s she stopped swimming in the Thames because 'it was seen as something not to do, and you had the alternative of a clean warm indoor pool. And one day I saw a steamer emptying its chemical toilet into the Thames and after that, never again!' Yet although river swimming fell out of fashion among the general public in Reading, clubs continued to hold races on the Thames, with organised competitions right through to the 1970s.

In the mid-1950s Tim Clark, who belonged to the Reading and Caversham Boys' Club, took part in an inter-club mile swim. The boys were 'taken up to what we call Fishery Islands, where you still see people swimming today,' explains Gillian, 'and then told to swim to Caversham Bridge. He was about fifteen. He was just told, "off you go". There was no big turnout of safety boats, just a "get in and swim". A mile is quite a long way if you're in the middle of the river and panic, but it was no big deal; it was what you did then.'

Today what swimming club would take teenagers into the Thames, let alone tell them to swim a mile without a major risk assessment, as well as public liability insurance, wetsuit requirements and accompanying kayaks and boats? On the other hand, Tim's 1950s race must have been regarded as enough of an occasion for him to be presented with a silver medallion, which he still has today, and to have his photograph in the local paper.

Organised river racing in Reading continued into the 1970s, with the local police holding a one-mile race in July, 'long after most people had deserted the river for the heated pools,' says Gillian, 'as they would have had to know how to jump in and rescue someone in trouble'.

John Humphries, a member of the Outdoor Swimming Society, remembers 'hundreds of people used to swim in the Thames at Reading in the 1970s during the annual music festival'. But others stopped swimming because of increasing numbers of swans, believed to carry avian TB, as well as the risk of larger boats, and illegal sewage discharge.

However, local people still used the various lidos into the early 1970s. At Scours Lane, situated in a sandy bay where the river was relatively narrow and cordoned off with pieces of wood chained together, there was a diving board, a safe area for children, changing rooms, lawns for sunbathing and picnicking, and Alf's Café for drinks and sandwiches. It closed around 1974, as did Freebody's and Cawston's, meeting the same sorry fate of many of the country's lidos.

Some twenty years earlier the King's Meadow men's pool had also closed, having been filled in and turned into a builders' yard. In the mid-1970s this in turn was demolished and replaced with housing. When in 1974 the women's pool was closed in order for new filtration units to be installed, it was never reopened. It was then leased to a sub-aqua diving club but after the lease expired it fell into disrepair. Yet in recent years campaigners have fought a determined battle to save the women's pool, said to be the oldest surviving outdoor municipal pool of its kind from the early Edwardian era. In 2003 there were plans to turn the site into a hotel, but then the ironwork supporting its partial roof gained Grade II listed status. Campaigners successfully blocked further development plans, clearing rubbish from the pool and holding open days. At the end of 2013 it seemed that Clifton Lido Ltd from Bristol would get the go-ahead to restore the site, with a year-round open-air pool, spa, restaurant and bar. But critics were concerned that the admission price would be too high, and urged the council to bid for Lottery funding, along with the King's Meadow Campaign, to keep the baths under public ownership. 'I will always feel sad that Reading Borough Council were so mercenary and heartless over it being a future community and youth engagement project,' says campaigner Bob O'Neill. 'They will end up with a private diners' club – fine while there are enough rich people to use it but when they move on, the pool as it has been proposed, will not be OK to cater for the needs of the "proletariat" in great numbers.' The campaign has drawn a lot of support on the lost lidos website, with many saying the pool brought back happy memories. 'I swam here as a small girl and would very much like to bring my grandchildren who live in Reading to swim here,' wrote one woman, while another commented, 'On the River Thames our Heritage [sic]! Beautiful river. We need to keep more Community Baths!'

To those like Bob O'Neill the crucial thing is to preserve this heritage – in the shape of the actual building, but also to connect us to the way we used the Thames in the past, in a town that once had pools and lidos, galas and clubs, where a group of winter bathers could send a telegram to the King and fully expect a reply and where the authorities went to great lengths to provide safe, clean areas in which to swim.

When Gillian sends me photos of the old King's Meadow women's pool today I'm taken aback by the way it's both beautiful

Campaigners have fought a determined battle to save King's Meadow women's pool, pictured today. It opened in 1903 and appears to have been the first women-only bathing spot on the Thames.

and decrepit. By the side of the bath are green pillars topped with ornate wrought-iron leaves, but although it's clearly being cared for the steps lead down into stagnant looking water where two ducks swim next to a cardboard box. The wooden changing rooms are missing doors; there are rubbish bins on the side and weeds around the edge. Yet there is something about the scene that makes me think of a stage set, as if it's just crying out to be revived, longing to be filled once more with novice schoolgirls learning to swim and the sound of women's laughter, this first ever pool that we were given on the River Thames in 1903.

5

5

Shiplake and Wargrave

'There is probably more than one Otter who harbours the idea
of returning to the tideway for a repeat of the great races of
Victorian and Edwardian times'

Otter Swimming Club, 1990

In the summer of 1888, some six miles downstream from Reading
at Shiplake, the Otter Swimming Club held its first annual
'Up-River race' on the Thames. This was a quarter-mile course with
eighteen entrants, and for many years the village would remain
central to the club's illustrious history.

Otter ranks among the earliest of British swimming clubs,
formed in London in 1869 with a spirit that was 'quite intangible
and indefinable', according to former president Dr Carmichael A.
Young, with 'fellowship and camaraderie' cementing the members
together. It's not the oldest club – the London Swimming Club was
formed in 1859 and the Brighton Swimming Club in 1860, while
the Serpentine Swimming Club started in 1864, based on the
Serpentine in London's Hyde Park with water originally pumped
from the Thames. But it is Otter SC that is one of the few survivors
of the dozens of clubs that once raced in the Thames, and still
swims there today.

I'm meeting current president James Stewart at the Lansdowne
Club in west London, an 'exclusive and traditional' private members'
club, with a very specific dress code. 'Ladies' dress' should be of 'a

A busy Edwardian scene at Shiplake Lock, near where the Otter Swimming Club
held its first annual 'Up-River race' in the summer of 1888.

conventional nature' – smart trouser suit, jacket, skirt or dress, and
definitely no leggings – and only when the ambient air temperature
exceeds 24 degrees C are gentlemen allowed to remove their jackets,
and even then they are not to be draped on chair backs.

The entrance to the club is so discreet that I don't even see
the name plaque until I'm right at the front door. Thankfully I'm
allowed in and I join James in the bar area, where adjacent seating
overlooks the club's swimming pool. He is an immaculately
dressed, broad-shouldered man in his early seventies and the
second longest serving honorary secretary in the club's history.
While early documentation is thin on the ground, he believes the
club was formed by members of Oxford and Cambridge university
swimming clubs and the Otters incorporated their colours, the
dark blue of Oxford and the light blue of Cambridge. The club's
first treasurer was William Terriss, a Victorian actor famous for
his appearances on the London stage, who also served as president
from 1870 to 1871. In 1897 he was murdered on the steps of the
Adelphi Theatre, where he was performing, by an out-of-work

actor who'd accused Terriss of 'persecuting' him; he was found guilty but insane. Today Terriss' ghost is said to haunt Covent Garden Tube station where a figure in a grey suit – some say an opera cloak – has been seen by more than one ticket inspector over the years.

Otters were founder members of the Amateur Swimming Association (ASA), having resigned from its predecessor, the Swimming Association of Great Britain, 'because they were admitting professionals and we were an amateur club,' explains James. This came after years of bitter argument, for the distinction between professionals and amateurs was an important issue in the late Victorian period, when only 'gentlemen' could afford to compete for honour rather than money.

Until 1869 there had been little distinction between amateur and professional swimmers, there were few baths and race meetings were of a 'rough and ready character'. Then the Associated Metropolitan Swimming Clubs was formed, and their rules defined a professional as anyone who competed for money prizes, wagers or admission money, or who 'made the art of swimming a means of pecuniary profit'. But an amateur could still compete against a professional for 'honour or for money' if they handed the prize over to the association. The group then changed its title, first to the London Swimming Association and then to the Metropolitan Swimming Association. But aside from lack of funds, the main problem was 'the frequent and apparently interminable discussions' as to what defined a professional swimmer. Volume nineteen of *The Badminton Library of Sports and Pastimes*, an edition devoted to swimming and published in 1893, has an entire chapter on the Government of Swimming and the history of the amateur movement. Its authors were William Henry (at one point vice-chair of the Reading Swimming Club) and Archibald Sinclair, who, along with Henry, was one of the founders of the Swimmers' Life Saving Society.

The Metropolitan Swimming Association decided an amateur could race against a professional for a 'prize or honour only', and in 1874 the group became the Swimming Association of Great Britain. But the bickering continued and 'wordy warfares' meant the 'better-class clubs held aloof from the association'. The professionals formed their own group, but this soon collapsed. By 1884 the Otter Swimming Club had had enough and resigned 'in consequence of a dispute on the vexed question of amateurism and professionalism'. Eight or nine other clubs immediately followed suit and formed the Amateur Swimming Union. There then followed a 'desperate struggle for supremacy' between the two, but eventually they formed a new organisation together and in 1886 the ASA was founded with a new code for the future government of swimming, with no fewer than 135 rules. It was now accepted that an amateur could not swim against a professional and the authors of *The Badminton Library* volume were happy to record that 'the tone of the sport has vastly improved'.

The amateur movement would come to control the sport, as in the United States, the ASA set the rules when it came to competing and those who swam for money were seen as less 'sportsmanlike'. But there was certainly money to be made. James Tyers, for example, a champion swimmer who won numerous ASA championships and turned professional in 1898, travelled the country netting 'a nice little sum' in prize money. The leading amateurs of the time tended to have 'no regular business' before joining the ranks of the professionals, noted *Pearson's Athletic Record*. When Tyers wasn't swimming he looked after a billiard room in a Manchester hostel, while Thames champion John Arthur Jarvis was a painter and paper-hanger.

When it came to the Otters, 'Our early members were upper middle class and mostly university graduates,' explains James, 'but one of the early presidents was a baths' superintendent. We're an eclectic club, for anyone who wants to swim.' The reason they held their first Thames race at Shiplake was probably because a member had a houseboat there, the *Dabchick*, a handsome two-storey vessel on which members posed for photographs in the early 1900s.

Racing was important in the early days of the club and for thirty-seven years the office of captain was decided by a 1,000-yard race at the Welsh Harp, a reservoir in Hendon, opened in 1835, and then, after 1886, a one-mile at Surbiton which continued until 1905. The Otter summer programme has always included an open-air quarter-, half- and one-mile race. The quarter was originally held at Shiplake; in 1888 it ran from a houseboat called the *Otter*, while in 1893 the course was from Shiplake Ferry to the *Dabchick*, a tradition that remained for the next forty-three years. The quarter-mile later moved to the Henley Sailing Club and then to various other Thames spots such as Hampton Court.

The half-mile was first held between the piers in Brighton, but from 1894 to 1898 it was swum at Shiplake as well and the winner received a gold cup, the most valuable of the club's trophies. In 1921 the half-mile was held at Walton-on-Thames and then, since 1969, at Henley Sailing Club.

The one-mile open-water trophy started in 1898 (presumably on the Thames, although it's not known where) and apart from during the First and Second World Wars it has generally been held every year up to the present day. One member went on to win gold in the 100 yards freestyle at the World Championships in 1906, while several have represented Great Britain at the Olympics even into the 1960s. In recent years the mile has usually been held at Windsor, although when the Thames proved too 'insanitary' it was held at Eton College's open-air pool.

James Stewart joined the club in 1962 after leaving school. 'I was brought up in Bombay and I swam competitively from the age of five. I was taught to swim at a Europeans-only club. A woman trained us up and told me, "you're good enough to get to the Olympics one day", although I didn't.' In 1951 he returned to the

Members of the Otter Swimming Club pose for a photo on the *Dabchick* in 1905.
The club was founded in 1869 and still holds races in the Thames today.

UK and took part in public schools relays in London run by Otter, who also ran the varsity match. 'I arranged for Otter to come and swim against us at the school and later my mother wrote to ask if I could become a member. So it's all thanks to Mum!'

His first swim in the Thames came the year he joined, when he did the mile at Windsor and the half-mile at Henley. 'I was worried most about my eyes and getting them infected. But the biggest difference between a river and a pool is that in a pool you can see the bottom and you can swim in a line. In the Thames I always do ten pairs of strokes, then I look up.' James was fast: in 1967 he was a member of the club's 4x110 yards freestyle relay team which won the ASA title. The following year he was the seventh fastest Englishman over 110 yards at the ASA championships, while he won the annual mile in 1967, 1968 and 1970.

In the mid-sixties the club stopped swimming in the Thames – 'the water was said to be a risk to health' – but returned to the river a few years later; 'we got a grant of £500 a year from Thames Water Board, we wanted to go back to the Thames and they wanted us to, to show it was cleaner'.

But while Otters were once the top men's club and national champions, in the 1970s they went into decline, coinciding with a general view that river racing was dangerous. In the 1990s, when the club celebrated 125 years, the future seemed uncertain. 'The nightmare scenario is one of stagnant waters, polluted seas and public baths in the form of kidney-shaped leisure centres,' noted the club's anniversary booklet. It bemoaned the closure of lidos and a 'woeful shortage of space for club swimming in central London . . . To be sure, we exercise caution in using the river, but there is probably more than one Otter who harbours the idea of returning to the tideway for a repeat of the great races of Victorian and Edwardian times.'

In part that has come to pass. Today the club has 375 members, 260 of whom are swimmers, and, as in the past, many are university graduates. And why do they still choose to swim in the Thames? 'Early swimmers started in open water,' explains James; 'it only really became a sport when there were indoor pools and lidos and people could race. Competitive swimming now is over timed distances, you need clear water and an appropriate temperature. Competitive swimmers never get out of a warm pool. But we're very traditional, we've never lost the Thames.' As for whether they wear wetsuits, 'No,' he says firmly, 'they are not allowed. No aids are permitted, as in Channel swims. I trained in a wetsuit for a triathlon a few years ago and gained twenty seconds each two hundred metres.'

Otter still runs its three annual swims, usually in the Thames. In 2012, twenty-four swimmers took part in the mile at Windsor, but the half-mile in Henley was only confirmed the morning of the race because of heavy rain, fast currents and 'excess debris' in the river. Around thirty to forty people enter each Thames race: 'it's a social affair with a dinner afterwards, a lot are London-based, and we have a coach that takes them to the race.' James has never known anyone to get ill, 'except once in the half-mile a man, a good swimmer, died of a heart attack. You're more likely to get sick if the river is low and there is stale water, there are no problems after heavy rain, and it will be a quicker race! We're competent swimmers, there is no reason for anyone to get hurt.' But there are more regulations now 'since Health & Safety reared its head'. In the 1960s, as with river races in Reading, competitors 'just dived off and swam, we were counted as we set off and the number checked when we got back. Today we get permission from the EA on condition we have boatmen, and river traffic is warned about the race.'

In recent years the club has regained some of its former glory: 'water polo has kept us going, and now we're one of the dominant Masters clubs in the country [essentially swimming for adults, as defined by G.B. Masters]. You still see the Otter name all over the place, even me – Charles James Stewart.' He's just returned from an ASA event where he competed as a member of the '280 squad', comprising four men with an average age of seventy.

Another major change is that the club is open to women. Their continuing exclusion 'reflected our Victorian antecedents,' says James, 'and led to some ridiculous situations'. At its annual dinner the club couldn't invite women guests and there was a crisis when the ASA elected a woman as president and 'we couldn't invite her!' Finally, in 1976, 107 years after the club was founded, women were allowed to join and the following year Dawn Eva won the one-mile at Windsor. James hands me a sheet showing the list of winners; everyone has initials only, except for Dawn because 'she wanted her full name, to show she was a lady'. I stare at the list, thinking how proud she must have been, and whether – intentionally or not – women were excluded from the Otter Swimming Club for over a century because the men were afraid of being beaten.

We leave the bar, walk to the seating area and look down on the Lansdowne Club's pool where three men are swimming leisurely. James points to the clock at the far end. 'There was a diving board there back in the 1950s when I joined the club, although it wasn't really deep enough to dive. There used to be a chute, too; things have certainly changed.' He believes the Otter Swimming Club has been strengthened by the growth of multi-sports events and many members compete in open-water events and triathlons, among them internationally known athletes such as Rachel Joyce. Susie Rodgers won three bronze medals for Britain's Paralympics swimming team in 2012, while the club's women's water polo team is ranked second in the British Water Polo League – and it all started at Shiplake on the Thames.

Others have loved swimming in this stretch of the river, too, like actress Margaret Rutherford who enjoyed bracing dips in the mid-1950s. It was at Shiplake that she taught a friend's grandson to swim – a young boy called Antony Worrall Thompson, now a well-known chef. 'She was a bit of an outdoor swimmer,' explains her biographer, Andy Merriman, 'she once told a friend, "I need some freedom" and then they went swimming. It lifted her sadness. If ever she saw water she threw herself in. Wherever she went, she was always swimming.'

A little way downstream, on the opposite side of the Thames, is Wargrave, which has a regatta that can be traced back to Victorian times, although it wasn't until the 1920s that swimming races were added. Demelza Blick grew up in Wargrave and took part in the regatta as a child: 'in between I would splash and swim. It has become too big an event now, but I felt a strange pull to the river and so I found other ways for me to swim. There are stretches further up that feel like my childhood river.' Her father retired when she was eight and in the late 1980s, during long hot summers, they went out together on the river where she remembers lots of freshwater mussels. As a child Demelza was sent for history lessons at people's houses where 'old river people would tell me which patches were stony, which patches were muddy, it was part of growing up. I get homesick now if I smell freshwater.' She says swimming in the Thames is very common around Wargrave and people don't bat an eyelid. 'There are river families who have been here for many generations. Gardens lead on to the Thames, and kids swim there after school. I haven't seen the river changing. The village has changed, with rich stockbrokers and retired film stars, but the people on the river haven't changed. Pubs have been renovated and turned gastro. Sunday drivers come and sit and look at the river, they are not engaging with it and old people and old families think it's a tragedy.' She tends to swim from April to October. 'I can't afford to fork out for a wetsuit, and otherwise the river can be very fast and cold.' She does, however, wear flippers, which means she can have two speeds and if a pleasure cruise appears she can get out of the way quickly.

Demelza wouldn't swim in central London: 'it's too dangerous and there are all the currents. I used to work on boats at Tower Pier and staff fell in and nearly drowned.' But she'll always continue swimming at Wargrave. 'People say, "oh, you're doing wild swimming, that's very trendy". That's odd to me, I'm not wild swimming, I'm just swimming.' Demelza is doing what people have always done: engaged with the Thames as swimmers. For her it is an obvious thing to do, to take to the waters on her doorstep, and so much a part of growing up that her education meant learning about the river from village elders. Similarly, James Stewart has been racing in the Thames on and off for over half a century, following in the footsteps of those eighteen men who, in the summer of 1888, plunged into the water from a houseboat at Shiplake. In many respects, the way we use the upper river in Oxfordshire hasn't changed at all.

6

Henley-on-Thames

'O, COME down to Henley, for London is horrid'

J. Ashby-Sterry, 'Henley in July', 1886

It's a sunny morning in early spring and the smooth, wide waters of Henley-on-Thames, three miles north of Shiplake, are empty but for a group of rowers just pulling off near the town's famous five-arched bridge. Henley Reach, north of the bridge, is the longest naturally straight stretch of the Thames (although it has been artificially extended) and at almost a mile long it's perfect for all sorts of races.

At the water's edge families feed ducks, a sign advertises twelve-seater 'Edwardian style chauffeured launches' for hire, and a weather-beaten boat called the *Aquaholic* is up for sale for £2,000. The water looks quite inviting in the sun; I could easily just step in, and at first it's hard to believe how packed this river used to be back in its Victorian heyday. But then comes a sound like wooden wings flapping, a loud shout of 'OK, guys!' and five men row past, followed by the roars from those on another boat, and then another.

I head along the river towards Mill Meadows where large boats rest at a line of piers offering one-hour boat trips; among them is Hobbs of Henley, established in 1870. The trips are year-round, but the piers are deserted today. As I walk on towards Rod Ait, with the headquarters of Henley Rowing Club on the opposite bank,

I see boats of all shapes and sizes, a clear indication of the town's glorious boating tradition.

Henley dates back to medieval settlements of 1179, and its riverside position meant that trade developed rapidly, with glass and malt manufacturers in the seventeenth and eighteenth centuries and a port supplying London with timber and grain. In the 1880s, with easy access by railway, Henley became a holiday destination where wealthy city folk moored their weekend houseboats. The town was only an hour's journey from Paddington and in the summer there were daily trips to Henley by train for a guinea. But it was the royal regatta, 'the most important gathering of amateur oarsmen in England', according to *Dickens's Dictionary of the Thames*, that made the town famous and the event ranked with Ascot as 'among the favourite fashionable meetings of the season'. The regatta started in 1839 – considerably later than the first formal Thames regatta held in London in 1775 – and received royal patronage in 1851, running from Regatta Island to Henley Bridge. Soon everyone it seemed wanted to come to Henley so that eventually the river was 'so inconveniently crowded with steam launches, house boats, skiffs, gigs, punts, dinghys, canoes and every other conceivable and inconceivable variety of craft, that the racing boats have sometimes the greatest difficulty in threading a way through the crowd'. The regatta was heavily dependent on the weather, however, and in 1869 the *Illustrated London News* reported that the two days' aquatic amusements were 'rather dull' and 'No steam-boats were this year allowed on the river'. The steam launches were no laughing matter to some visitors, among them the narrator of *Three Men in a Boat*: 'I hate steam-launches; I suppose every rowing man does. I never see a steam-launch but I feel I should like to lure it to a lonely part of the river, and there, in the silence and the solitude, strangle it.'

After the Second World War Henley was still a place of play and pleasure. John Betjeman's 1948 poem 'Henley-on-Thames' is a mournful work, yet as the speaker stands 'house-boat high' surveying the upper Thames there are still dives and shouts, boats for hire, the sounds of 'cheerioh' and 'cheeri-bye'.

Today the introduction to the town's website resembles Victorian descriptions of the place: 'Henley-on-Thames is a pretty riverside market town on one of the most beautiful stretches of the River Thames . . . making it ideal for a day trip or for a long weekend away from the madding crowd.' Travellers from London still leave from Paddington, and with only a handful of direct evening trains the journey means a change at Twyford, so it still takes around an hour.

Such is Henley's renown for rowing that it has its own museum, one of only two devoted to the River Thames. It's also home to the Thiess International River Prize, administered by the International River Foundation, and awarded to the Thames in 2010 as one of the most improved rivers in the world. The River and Rowing Museum is a large, bright riverside building with famous boats, tales of sporting prowess, sections on wildlife and weapons offered to the sacred river in ancient times. But a 1930 photograph of a family in smart Jantzen bathing costumes is the only sign of any swimming on the main floor. While the museum holds around 20,000 objects, there are just a handful of photos and artefacts related to bathing. 'Swimming is a bit of a side mention, our focus is rowing,' explains assistant curator Lindsay Moreton; 'perhaps swimming history has been buried because Henley is famous as a rowing town.' She takes me to the Thomas Keller Library, a small, sunlit room on the second floor where the shelves are lined with Thames books, many of which are hundreds of years old. But even among these, Lindsay warns, there is little to be found on swimming. The first book in my pile is *Walker's Manly Exercises*, published in 1847, in which swimming is described as a beneficial exercise for muscular weakness, with the added benefit of 'tranquillizing' the nervous system. Like other books and pamphlets of the time a good deal of space is taken up with the correct actions of the hands and feet, and the author bemoans the fact that when Athenians wanted to 'designate a man as fit for nothing' they would say 'he cannot even swim' or 'he can neither read nor swim'.

The best time to bathe is between May and August, before breakfast, and, as with Steedman's manual, evening swims were frowned upon – 'the hair is not perfectly dried, and coryza [a head cold] is sometimes the consequence'. Swimmers also risked catching a cold if they bathed while it was raining, and were advised not to swim 'before digestion is finished'. As for clothes, bathers 'should use short drawers', but it was also of 'great importance to be able to swim in jacket and trousers'. No mention is made of what women should wear, because in 1847 they were not expected to be able to swim. When it came to recording swimming feats, *Walker's Manly Exercises* found very little of note. Men had been 'known to swim in their clothes a distance of 4000 feet' (around three-quarters of a mile), while 'others have performed 2200 feet in 29-minutes'. It concludes that 'this art . . . has made little if any progress from the earliest records that we possess of it'.

Next in the pile is *The Encyclopaedia of Sport*, volume II, 1898, which provides an explanation of the strokes alongside photographs. I'm beginning to think there is little here related to Henley, when I lift another book to find a copy of an old sepia postcard of the Henley Baths. They were established on the Thames in the early 1870s next to Wargrave Road, on an area of land known as Solomon's Hatch. Like the King's Meadow pool at Reading which existed some thirty-six years earlier, the Baths were 'open to the public' (in other words men), from 6 a.m. to 8 p.m., although in Henley there were two hours set aside for 'ladies'.

The Oarsman's and Angler's Map cited 'good bathing at all hours at Solomon's Hatch' as did George Leslie in his 1881 book *Our River*. But as to its name, 'I never could find out who the particular Solomon was that the place is named after, and I know of no hatches or little sluices about here, but the bathing-place is a capital institution for Henley; the water is clear and the bottom sandy. Between the hours of 11 and 1 in the morning it is reserved for ladies only, and I am glad to say a good many avail themselves of this opportunity of learning the art of swimming; the bathing-place is in a backwater, separated from the main stream by a long eyot, and I believe during the ladies' hours quite safe from intrusion.' Intrusion was an important concern when it came to women swimming outdoors: 'there are not many lady swimmers who bathe in open fresh water,' explained author Archibald Sinclair in 1893, 'privacy being somewhat difficult to obtain.' The Henley Baths consisted of two large blocks of changing rooms between Hobbs Boathouse and Rod Ait, the island in the Thames opposite the Baths.

There was a diving board, deckchairs and a series of steps into the water. The postcard dates from around 1910 and it shows swimmers sitting on a boom; the pool appears to be segregated, with women in one area and men in another. The river is busy with people splashing and the water looks relatively shallow; some bathers appear to be standing up, while in the foreground a man is doing front crawl right next to a punt. In the early days the Henley Swimming Club, formed in 1894 'to encourage the most necessary accomplishment for all who love boating and fishing', swam and competed at the Baths. Their first president was Mr R. Ovey, who lent his name to the Ovey Challenge Cup, a monthly 100 yards race starting at 7 p.m.

Some twenty years after the Baths were built a new weekly magazine, *Lock-to-Lock Times: The Journal of the Thames*, was launched. It included profiles and sporting news, a regular 'Fashion on the river' section – the text fully illustrated and often covering an entire page – and advice on 'house-boat etiquette'. I pick up its very first edition, dated 9 June 1888, which has an 'In the Swim' section, though this was later dropped. It includes a report on Madame Darnley Mitchell, 'accomplished swimming mistress of

Kingston baths' who on 14 June 'took her first swim in the river this year', all the way from Ravens Ait in Kingston upon Thames to the Henley Baths. The distance itself is impressive (Kingston to Henley is twenty-seven miles as the crow flies), but Madame Mitchell also performed tricks on the way, eating and drinking underwater, sinking to the bottom and passing through a hoop. Despite the continuing need for privacy for 'ladies' bathing outdoors, by now several women were earning a living as swimmers, demonstrating their skills in indoor pools, diving from seaside piers, immersed in music hall tanks, and in the Thames. While I can't find any other reference to Madame Mitchell, if she had swum any distance over twenty miles she would have set a new world record for women.

Next in my pile of books is *The Field, the Country Gentleman's Newspaper*, which has swimming reports tucked away amid articles on polo, shooting and golf, the habits of tigers, and a performance of chess with living pieces.

While swimming races were mainly held in indoor baths, in 1891 the Ilex Swimming Club's annual handicap was '150 yards straight

The Henley Swimming Baths were established in the early 1870s on an area of land known as Solomon's Hatch where there was 'good bathing at all hours'. This postcard dates from around 1910.

away from opposite Solomon's Hatch bathing place' and twenty-one people took part. Ilex was founded in 1861, with members from amateur rowing, yachting, canoe, cruising, athletic and football clubs. Its headquarters were at the Lambeth Baths in London and the position of club captain was annually swum for in the Thames.

Some thirty years later and Solomon's Hatch was still well used, this time by the boys of Henley Royal Grammar School. The school magazine, *The Periam*, reports 'a good entry of 9 for the long swim' in the summer of 1921, although there was 'no current and plenty of weed'. The course was across from the Baths to Hobbs lower boathouse, and, aside from the long swim, there was also an Old Boys' Cup, a Phyllis Cup and a House Competition. But senior boys had proved themselves 'not very keen', and the school authorities strongly urged that all boys should master the 'science' of swimming.

The following year seven boys took part in the long swim; it was 'accomplished in good time' and for the third year in a row everybody who entered 'passed the test'. In 1923 the Old Boys' Cup was difficult as 'weeds on the course were rather bad', but nine boys took part in the 'long test' on 23 July which is now described as being from the Baths to New Street – further downstream past Henley Bridge. Eight finished the course; it's not recorded what happened to the ninth.

Bad weather the next year meant there were very few senior boys 'who would pluck up the courage to go down to the Baths', as well as 'very few competitors for the Old Boys' Cup'. Only five took part in the long swim, suggesting the tradition was already beginning to die out. It's not clear when people stopped using the Baths; like the King's Meadow pools at Reading they appear to have lasted into the 1950s and by the 1980s were derelict.

It is this loss of a swimming heritage that, until recent years, has been the story of the Thames in Henley, both the closure of Solomon's Hatch and awareness of the Victorian club that once raced here.

Lindsay takes me on to the museum's indoor walkway and points through large windows to the island of Rod Ait, now with houses on it. Behind the Ait is where the Baths used to be, only now it's the home of the Henley Rowing Club. 'Swimming was replaced by rowing,' Lindsay says, 'that's how it is in Henley.' And unlike swimming, rowing has an almost unbroken tradition: 'the regatta has never been missed except during war. Perhaps we lost our swimming history because of Health & Safety? Swimming died out, but now it's coming back and soon we're hosting a small exhibition on the Henley swims.' Inside the Henley Gallery is the original wrought-iron entranceway to the Henley Baths, a selection of swimming postcards and two impressive Victorian silver challenge cups. It's here that I'm meeting Tom Kean, who, along with Jeremy Laming, is the founder of the modern Henley swims. A lean man wearing a Henley Swim t-shirt, with cropped hair and a pair of sunglasses on his forehead, he's crouching in front of the cabinet, admiring the cups. 'We've adopted them,' he explains, 'they're beautiful, solid silver and we asked the museum if we could

THE SWIMMING POOL, HENLEY-ON-THAMES.   H.2429.

A more modern scene at 'Henley's Thames swimming pool', which appears to have lasted into the 1950s.

name our races after them because we wanted to create a culture of swimming in the Thames again. We thought, blimey, Henley used to have a swimming club, they had boomed off areas to swim in, they had competitions and trophies, and we're resurrecting that. People have never stopped swimming in the Thames, but now we're doing it properly again.'

Tom believes river swimming went out of fashion because 'we live in centrally heated homes and we've been indoctrinated with Health & Safety. Cold-water swimming is a habit that we've lost. There were hundreds of swimming clubs in the past, now there are virtually none.' But thanks to Tom and Jeremy this has now changed and a pre-dawn swim taken for fun some ten years ago has led to the birth of three major annual swims – the Henley Classic, the Henley Mile and the Bridge to Bridge – and the formation of the Henley Open Water Swimming Club.

As a young man Tom took up rowing like his father, but after suffering a back injury he had to give it up. By now he was familiar with the Henley regatta course, which he had rowed a dozen times, and along with Jeremy belonged to the Marlow Rowing Club. Then in 2004 Jeremy had an idea. 'He wanted to get into triathlons', explains Tom, 'and he knew I used to swim, so one day he said, "do you fancy an open-water swim?" I'd never done it, so we both got wetsuits because I don't like the cold.' The two men decided to swim the regatta course, wanting to 'get the unique perspective you get on a dead straight course, framed by booms'.

'As oarsmen we knew what rowers are likely to do. I've never rowed before 6 a.m. so we knew to swim before this time would be low-risk, and we wanted to do the regatta course as it was all set out. Friday afternoon are the qualifiers, the next four days are training, and then the regatta begins on a Wednesday. So we knew 4.30 a.m. at first light on the Sunday would be relatively safe', and they persuaded a friend to accompany them in a canoe. 'It was pitch black. I thought, what the hell are we doing? We thought we were being so daring, and we thought that when we got out at the secure area where the boats are we'd be arrested. But the guards just looked at us and gave us a nod and a "morning".'

It took the pair about an hour to swim the course. 'We were faffing around, and stopping to chat with a fisherman', and while their swim was covert to begin with, 'early morning seems to appeal to people, it caught people's imagination'. In the second year around twenty other swimmers, mainly friends, joined them, and the year after that it had risen to fifty. In 2008, with so many people taking part, they decided to formalise the event and to charge an entrance fee. Tom runs his own financial advice business, while Jeremy owns a business simulation company: 'we both have fairly boring jobs, with the swim we're building something we're proud of.' While it may have been 'an accidental process', the Henley Swim is now a proper events company, while the swimming club has around thirty to forty members. As for getting permission to hold the swims, 'for the first couple of years of the Classic we didn't seek permission from the EA but we certainly do now', while 'the regatta people are charming and helpful, they grudgingly accept our existence'.

At first they tried to ensure that swimmers wore wetsuits, of which Tom is a big fan. 'There is a snobbish anti-wetsuit attitude, but it means you can swim in comfort, and you're quicker and more buoyant.' If entrants wear wetsuits then fewer safety canoes are needed, and even insurance is cheaper.

'When it dawns on the masses how good wetsuits are people will want to do it, it's a lovely bit of kit,' says Tom, who believes the resurgence in open-water swimming is thanks to wetsuits: 'if you wear one then if you get into trouble you will float.' But many swimmers were horrified at the idea. 'We tried making wetsuits compulsory but the venom and the vitriol! The "skins" wrote saying how pissed off they were; they said, "it's ridiculous, we pay good money . . ." We got lots of emails.' So now wetsuits are optional, unless the water is below 14 degrees.

Henley today hosts a series of annual river races, thanks to ex-rowers Tom Kean and Jeremy Laming whose pre-dawn dip in 2004 led to the formation of an open-water events company.

The Classic is a 2.1-kilometre endurance upstream swim, held over the regatta course, and competitors have included multiple winner Greg Whyte, four times Iron Man legend Chrissie Wellington and Olympian Toby Garbett. The Henley Mile is an upstream swim, and more of a family day with children's events, while the Bridge to Bridge is fourteen kilometres from Henley-on-Thames to Marlow. The Bridge to Bridge is now becoming as popular as the Classic; in 2012, 176 competitors took part, with finishing times ranging from two hours fifty minutes to just over six hours, but it's 'more about the personal challenge and team spirit, rather than a race'. Swimmers are organised into groups of approximately twenty, based on the speed with which they reach the first lock at Hambledon. The swims have various categories – elite, performance (men and women), then open men and then women. To begin with the elite was split into men and women, but the faster women were catching the slower men and weren't getting a good race, 'so we changed it, each year we're learning something'. People declare their time beforehand, in order to get into the right category, but men often overestimate their time, while women tend to underestimate theirs.

While some are put off by weeds and mud – and the sensation of weeds underfoot can cause panic – it's the possibility of drowning that is the real fear for the organisers. 'What we expect is that someone will drown,' says Tom, 'what is likely is hypothermia. What may happen is a heart attack.' They have already had people with hypothermia. 'The Bridge to Bridge swim can be quite long and we had to nearly haul one woman out, and have the medics ready. You can get hypothermia even in warm water because the body is losing heat.' One year a woman got knocked on the head during a scrum at the start. 'She said she didn't see the starting line, although it had a laser light on it, and she found herself at the front end of a wave of people. Someone swam on top of her, clouted her on the head and she went under and swallowed water. She came to the side and started throwing up. She was very close to being drowned. She recovered and said she was fine to carry on but the safety guys said no. She later collapsed in the shower with concussion, and was grateful we'd stopped her. Usually people drown because they're doing something silly, then they panic and when you panic you're done for. Panic is like temper, you have no control.'

But as for currents and streams, Tom says they are minimal; 'there are myths and misunderstandings but if you're not drunk and showing off then it's fine. If you're a sober and sensible swimmer then it's not true about the currents, but if you're cold and drunk . . .' He has written to the press to challenge assertions from the PLA that the Thames has fast-running tides and eddies that can drag you under. 'It would be very helpful to dispel some of these urban myths . . . we are seeing a massive increase in interest for "wild swimming", and it is only a matter of time before someone gets injured or worse. If we can highlight good river etiquette, we may save the odd life. Joining a club is the first and easiest thing to do.'

As for the quality of the water, he is 'a keen believer that what doesn't kill you makes you stronger. I've never had Thames belly and I swim all the time. In ten years I've never been ill because of the river. I don't get cut, I've never swum into something dead, I've never seen major litter, but people have to realise it's a living, breathing environment.' The Henley Swim now pay a private company to test the water, 'because people expect us to. There's going to be stuff in there and people need to accept that. It's a moderately organic tasting and smelling environment. It tastes and smells like it looks, a live habitat, it's not chlorinated.'

Henley Swim was recently invited to join the Marlow Rowing Club and create a hub for water sports; 'we have funding from Sports England and planning permission for a state of the art club by the bridge,' says Tom. 'It's the dawn of a new era of swimming clubs.'

I leave him in the museum's café and head back to the station along the river. While the old swimming spots have been closed down in Oxford, and river racing has died out in Reading, the story of the Thames is slightly different in Henley. This is the first place I've been where a club has been formed especially for swimming in the river and where a swim taken just for fun between two friends now attracts hundreds of people every year. Henley once again has a culture of swimming, and it hasn't been replaced by rowing after all. Instead, two rowers have reintroduced people to the river and, with their annual swims, created a new 'capital institution for Henley'.

7

Marlow–Cookham–Maidenhead

'For, O, the water's deep and clear
That flows by Marlow town!'

J. Ashby-Sterry,
'A Marlow Madrigal', 1886

In Victorian times there was 'no more fascinating spot' on the River Thames than Marlow, declared *Dickens's Dictionary of the Thames*. It was the perfect place for boating, camping holidays or 'sketching purposes', and the water teemed with fish. Jerome K. Jerome found Marlow 'one of the pleasantest river centres I know of', where people 'bathe before breakfast'. Yet while the town, eight miles downstream from Henley along the Thames Path, had tennis, cricket and football clubs, as well as a river regatta, as with Lechlade I can find few archival references to swimming.

In the summer of 1866 a one-mile race was held on the Marlow Reach, as well as 'several other swimming and diving matches from the Suspension Bridge', although the Annual Regatta and Aquatic Sports in the 1890s included only one swimming event, 'the Canadian Canoe Race', in which competitors had to stand and 'paddle to the ryepeck', and then swim back with their canoe. Other mentions of the Thames at Marlow tend to concern drownings, such as the family tragedy that occurred in July 1906 when a father

Marlow is the modern setting for a mass-participation swim organised by Human Race, whose founder John Lunt says the Thames is 'the cleanest metropolitan river in Europe'.

and his two sons, all accomplished swimmers, went down to the river. One of the sons sank suddenly 'while attempting to swim the river a second time' and his brother and father perished while trying to rescue him.

In more modern times, however, Marlow is notable for two reasons: an official ban on swimming in the Thames, and more recently the launch of a mass swimming event. In June 1960 the *Daily Mirror* reported, 'Education chiefs last night BANNED school bathing at a Thames beauty spot. The order went to head teachers of schools at Marlow, the picture-postcard Buckinghamshire market town.' Samples of river water had been 'analyzed and found to be POLLUTED'. The Education Authority had acted on the advice of the Medical Officer of Health; parents were urged to stop their children swimming in the Thames, which was 'filthy', and where they risked 'dreadful diseases from sewage'. While schoolchildren had long been taught to swim in the Thames – at Tumbling

Bay in Oxford, King's Meadow in Reading and Solomon's Hatch in Henley – and although Marlow residents once bathed before breakfast, now they were being actively warned to stay away from the river or risk dreadful consequences.

But we never seem to stay away for too long and thanks to the rise in triathlons today Marlow is the setting for a swim organised by Human Race, the largest mass participation events company in the UK, who promise that 'taking to the water from the grassy banks [will be] an unforgettable experience'. Human Race runs triathlon and cycling events, as well as six open-water swims, three of which are held on the Thames – at Marlow, Windsor and Hampton Court. 'We chose the Thames because of a whole raft of reasons,' explains John Lunt, who founded the company in 1990, including the fact the river was on his doorstep and he knew it well. An experienced triathlete who has raced 'all over the world', he's originally from Lancashire but moved to Kingston in 1983. 'The Thames is the cleanest metropolitan river in Europe,' he says, 'we knew salmon had been seen, and there is less industry now, and we thought, let's go for it . . . And now we've been doing it for twenty-four years.'

In the early days, 'people thought swimmers were a bit mad, the running boom had just started and when the London Marathon was first held in 1981 triathlon was in its infancy, people thought you were crazy even if you jogged on a street. River users had learnt to swim in the Thames when people couldn't afford pools, and they weren't surprised by our swims, but now there is a more risk-averse culture.'

Around 2,000 people take part annually in Human Race's swims on the Thames. Competitors vary: 'the madcap open-water swimmers do it for the hell of it, anywhere, any time, any place', then there are general swimmers who want a new challenge, as well as novice open-water people. Human Race's official charity is Cancer Research UK and entrants are invited to make a donation and offered a charity fundraising pack. While most people do raise money, 'they are not compelled to, it's secondary to the challenge'.

Ninety-nine per cent finish the set course and he says it's rare that anyone drops out, because 'if people are not happy then they don't start'. Ten to 20 per cent are no-show, usually because they 'haven't trained enough', but once they start they finish. There have been no heart attacks, 'touch wood, and no near-death experiences'. John believes one reason for this may be that 'our database is more the hardcore swimmers' whereas in other mass events entrants 'may be less well conditioned and possibly less prepared'.

At Marlow there are three events, 750 metres, 1,500 metres and three kilometres, all starting and finishing upstream from the bridge. There are minimum age requirements, as well as cut-off times, and entrants must sign a declaration that they are aware of 'a risk to health associated with swimming in open water and that there is a chance that participants may contract illness from competing in such water'. They need to be 'aware of the physically strenuous nature' of the event and fit and healthy enough to take part.

'When we started there were hardly any mass swims in the Thames,' says John, 'there's been an explosion in the last two years. Other race organisers thought it would be easy, but there is a wide range of safety cover levels.'

F3 Events also run mass swims at Marlow. The company was established in 2006 and the Thames was chosen because 'all our staff are born and raised in the Thames Valley with an interest in triathlon,' explains a spokesperson. He says safety is 'one of the main items on the agenda' and 'we go overboard with safety boats when swimmers are in the water'.

In 2012, when the Thames was 'red boarded' (with warning signs placed on locks to advise boat users against using the river), they 'held off till the last moment as it was the day of our Olympic/ standard triathlon in Marlow. We waited thirty minutes prior to the race start to get the last official word from the EA before proceeding; we also shortened the course on safety grounds'. F33 hold swims at Henley-on-Thames and Windsor and on average

350–500 people compete in each event. 'We get a mixed bag, from total amateurs to the most experienced elite athletes and celebs; in the build-up to David Walliams' swim he attended many of our river swims as training.'

Downstream from Marlow, the village of Cookham is another favourite spot for swimmers. This was 'earthly paradise' for artist Stanley Spencer who painted numerous river scenes and wrote in 1917, 'we all go down to Odney Weir for a bathe and a swim . . . I feel fresh, awake and alive; that is the time for visitations.' Ella Foote, who recently moved to Cookham from Maidenhead, says there are lots of beaches where it's easy to walk into the river. She used to go canoeing on the Thames, but as a child she was told it

'Swimming in the Thames was a thrilling experience': Ella Foote pictured at Pinewood Studios during her 30 Memorable Swims Project.

was a dirty place and didn't think of swimming in it. When she first started outdoor swimming around 2007 there were few mass swims open to people of different abilities; 'it's gone a bit mental in the last three years, before that there were elite swims and you needed wetsuits'. Her love of Thames swimming came from a desire to raise money for charity. 'I did a Race for Life run and hated it. I thought there must be another way to have a challenge and do something that's actually enjoyable. The British Heart Foundation were doing a swim in Brighton, it was the only charity offering a swim then, but the tide changed, I was inexperienced and doing breaststroke and I was told by security to get out! So then I really started looking for other ways to swim.'

About two years ago Ella joined the OSS and took part in a swim upstream on the Thames at Sonning. 'I thought, why haven't I done this sooner? It was just lovely. I was really surprised how clear the water was. It looks very still, it's only when you get in you realise there are strong currents underneath. I was a little frightened by boats. We wore bright swim hats, but when a long narrow boat is coming at you, they don't know you're there.' But overall she found it 'a thrilling experience and I was hooked. I was nervous about weeds but apart from the shallow area, it was fine. I have to say I am a nervous Thames swimmer when the river is high and fast – I prefer it a bit calmer.'

Ella joined the Henley Open Water Swimming Club, which helped with her training for a Channel relay swim in 2012. The following year she completed thirty swims to celebrate her thirtieth birthday, including some in the Thames such as the Henley Classic. 'I've made so many friends through random swimming. It is slightly risky, the water is cold, there's a fast flow, and, let's face it, it's taken a few people's lives, and you're doing it with people you don't know. But it's comforting; it's a community of swimmers.'

A couple of miles downriver is Maidenhead, which, unlike Marlow, has a long river-racing tradition and a club that was formed in Victorian times. This was once 'the haunt of the river swell and his overdressed female companion', according to Jerome K. Jerome, and 'the witch's kitchen from which go forth those demons of the river – steam-launches'. Boulter's Lock, just east of Maidenhead, first built in 1772 and then rebuilt in 1828, was certainly a busy place in Victorian times and the press reported several 'Alarming Accidents'. On one Whit Monday, 1,200 boats and punts and 106 launches passed through the lock and several holidaymakers ended up in the river when their canoes capsized or were 'run into' by a steam launch. The artist Edward Gregory spent several years painting the spot in the late 1880s and his *Boulter's Lock, Sunday Afternoon* shows a traffic jam of boating parties passing through the narrow lock, a scene of happy mayhem with oars, punts and sails, and everyone decked out in their Sunday best.

As for swimmers, during a 'Volunteer Encampment' in 1863, 500 men pitched their tents at Maidenhead and 'owing to the close proximity of the river Thames, it is expected a cold bath will be the order of the morning'. Weeds had 'been cut for some distance, and a portion of the water roped off for those who cannot swim, added to which men will be in attendance each morning with boats'.

But far more organised was the 'River Race' or 'Long Swim', run by the Maidenhead Amateur Swimming Club. The club appears to have been formed in the early 1890s, around the same time as Reading's, first holding swimming entertainments at the Grand Hall Swimming Bath. By 1894 it was running an annual sports day in Kidwells Park to raise funds, where 1,200 spectators watched a one-mile handicap and a 'consolation race'. Then in 1897 the club decided to switch venues, agreeing at its annual meeting that 'members should leave the Grand Hall Bath, and bathe and swim in the river instead'. They were now negotiating with the Rowing Club 'for the use of their boathouse' in the early mornings, and a few months later the club held its annual event, called the Swimming Competition, Carnival, and Cycle Gymkhana, in the grounds of

'The Fishery'. Events included a tortoise race, swimming handicaps, diving, a clothes race and 'a splendid exhibition of swimming by Mr. W. Jenkins, formerly of Maidenhead, including imitation of torpedo, swimming on chest feet first, and many different styles of swimming'. This was followed by dancing and an open-air concert on the riverfront.

The club's move to the Thames was highly successful and their river races were held every year until the late 1960s, except in wartime. It began with a two-mile course for men and then a one-mile course for women, both usually held in the evening in late summer to mark the end of the season. The original course for the men's race, up until 1914, was from Cookham to Boulter's Lock, there was then a break until 1923 when the course was changed to run from Boulter's Lock to Bray, while the women's race ran from Boulter's Lock to Maidenhead Bridge. Now women weren't just swimming in the Thames during segregated hours at official bathing spots – they were racing against each other, too, with competitors diving in from the Boulter's pontoon, each accompanied by a safety boat.

In 1923 L. Badcock, Superintendent at the Maidenhead outdoor pool, completed the two-mile men's course in forty minutes and won the Dunkels Cup, named after Ernest Dunkels, a wealthy local resident and former president of Maidenhead Football Club. After the war it was the turn of Badcock's sons, George, Eddie and Derek, to dominate the event. They were also members of the Maidenhead Swimming Club, and used to train by swimming against the flow from the Sounding Arch to Boulter's Lock. In 1950, at the age of fifteen, Cynthia Brooks won the women's event, having first taken part when she was eleven. She was a member of the Hammersmith Ladies Swimming Club and in 1948 travelled to Belgium to take part in a sports event aimed at restoring friendly relations after the war. 'It was a great experience,' she later recalled, 'and the first time I'd seen either ham or iced cakes.' She went on to win numerous swimming events at both county and national level and was presented with Maidenhead's 'Woman of the Year' award.

River traffic was still an issue on the Thames at Maidenhead, however, as the Jackson family discovered one sunny bank holiday in 1954 when Margaret and Ken and their five children hired a rowing boat. When a 60-ton steamer appeared, Ken, who was rowing, pulled their boat over to the side, but they were sucked back by the current right into the path of the steamer, which ploughed straight into them and cut their boat in half. 'My husband and the older kids went one way and I went the other,' Margaret, who couldn't swim, later told the *Bucks Free Newspaper*. Then a fifteen-year-old 'schoolboy swimming champion' heard her screams and dived in. 'He came for the baby. I can remember grabbing hold of him and I can remember him saying, "I can't take you both. I'll take the baby".' But in the end everyone was rescued and their story made national news.

Open-air swimming continued to be a popular pastime in Maidenhead, with the annual river races held from about 6 p.m., after the boat traffic had finished for the day. By 1966, however, increasing costs meant there were only a couple of safety boats for the entire race. 'We swam in costumes only,' remembers Derek Harris, 'no wetsuit, goggles, earplugs, swim hat. The speed of the river's flow had a major effect on race times. I seem to remember winning one year in less than thirty minutes. As for preparation and training, there really was none for me, other than being in the swimming pool all summer with friends and playing water polo.'

But as with Reading, in 1969 the river races came to an end; numbers were down and the great tradition was abandoned. However, in a similar way to Henley, and again thanks to a group of rowers, things have now been resurrected, with a new Boulter's to Bray Swim, run by the Royal Borough of Windsor and Maidenhead.

The idea came from three members of Maidenhead Rowing Club, Tom Jost, Rob Davies and Keith Dixon, who wanted to swim on the Saturday morning of the annual Henley Regatta, just 'as a bit of fun' from the Rowing Club to the Waterside Inn in Bray. Tom mentioned the idea to fellow rowers and one said, 'hang on, I think it used to be a regular thing', explaining she'd spotted an old trophy for a swim from Boulter's Lock to Bray in an antiques shop. Just like Tom Kean and Jeremy Laming in Henley, they'd discovered a lost tradition.

Tom Jost decided to investigate and placed a small article in the *Maidenhead Advertiser* and soon people who had competed in the 'Long Swim' got in touch. The three men then decided to organise it as an official event, but first they did the swim themselves, with fifteen participants following the Boulter's to Bray course. 'One of the swimmers worked for the council,' explains Ben Collins, an ex-army officer who used to row for Maidenhead, 'and she said "why not make it a council event? Then you'd be covered through their insurance." The council have been great.' Ben has also been doing triathlons since 2009 – 'old rowers don't die, we become triathletes' – and with the Long Swim 'I suddenly realised we were taking the lid off something massive and historical and significant. Once the swim was announced and word got out we discovered all this history. The Babcock family got in touch and people remembered it fondly; it was a significant community event and we wanted to retain that ethos by forming a charity.'

The first official event was held in 2012, starting at 6.15 in the morning before river traffic commenced, and 120 swimmers completed the course, including seventy-four-year-old Mike Hughes who had won the men's Long Swim in 1967 and 1968. Cynthia Lockie (née Brooke), who won the women's race in 1950, brought her family along to watch. 'She told us there used to be a big house near the river and they would open up their garden and people got changed there,' explains Ben. 'It may have belonged to

Ernest Dunkels. She was thrilled to see the swim and she presented one of the trophies.'

Today the distance is 2.8 kilometres and there are three categories: Open, Masters 49+ and Junior 15–18. 'Lots of people who enter are rowers but I try to get anyone to enter,' says Ben. 'People ask "is that safe?" They are worried about pollution and the cleanliness of the water and there was a bit of a worry in 2013 when river treatment works upstream overflowed a couple of months before our swim. But I used to work for the EA; we know the river is cleaner because of the wildlife.' As for wetsuits, if swimmers sign a disclaimer and prove they are competent they don't have to wear one.

The Boulter's to Bray Swim Trust is now a registered charity with five trustees, including Ben, with the objective of promoting local sporting projects. 'For triathlon you need expensive kit, so it becomes exclusive,' he says. 'I'd love to see open-water swims more accessible. Lots of commercial outfits do Thames swims, but newbies can be put off, and we're community-centric, the money we make goes back into local amateur sports projects.' This means that for a £33 entrance fee Maidenhead residents can enjoy the river just as they did some 120 years ago, and with the full backing of the council.

But what puzzles me is not so much how we lost the tradition of swimming in the Thames, but how we lost the *knowledge* of this tradition. In the late nineteenth and early twentieth centuries there were well-organised river races at Oxford, Reading and Henley. They were regularly covered in the press; there were medals, prizes and certificates. Champions were created, records were broken. How could all of this have been so easily forgotten? Perhaps because people left the river in favour of warm indoor pools, old bathing places closed, other sports such as rowing replaced swimming, and bathers were put off by fears of pollution or by outright bans. If an old trophy for a swim from Boulter's Lock to Bray hadn't been spotted in an antiques shop, would hundreds of people now be swimming the very same course that existed in the 1920s? Time and again we are drawn back to the Thames where we discover our lost heritage, re-enacting history and finding out a simple truth: we swim in the river because we belong there.

8

Windsor and Eton

'Say, Father Thames, for thou hast seen
Full many a sprightly race
Disporting on thy margent green
The paths of pleasure trace'
   Thomas Gray, 'Ode on a Distant Prospect of Eton College', 1747

Windsor and Eton have a unique place in the story of Thames swimming because, unlike other riverside towns, the tradition of bathing, among royalty and privileged Eton College boys, has been well documented here for hundreds of years. In 1303 the eighteen-year-old prince who would later become Edward II injured his Court fool, Robert Bussard, while playing 'a trick' on him in the Thames one winter's day, and had to pay four shillings' compensation. By the 1500s pupils at Eton, founded in 1440 by Henry VI, were bathing at numerous places along the river, while it was a group of Old Etonians who helped form an outdoor bathing group, said to be the first swimming society in England. Less well documented, however, is the swimming tradition among the townspeople, who were keen river users as well, with a public bathing place on the Thames as early as the 1850s, followed by local swimming clubs for both men and women.

The train from Waterloo to Windsor & Eton Riverside is busy with tourists; next to me a German woman and her daughter are consulting maps, while three Japanese visitors take snaps of the

A newspaper illustration from the 1880s showing Eton boys at Athens and Boveney, two of the college's swimming spots on the Thames. In theory bathing drawers were compulsory.

Thames from the window. They are presumably all on their way to the castle, the Queen's official residence. The Thames is a short walk from the station and the water looks icy cold and grey; to my left is Windsor Bridge, to the right a large red DANGER sign in the middle of the river.

I reach the porter's lodge at Eton College where I'm asked to sit in a chair to have my photograph taken. 'Bit royal all of this,' smiles the porter as he makes my ID card and I turn to stare at a picture of Princes William and Harry on the wall. I walk into the college grounds; the schoolyard is surrounded on all sides by ancient buildings, making it feel a bit like an exclusive barracks. There is, as Henry Skrine wrote in 1801, 'an air of superior grandeur and propriety' about the cobbled square, deserted today because it's half-term. I head under an archway and through a small wooden door pitted with iron studs. My destination is the college archives, which has manuscripts dating back to 1091. I produce my passport and driving licence (getting into the archives is no easy matter) and the archivist, Penny Hatfield, lets me into a compact, book-lined room. I am the only person there but for an elderly man who appears to be studying cloth scrolls.

I sit down at the wooden table, carefully pulling my chair across the parquet floor. Tall windows let in the midday sun, providing a glimpse of blue sky, Gothic spires and a distant flagpole. All I can hear is the soft breathing of my companion who then tells me quietly that he's researching fifteenth-century Fellows of Eton College. I open the first book Penny has laid out for me on the table, *The Eton Book of the River*, published in 1935. It's a weighty tome with pages that have turned a pale yellow over the years, and while its focus is the evolution of boat racing there are two chapters on bathing. The first, 'Bathing up to 1840', is significantly subtitled 'a chapter of accidents'.

Despite 'the insanitary state of the river', bathing took place at Eton 'from a very early date', with one boy drowning in 1549 after he'd gone to bathe from the playing fields. By the 1770s the college had hired 'watermen' with boats and one pupil, writing to his father in 1796, offered the following reassurance: 'I hope you will not make yourself the least uneasy about my going into the water, as I do really assure you that I never go in without proper people attending.' Another pupil remembered his swimming experiences a decade later: 'Sooner or later all swam. Men were stationed at particular bathing places, to prevent accidents (to bathe elsewhere was a flogging), and they taught swimming at a guinea a head.' But when he wrote to his father asking for the guinea, he 'received an angry answer that in his time boys taught themselves to swim, and I might do the same'. It took him three days, 'terrible work it was', but this was followed by 'great fun by land and water'. Some 'little fellows' had an unusual way of drying themselves, 'catching a cow by the tail, using the towel for a whip, and making the animal gallop them about the meadow till they were dry'.

Within a few years the arrangements for bathing at Eton had been further improved. One pupil recollected, 'those boys who are not able to swim are debarred from ablution except at particular places, where it is almost an utter impossibility from the shallowness of the water, that an accident can possibly occur'. Excellent swimmers appointed by the headmaster were 'regularly paid by the boys' to prevent mishap, and by now there were seven bathing places along the Thames: Sandy Hole, Cuckow Ware, Head Pile, Pope's Hole, Cotton's Hole, South Hope and Dickson's Hole. 'This use of the word Hole has died out in England,' explains *The Eton Book of the River*, 'but a bathing hole is still a common name for a bathing place in the United States; it has no derogatory sense such as it now suggests to us.'

Eton was also the centre for a number of swimming societies. In 1828 the Philolutic Society was formed, with members from Cambridge, Windsor and Eton. It was divided into two sections, the Philolutes and the Psychrolutes, 'lovers of bathing and lovers of cold water'. The latter bathed outdoors daily between November and March, while members of both societies were called the Philopsychrolutes.

The Philolutic Society's accounts book from 1829 to 1833 includes weekly fines for 'non-bathing' at a cost of two shillings and sixpence. The group's treasurer and first president was the Right Honourable Sir Lancelot Shadwell; then nearly fifty, the former barrister and MP had been educated at Eton. In 1827 he'd become the last Vice-Chancellor of England and was knighted soon after. He was known to bathe every day, whatever the weather, in a creek of the Thames near Barn Elms where he once apparently granted an injunction during a swim. The society certainly had some prominent members; the list begins with Queen Victoria's husband,

HRH Prince Albert, HRH Prince George of Cambridge, the Earl of Denbigh and HRH the Duke of Cambridge. In total there are 183 members, some resident near Eton and others occasional visitors, but after a few pages it descends into pencil-scribbled surnames.

Next I pick up the 1828 *Book of the Society of Psychrolutes*, a large publication with pages set out like a ledger, and I turn them until I come to a chart listing 'Rivers, Lakes and Streams bathed in by this Society'. The page is divided into columns, giving the name of the river or lake, which members bathed there and what, if any, were the remarks. First is the Thames, frequented by 'most of the Club' and 'In all parts Superb!' The Cam, 'passable at Granchester but elsewhere, vile', is also used by 'all of the Society'. The Medway was 'fair', the Cherwell 'Better than nothing', the Wandle, 'Cold. Insipid. Small', and the Clyde 'uncomfortable'. Members swam in rivers abroad as well, including the Seine and the Rhine. The book also features a full-page hand-drawn human skeleton with the caption, 'This gentleman was Not a psychrolute' and on the facing page, a rugged mountain of a man somewhat resembling a Roman soldier: 'This gentleman *was* a psychrolute'.

In the following decades swimming for Eton pupils became even more organised, thanks to William Evans and George Selwyn who introduced classes under Evans' tuition. Evans was drawing master, while Selwyn was a private tutor and a keen swimmer who would become Bishop of New Zealand. His feats included diving 10 feet over a thorn bush overhanging the river above Windsor, and while 'going down in a sinking boat' standing up on his seat and taking 'a dexterous header before the boat disappeared'.

Until 1839 there had been 'no systematic attempt to teach swimming' at Eton, according to *The Badminton Library*, but that year a boy named Montagu drowned after being 'dragged out of his boat by a barge rope'. As a result, Selwyn and Evans 'prevailed' upon the then headmaster, Dr Hawtrey, that all boys should pass an examination before they were allowed to go out in a boat. Just as

A 'pass' in progress at Eton, a regular summer event that included diving, swimming and treading water. In the 1890s around 200 boys passed each season.

would happen later at Oxford, the impetus for learning to swim at Eton came from the need to improve the safety of rowers.

The various tests, which became known as 'passing', or 'the Eton pass', included 'a header' (dive) from two or three feet above water, and a 100 yards swim, fifty with and fifty against a slow stream. Each boy also had to tread water and 'while doing so, to keep his hands up to the level of his head or higher', and to swim on his back. Only breaststroke was allowed, for the swimmer needed 'a clear view all round him,' explains *The Eton Book of the River*, 'and this is in some circumstances essential for the avoidance of a blow on the head from the oar or scull of a passing coxswainless boat'.

Eton pupils became known as accomplished swimmers and the swimming school passing certificate from 1846 includes a quote from the eighteenth-century poet James Thomson, 'This is the purest exercise of Health,/ The kind refresher of the Summer heats'. The poet and novelist Algernon Charles Swinburne later wrote that his only 'really and wholly delightful recollection' of his time at Eton was 'of the swimming lessons and play in the Thames'.

Over the years some of the old bathing places were abandoned, but Cuckow Ware – or Cuckoo Weir – and South Hope remained in use. In 1856 Evans was granted a land lease which stipulated he was to 'permit and suffer the Masters and Schollars [sic] of Eton College to have free access through and over' the land around Cuckoo Weir to the stream on the south side 'for the purpose of bathing as heretofore accustomed'.

In 1860 Edmond Warre, an assistant master, took over from Evans and Selwyn, again improving Cuckoo Weir as well as two other swimming spots, Boveney and Athens. 'Great credit is due to the authorities at Eton,' wrote Henry Robertson in his 1875 book *Life on the Upper Thames*, where nearly every boy was a competent swimmer, 'the result being that out of a school averaging eight hundred, not one case of drowning has occurred for many years; and this, at a place where everybody seeks the river as his natural out-of-doors home, makes Eton probably the first gymnasium for swimmers in the world.'

The next River Master was Walter Durnford, who reigned over the bathing places from 1885 to 1899, during which 'trouble became rather acute with the Thames Conservancy owing to the objection of the innumerable Mrs. Grundies of those days to the sight of youth disporting itself naked and unashamed in the river and on the banks'. So bathing drawers were introduced and screens put up at Athens.

In the 1890s, 'passing' was held as soon as the water became warm enough, generally towards the end of May, at Cuckoo Weir. Much attention was paid to style, noted *The Badminton Library*, with the event repeated once or twice a week during the summer term, with 200 boys on average passing each season. The taking of 'headers' formed a characteristic feature of Eton swimming, with one 'famous exponent of the art as a boy' being the politician and cricketer Lord Harris, who was sent to Eton in 1864.

Once Edmond Warre left, a duumvirate was set up, the authors of *The Eton Book of the River*, L.S.R. Byrne and E.L. Churchill. Their first task was to try and restore 'something approaching to the old proportion between the bathing accommodation and the number of boys in the school'. Cuckoo Weir had for years been used by Lower Boys and Non-nants (as non-swimmers were known), Athens by the 600–700 boys of the Fifth Form, while Boveney Weir stream was confined to a 'select few'. It was then decided to widen Cuckoo Weir, which would later become known as Wards Mead Bathing Place.

The duumvirate ended shortly after the First World War, when Athens was bought for the college. Up to that point, the bathing spot had been rented from the Crown but in 1917 an Eton pupil, John Baker, was killed in a flying accident. The Commissioners for Crown Lands agreed to sell the land to his father, who gave it to the school in memory of his son, a 'regular water baby'. Today there is still a stone tablet at Athens, opposite the Royal Windsor Race Course, in memory of young Baker, 'a brilliant swimmer who spent here many of the happiest hours of his boyhood'. On one side of the stone is a sign outlining BATHING REGULATIONS AT ATHENS, as taken from the 1921 School Rules of the River. There was to be no bathing on Sundays after 8.30 a.m. and 'boys who are undressed must either get at once into the water or get behind screens when boats containing ladies come in sight'. Boys were also not allowed to 'land on the Windsor Bank or to swim out to launches and barges or to hang onto, or interfere with, boats of any kind'; anyone breaking the rule would be 'severely punished'.

Swimming at Eton had certainly evolved over some 150 years, becoming safer, more skilled and far more regulated. Gone were the days of naked boys paying a guinea to learn how to swim; now pupils needed to obey rules restricting swimming to certain places at certain hours and to pass an exam, just as in other subjects.

By the 1920s Cuckoo Weir was used by other boys as well. A Pathé News clip shows 'A Boys' Camp at Cuckoo Weir'. It opens with camp leaders in pyjamas striding past a row of wigwam tents; they then burst into the tents, wake the boys, drag some of them out on their blankets, swing them by their hands and feet and toss them into the river. Later in the day there's a swimming race, and after lunch the boys wash the dishes in the river.

By 1935 the Eton bathing spot at Boveney had been given up, although pupils still swam downstream from Boveney to Rafts, and the former 'Masters' Bathing Place' at Romney Weir was used by both masters and the 'more prominent boys in the school'. But the days of swimming in the Thames came to an end, at least officially, in the 1950s. Penny tells me this was partly because an outdoor pool was built, and also because of fears of pollution and polio. The highly infectious polio virus was a frequent cause of death and paralysis in the 1940s and 1950s, especially among children, who were warned to stay away from ponds and rivers.

I stack the old swimming society books into a neat pile and head back through Eton, stopping at an antique bookshop to ask the man behind the counter if he has any prints depicting bathing; he says someone came in the week before and bought them all. And would he ever swim in the Thames? He pulls a face: 'I've seen the rats, and the current is really strong, especially around Windsor Bridge.' He's right; standing on the bridge a few minutes later I watch gulls floating speedily along like bath toys, the water rushing under the stone arches. Down on the Thames Path people are feeding the swans – throwing entire slices of bread – while others board a French Brothers' boat. I walk along the path where the honking of geese is deafening, the landscape busy with bridges, a viaduct and various channels. There are plenty of signs: 'river users' are told to 'take extreme care at all times' particularly near the bridge, while danger signs warn of shallow water.

Under the viaduct bridge, and just before the modern Windsor Leisure Centre, is a sign to Baths Island & Pleasure Ground. A wooden bridge leads to the island, a wide stretch of grass deserted today but for a solitary man on a bike. It's here that the town's outdoor swimming baths were first built and on 1 May 1858 the press reported the opening of the Windsor Subscription Baths, 'Season Tickets 8/- Gentlemen under 17 years of age 6/-. Great improvements have been made. An experienced Waterman with a punt will be in attendance and swimming taught. W.F. Taylor.' Taylor had a shop opposite the parish church and was also known to run 'peep shows' of the Royal Apartments.

Then, in 1870, the baths were moved. 'Queen Victoria was looking out of the castle windows one day and she saw all these half-naked men,' explains long-time Windsor Swimming Club member Leslie Sturgess, 'so it was moved to the other side of the railway bridge.' The new site, between Jacobs Island and the riverbank, was known as Boddys Baths. It was home to the Windsor Swimming Club, founded in 1883, with a clubhouse on the island. There are earlier references to 'the Windsor and Eton Swimming Club', which had thirty-six members in 1881, but Leslie says this was a water polo club.

The Windsor Swimming Club, founded in 1883, held annual competitions which included Walking the Slippery Pole, with the winner receiving a butter dish.

The Windsor Club held annual competitions; with the winner of the 50 yards Novice Race being awarded a silver pencil case, and the winner of Walking the Slippery Pole receiving an 'oak electro butter dish'. In July 1886 the press reported that the 'first race for the championship of this rising Club came off in the river Thames early on Monday morning when, despite inclement weather a fair number of spectators assembled in the Eton Brocas to witness the event'. The course was from the Great Western Railway Bridge to the Swimming Baths, a distance of about 400 yards.

The club's fourth annual competition included a 100 yards handicap final, a 50 yards handicap boys, running headers and Walking the Slippery Pole. This time there was a 'numerous company of spectators present' and Mayor Mr J. Lundy said he was 'surprised and pleased to find ladies present'.

Sometime around 1896 the club was wound down, but was re-formed in 1909 at new baths built in 1904 and known as the Eastern Baths. This also appears to have been when a separate bath was created for women. In 1912 the Windsor Ladies Swimming Club was formed, one of many Thames-side clubs for women in the period. The press reported that within just a few months 'its path has been paved with prosperity. The members have displayed the utmost enthusiasm, with the result the members have increased until at the present time it is a really healthy club doing an excellent work in the cultivation of the art of swimming.' The year 1912 was a significant one for women: they were allowed for the first time to compete in Olympic swimming and diving events. Diving had become an Olympic sport for men in 1904, and swimming in 1908, but it was only at the Olympic Games in Stockholm in 1912 that women could take part and when Londoner Mary Belle White won bronze in the ten-metre platform event.

The object of the Windsor Club was 'the encouragement of the art of swimming and life saving,' explained its yearbook for 1923; fixtures included the mile, the half-mile and the 100 yards handicap, and any member found guilty of 'regrettable behaviour' would be expelled. While such behaviour isn't defined, it may have had something to do with clothing, for the yearbook reminds members that at meetings of 'both sexes' and in all Amateur Swimming Association (ASA) championships competitors 'must wear regulation bathing costumes and drawers'. By now there were numerous rules as to what women, and men, could wear while swimming at official events. The first ASA costume rule appeared in 1890, by which time costumes were being manufactured, but it applied only to men – the first ASA championships for women weren't held until 1901. But already in 1899 rules on women's costumes had been added; they were to have 'a shaped arm, at least three inches long' and the costume 'shall be cut straight round the neck'. By the following year costumes could now only be black or dark blue, presumably because these were less transparent when wet. Men who didn't wear the regulation costume when 'ladies are present at Galas' and who 'swam without drawers' were disqualified. Nine years later the rules were again revised, and now there was specific reference to 'Ladies' races in Public'. At competitions where 'both sexes were admitted' females over the age of fourteen had to wear 'on leaving the dressing room, a long coat or bath gown before entering and immediately after leaving the water', a rule that continued for decades. Women might now be competing publicly as amateurs and winning medals for Olympic diving, but social constraints meant they had to be appropriately dressed, the cut and length of their costume clearly defined, their bodies shielded from view until they got in the water and covered up again the moment they got out.

By 1930 things had changed somewhat and the Windsor Ladies' life-saving competition now required competitors to swim 30 yards wearing clothes, 'take off clothes in water. Dive for object 4ft, and bring same to bank on back.' They also had to plunge in from the bank, save someone 'by one release method and carry her

30 yards by one rescue method'. The women swam from Boveney Lock to Romney Lock, a distance of two miles and 572 yards, for which they received a lock-to-lock certificate.

Boys from Windsor Grammar School also took part in school swimming and diving sports at the public baths in the 1940s. By now mixed bathing had been introduced and diving boards installed, but the baths, like those at Reading, appear to have become derelict by the end of the war when they were full of rubbish. 'Indoor pools were built around the area, at Slough and Maidenhead,' explains Leslie Sturgess. 'Our club had a hundred-year lease on the island but we were forced to close the clubhouse because of Health & Safety; the council said we had to do the place up and we couldn't afford it.'

Windsor Swimming Club still exists, however, and its website explains that members have 'achieved frequent success at County, Regional, National and International levels. Windsor has become one of the most admired clubs in the south of England, with a growing reputation.' Their focus is 'competitive development', with training no longer held in the Thames but at various local indoor pools.

Human Race chose Windsor as the location for one of its annual swims, with the background of the iconic Windsor Castle.

But if swimming in the river at Eton and Windsor fell out of favour after the 1950s, today, as at Henley, Marlow and Maidenhead, it's a popular place for mass-participation events. 'Windsor is such an iconic centre,' says John Lunt, founder of Human Race, 'it has the castle and it's great geographically and historically.' When he launched the Windsor Triathlon in 1991, 'we needed a place to swim; if there had been a lake in Windsor it would have been in a lake, but as the River Thames goes through the town it was perfect'. Places for the televised triathlon, named Event of the Year by the British Triathlon Foundation seven times, sell out in weeks.

Windsor has also been a memorable spot for those passing through the town after days submerged in the river. For Lewis Pugh arriving here in 2006, having swum from Lechlade, it was definitely a high point. 'The Thames gradually descends; the source is only 110 metres above sea level and it has a long way to slowly descend across fields and meadows to the North Sea. It's not like the Ganges, for example, which descends from high in the Himalayas and on either side there are valleys, glaciers and temples. I was struck by the sensory deprivation in the Thames, the water was mud-brown so I saw little underneath me and when I took a breath there was nothing except six foot of muddy banks on either side, that's it . . . but then I hit Windsor and came round a bend in the river and saw the swans and there rising out of the mist was Windsor Castle! I told the Queen about that later, and her face lit up.'

Charlie Wittmack had a similar experience during his world triathlon in 2010: 'when you swim your head is in the water, you can't see anything all day, you can't hear anything all day. All you're left with is your thoughts and those thoughts can be really really tough, especially when the plan is to swim eighteen miles or more. There's nothing to look at, listen to or smell all day long. One day I stopped and popped my head up out of the water and looked over and I was right outside of Windsor Castle! I hadn't seen or heard anything all day and there it was, that was a fun surprise.'

9

Hampton Court–Molesey Lock–Sunbury–Kingston

'Should you fall into the water, you will find swimming of more use than mathematics'

Revd Charles Haddon Spurgeon,
Baptist preacher, 1834–92

It's a bitter April morning as I approach Hampton Court, on board the *Richmond Royale*. It's the first time I've seen the Thames so uninviting; even the seagulls look frozen. Inside the boat the sides are lined with red leather seats, the floor covered in patterned carpet like an old-fashioned pub. It's so cold I can see my breath in the air. I chat to a crewmember, a young man who lives locally but has never swum in the Thames. He knows of three people who ended up in hospital recently after jumping into the river. One incident happened downstream at around 8 p.m. on a hot day: 'we saw a man in the middle of the river, with his mates outside a pub cheering him on, then on our way back we saw an ambulance and he was being given CPR. He died the next day. It's the shock of the water when you're drunk.'

Outside the snow-splattered window the river looks like dull scratched metal. I go up on the top deck, where there's a bit of a blizzard blowing, just in time to see Henry VIII's magnificent palace, originally built for Cardinal Wolsey. There's a glint of gold at the grand Tudor gates and further on, beneath the turrets, a hand-painted sign that reads 'No Mooring'. In the summer of 1718 three gentlemen arrived here from London on horseback and 'it being excellent hot they went to bath themselves in the River of Thames. And not being skilled in Swimming, they were all drowned.' But others found it a perfect spot. 'If there be a situation on the whole river between Staines Bridge and Windsor Bridge pleasanter than another, it is this of Hampton,' wrote Daniel Defoe in 1724. 'The river is high enough to be navigable, and low enough to be a little pleasantly rapid; so that the stream looks always cheerful, not slow and sleeping, like a pond. This keeps the waters always clear and clean, the bottom in view, the fish playing and in sight.' There is little cheerful about the scene today and no bottom in view as I step off the boat. There's no sign of any fish playing either, although porpoises were recently reported downstream at Twickenham, where sightings go back to at least 1896, when the press warned it was illegal to shoot them and that 'porpoise meat, though doubtless nourishing and perhaps toothsome, has long gone out of fashion'.

In the 1880s city holidaymakers enjoyed regattas at Hampton, just as they did at Henley, along with river festivals and other 'primitive amusements', while hustling photographers stood at vantage points to take pictures. In 1890 Henry Bran, 'swimmer, waterman and ferryman at Hampton', escorted the American Davis Dalton in his attempt to swim the Channel, accompanying him in a small punt. When Dalton arrived in England he fainted on the beach at Folkestone after a twenty-three-hour crossing, the British press disputed his swim and it was never officially recognised. The following summer, however, Dalton was in the Thames, this time swimming all the way from Blackwall to Gravesend on his back.

Today this part of the river is also the site of an annual mass swim, 2.25 miles from Hampton Court Palace to Kingston upon Thames, again staged by Human Race and described as one of the more challenging events in the open-water swim series. 'It's a linear

Victorian holidaymakers enjoyed regattas at Hampton Court, while in the 1920s there was a resort for swimmers known as 'London's Palm Beach'.

course, the start and end points are in different places and we have to move people's kit,' explains John Lunt, 'but for spectators they can walk along the towpath so there is the tourism element; if you were in the middle of a lake no one could see you.' The first swim took place on 1 August 2010 with 1,200 swimmers, including Olympic silver medallist and open-water swimmer Keri-Anne Payne and Olympic rower Toby Garbett (who also swims the Henley Classic), and the race raised £10,000 for WaterAid. In 2011 it was renamed the Speedo Open Water Swim Series and the following year a non-wetsuit option was introduced (if the water is over 15 degrees). The event is now billed as the UK's largest river swim, although, as with all Thames events, the actual dates are dependent on the weather.

In 2012 the race was postponed from July to October after heavy rainfall and flooding, and in a survey conducted after the event almost half of the 700 entrants reported falling ill. Public Health England concluded that poor hygiene and swallowing river water may have been to blame, but it also found that those who had previous recent experience in an open-water river event, and those over the age of forty, were less likely to get ill. It recommended cleaning wetsuits after swimming and so Human Race put new measures in place – including hygiene stations where participants can soak their wetsuits in sterilising Milton Dip, as well as gel pump dispensers. While most people don't get sick from swimming in the Thames, in the modern world precautions are always being improved and refined.

I cross the handsome three-arched Hampton Bridge, where a sign tells me it's 147 miles to the source of the Thames. As I turn right towards Molesey Lock I consider the distance I've come and how the landscape has changed over nearly seventy miles, from a waterlogged meadow in Gloucestershire, to a winding waterway through the city of Oxford, to the rowers' delight that is Henley, the grandeur of the Thames overlooked by Windsor Castle, and now I'm here in Surrey, just entering Greater London.

First built in 1814 and then rebuilt in 1906 and enlarged to let 200-foot-long naval craft through, Molesey is still a working lock today. It's lined with well-trimmed grassy banks, although now it's snowing so hard I can barely see a thing. Back in the 1890s this was the busiest lock on the Thames where visitors couldn't even see the water for all the 'bright blazers, and gay caps, and saucy hats, and many-coloured parasols'. On a fine Sunday, 'all the inhabitants of Hampton and Molesey 'dress themselves up in boating costume,' wrote Jerome K. Jerome, 'and come and mooch around the lock with their dogs, and flirt, and smoke, and watch the boats . . . one of the gayest sights I know of near this dull old London town'.

The lock was also the site of races, such as those carried out by the Ilex Swimming Club. In the summer of 1873 the banks were crowded with spectators – the press noted 'amongst whom were many ladies' – as swimmers competed for four prizes offered by an Ilex club member for a three-quarter-mile handicap. Twenty-three men took part, starting at 6 p.m. on a barge moored above the Hampton ferry, swimming downstream to a flagstaff opposite the headquarters of the Molesey Boat Club. It was won by the aptly named Mr Leader who 'had all the race to himself'.

River races were also held a few miles upstream at Sunbury where in 1907 the Clapton Ladies held their second quarter-mile handicap. The *Daily Express*, which by now often featured photos of 'lady swimmers in the Thames', reported on a 'keen contest, in which the competitors were started from a big punt in mid-stream'. Sixteen women took part, with the winner, Miss Thistle, finishing the 'hardy-fought race' in just over eight minutes.

As late as the 1970s families still spent summer Sundays and school holidays paddling in the Thames at Sunbury, for example at Rivermead Island. One bather remembers, 'It was considered a normal thing to do. Is the Thames worse than it was? Are we more sickly? Or simply more careful?'

Others swam a couple of miles further upstream, at Walton-on-Thames. 'My grandfather, on leave from the navy, used to dive off Walton Bridge for coins tossed from the boats,' says Ray Kennet. 'There used to be a lot of picnics, swimming, musicians, all the poor people enjoying themselves in the water.'

A 1909 postcard of the swimming baths at Walton-on-Thames. In the 1940s families would picnic and swim near the bridge.

He recalls one particular Saturday in 1945, a blazing hot August day, when the family, who lived on a council estate in Hersham, had just enough money to get the bus to Walton Bridge for a picnic and a swim. Fifty or so others were already there, shirtless men with knotted handkerchiefs on their heads, women sitting on old army blankets cutting bread for watercress sandwiches. 'It cost nothing and was a day off from the factory, or cooking and washing clothes,' explains Ray. 'Modern folk may have to imagine this, the people were happy.' He was then five years old, could already dog-paddle and was anxious to show off. 'The adults are seated on the grassy bank just downstream of the bridge where the water is shallow and safe. I dog-paddle past the crowd but I am not noticed. No one shouts, "look, he's only five and can swim already!" Frustrated, I wade out a little further and repeat my swim-by. Still no cries of praise. I keep going until I run out of breath and reach for the bottom with my toes. The riverbed is not there, no gravel to support me. I am aware of seeing a blurred underwater vision of death, I thrash wildly, a great bright sky glows down, everything becomes blurred again. I go into shock, my mind says, very clearly "so this is what death is, it is like this." One final desperate thrash, everything turns bright. I hear a piercing scream. I realise later that it was my mother, who raced into the tranquil Thames and fell flat on her face.' But then some strong-armed men grip him just in time. 'I remember one last thing, all these decades later. I had been wrapped in a towel and my mother is crying. She pulls herself together and snaps, "you stupid little bastard." My mum lived to be eighty-six and it was the only time I ever heard her swear.'

Some thirty years later Chris Dane also used to swim at Walton, to the west of the town's bridge at a place known as Cowey Sale. 'Mum used to take us when it was hot, there was a grassy beach and a slipway for boats which meant you could get in. We did it to cool off and we weren't the only ones, there were people sunbathing, people with kids . . . I remember mum was always careful, she'd say "don't go too far", but there was a low current. I can't say it was pleasant but it was cool. It was dirty, but not polluted. There was boat oil, and people cut their feet on broken bottles, but it was needs must when it was hot, especially the summer of 1976. I was around ten and a good swimmer, the current didn't seem strong, but it was horrible and silty underfoot so the idea was to get swimming as soon as possible.' Chris went back in his late teens, 'splashing round and being stupid with mates', and again as a student in the 1980s, but he now lives in London. 'I don't know if people still swim there at Walton, parents would probably frown on it.'

I leave Molesey Lock thinking of the crewmember on board the *Richmond Royale* who lives locally but has never swum in the Thames, and knows only horror stories. Yet swimmers have used this stretch of the river in many ways over the past century; where once this lock was crowded with spectators in bright blazers and coloured parasols watching life on the Thames, today wetsuited swimmers gather nearby at Hampton Court each year to race in the river itself.

I get the train to Kingston upon Thames, around three miles downstream, and whose inhabitants similarly have a grand tradition of using the river – with a floating platform in the 1870s and a mixed bathing pontoon in the 1920s. Kingston residents have fought for the right to bathe in the Thames and the town was also the training ground for two very successful women's swimming clubs whose members included once famous long-distance swimmers largely forgotten today.

There's not much to see from the train window but the backs of houses and a fox curled up asleep on an old pillow, and when I get out at the station the wind is icy and it's snowing again. I dodge through road builders down to the river and a bleak stretch of iron that is Kingston Railway Bridge, then along the riverside and on to Queen's Promenade and Charter Quay, a recent development with bars, cafés and luxury apartments. Turning left, I find myself in a market, which in today's weather is dismal. A man shouts out the price of avocados but there are virtually no customers to hear him; a nearby stall advertises rump steak, ostrich and zebra meat. Kingston is known for this ancient market place, along with its royal connections as a place where Saxon kings were crowned, while its three-mile stretch of the Thames is the focus of an annual regatta now around 150 years old. More sinisterly, the river once also featured ducking stools used for punishing women. In April 1745 the *London Evening Post* reported, 'a woman that keeps the Queen's Head ale-house at Kingston, in Surrey, was ordered by the court to be ducked for scolding, and was accordingly placed in the chair, and ducked in the river Thames, under Kingston bridge, in the presence of 2,000 or 3,000 people'. When the characters in *Three Men in a Boat* set off on their trip along the Thames, it was at Kingston that they began, picking up their boat just below Kingston Bridge. The town in those days was a place of quaint backstreets, a 'glinting river with its drifting barges', a wooded towpath and trim villas. As with elsewhere on the Thames, it had become popular with city day trippers and boating enthusiasts, with regular fast trains from London.

Today people often leap off Kingston Bridge for fun, and then post their dives on YouTube. A recent clip shows 'students Kay and Kaleem' jumping from the bridge on the last day of college, to cries of 'oh f**k'. Others, filmed by passers-by, show people jumping off the 23-foot bridge to roars of 'go on, mate!' and 'hurry up!' In one case a man does a backflip, and then appears to break his back when he hits a shopping trolley.

Inside Kingston's Local History Room it's blissfully warm. History officer Michele Loose has dug out some documents relating to swimming and I sit facing a table with boxes of card catalogues, on top of which is a small brown stuffed mouse. It appears to be watching me as I start to look at maps, archive newspapers, a leaflet from the Court of Chancery, and local history books.

The first public swimming pool in Kingston was a floating platform on Steven's Ait, to the south of the town. It was officially opened in 1872, after the council obtained a seven-year lease and put up a canvas screen to shield passers-by from nude bathers, just as at other Thames spots. It was for men and boys only, and was said to be deep with a strong current. But locals had used the river as a bathing spot long before the floating platform. In 1865 the Attorney General went head to head with the Mayor of Kingston, Aldermen and local burgesses over whether the town should be allowed to drain all its sewage into the Thames. The Thames Conservancy Board, which had taken control of the river from the Corporation of the City of London in 1857, wanted to take out an injunction to prevent this, but it was argued that the volume of water and the rapid stream meant there would be no serious ill effects. The Thames had been 'used from all time' for drinking water and fishing, although when it came to bathing it was unclear 'as to the degree of right acquired by the public'. While a gentleman wishing to bathe who 'chose the particular spot where the sewer drained into the river, might find it exceedingly inconvenient', it was 'not on that account necessarily a nuisance'. The conclusion of the Court of Chancery was that 'everybody has a right to employ the water of a large public river as he thinks fit', and the injunction was dismissed.

In 1880 the council gave local engineer John Dixon £1,000 to build a new swimming place where women would also be allowed, as in other riverside towns, for a few hours a week. This was a pontoon, accessed by steps near Kingston Bridge, but the Thames Conservators objected to its location so it was towed upriver to Town End Wharf, moored just off the Anglers pub and opened in July 1882.

Again the Conservators objected, but when they wanted the baths moved once more, downstream and near the tannery, the council refused. It was then that a 'miniature war' broke out, reported the *Surrey Mirror* on 19 August 1882: 'An unseemly squabble, ending in something like a fight between officials representing the Thames Conservancy and members of the Corporation took place on Friday morning last at the river side.' The 'cause of the disturbance' was the swimming bath, which the paper insisted was 'in no way interfering with the navigable part of the river'. At 8 a.m. a tug called *Queen* arrived on the scene and its crew tried to moor on to the bath. The Borough Surveyor, with plenty of assistants, stopped them. An hour and a half later conservancy officials arrived and one of their representatives, a Captain Little, was allowed on to the bath. There was then a dispute over who was in charge, resulting in a 'scrimmage'. The Borough Surveyor won.

By now a large crowd had come to watch, as well as the Mayor and several councillors. The officials held a 'parley' on the tug, when Captain Little 'tripped' the two anchors at the stern of the bath. His men were about to cut away the chains holding the pontoon when deputy mayor Alderman Frederick Gould 'showed resistance'. In the resulting dispute 'boat hooks were freely used', one of which tore Gould's trousers and injured him on his left thigh. As soon as 'the miniature war' was over, Captain Little held 'another conversation' with the borough authorities, which consisted mainly of threats to sue them.

The *Surrey Mirror* appeared proud of the outcome, reporting that as the tug turned 'her head down the river, and as she steamed away cheers . . . were given for Alderman Gould and the Borough Surveyor for their present victory over the Conservancy'. The swimmers had established their right to bathe where they chose, and demonstrated the lengths they would go to in order to protect this right, and the floating pool remained. A week later David Pamplin, former teacher and examiner of swimming at Wellington College, and now at the Kingston Floating Swimming Bath, wrote to the press to 'induce the Kingstonians to avail themselves in greater numbers than they now do of the opportunity they have of bathing and learning to swim'.

After an explanation of the best strokes to use, and the importance of life saving, he ended with a quotation from the Revd C.H. Spurgeon: 'Should you fall into the water, you will find swimming of more use than mathematics.'

But in the coming years the cost of maintaining and improving the bath proved too high for the council. By the early 1890s it had closed, although the 1893 *Oarsman's and Angler's Map* still has a 'bathing place' noted on the Hampton Wick side of the river. People clearly liked a swim in Kingston, though. At three o'clock on a September morning in 1893 a local domestic servant found the back door of her employer's house open and a pile of her master's clothing on the grass near the river. She at once alerted the police. However, it turned out her employer, a tradesman in the high street, had fancied a bathe at 2 a.m. He had 'got to the Middlesex side' but was not able to get out, so he was 'obliged to walk in a nude condition' through Hampton Wick all the way to a friend's house to beg for some clothes.

In 1897 Kingston's first indoor swimming pool opened, the Corporation Baths, and it was here that the Kingston Ladies, one of the earliest swimming clubs for women on the Thames, was formed. They held their first meeting in May 1898 with twenty-four members and a few months later performed an 'entertainment' in front of an all-female audience of fifty. 'At first it was decreed that competitors should race in long dresses,' explains local historian June Sampson. 'Mercifully for them, this idea was dropped and they presumably wore the uniform club swimsuit instead. This was a knee-length garment in brown serge, with frilled sleeves, high neck, and shoulder flounces edged with gold braid.' In 1901, however, competitors had to wear stockings 'because husbands and fathers were present'.

How crazy this seems today, and how difficult and uncomfortable it must have been to swim in both knee-length serge and stockings. But this certainly didn't stop the Kingston Ladies and they were one of several clubs that would dominate the river-racing scene in the early 1900s, fielding a number of champion swimmers. In the summer they swam in the Thames, in the winter they held galas indoors. In July 1901 five club members entered the Thames 'opposite the Swan at Ditton' and swam to the railway bridge at Kingston, just over two miles. One added a further half a mile by carrying on to Corporation Island in Richmond. The following month Florence Harper was reported as having 'broken all records' by swimming from Hampton Court Bridge to Teddington Weir in four hours, while in 1905 Ethel Littlewood made a record nine-mile swim from Hampton Court Bridge to Richmond Railway Bridge in five hours. The following year she set another record, swimming sixteen miles between Sunbury and Richmond locks in eleven hours, beating seven male competitors.

There was also a junior club for women, the Kingston Cygnet Swimming Club. At their annual long-distance race in 1906, seventeen-year-old Claire Parlett, along with twelve others, left Sunbury Lock at 11 a.m. The 'wonderful girl swimmer' didn't leave the water until 7.30 p.m., after swimming thirteen miles in eight and a half hours, a feat that 'beats all previous records for lady swimmers in the Thames'. It must have been a round trip, for she was loudly cheered as she passed through Molesey and Teddington locks before ending at Kingston Railway Bridge looking 'quite fresh and well'.

Kingston was a focal point for women swimmers at the turn of the century, Reading may have had a club in 1904, and other Thames towns had designated bathing places, but aside from racers in Maidenhead in the 1950s this is the first time I've come across so many champion women in one place. The Kingston Ladies fielded both national and international stars; Violet Morgan won the Southern Counties ASA Girls 100 yards freestyle championship in 1910, while in 1924 Audrey Clemons, 'still in her teens', swam a twelve-mile race in the Thames, lasting five and a half hours in water that was 'exceedingly cold'. Three years later Olive Bartle, aged fourteen, won the club's mile race in the Thames in twenty minutes forty-eight seconds. The fact that 50 per cent of Thames lightermen couldn't swim at the time must have made such an accomplishment even more impressive. In 1934 Bartle won bronze in the 4x110 yards freestyle relay at the Empire Games and represented Britain in the European Games in Germany. She later gave a special exhibition at Holborn Baths, where competitors were supplied with Bovril, which, the programme promised, 'prevents that sinking feeling'.

The Kingston Ladies stopped racing in the Thames in 1939, although the club kept going through the war; races were then briefly revived in 1943, but ceased in 1949. After the war, the club gained national renown for its Rhythmic Swimming Team which performed water ballet routines, and continued as a successful competitive club until the Coronation Baths closed in 1980. In 1989 it reopened at the New Malden Centre as Surrey's only Synchronised Swimming Club and now has around fifty members. The Silver Lifebuoy Trophy, awarded annually for services to the club, was originally won by Daisy Littlewood in 1908 and a lifebuoy is now the club's logo.

Another women's club, the Surrey Ladies, was formed even earlier than the Kingston Club, for in 1880 they held their 'sixth annual entertainment' at the Surrey County Baths, where they gave displays of 'elegant and rapid swimming' competing for a writing desk, a lady's toilet case and a tête-à-tête tea service. As with the Kingston Ladies, they also swam in the Thames and the Surrey Ladies may well be the river's oldest, and possibly first, club for women. In 1912 they held a long-distance race from Molesey Lock, while in the summer of 1919 Ivy Hawke swam just over eleven miles from Raven's Ait to Chiswick church, spending six and a half hours in the water. Eighteen women started the race; just nine reached Teddington Lock. In 1931 a mother and daughter took part in a Surrey Ladies' Thames swim; K.E. Roberts won the endurance race for the fourth consecutive year, while her fifteen-year-old daughter, Lorna, won the club's quarter-mile Thames race twice.

Women dive off a barge at the start of the Surrey Ladies' annual river swim in 1917. The winner was fourteen-year-old Ivy Hawke.

Just who were these women who braved the often freezing Thames, who swam for hours, mile after mile, setting new records for speed and endurance, winning championships and representing their country abroad? History officer Michele Loose inserts a memory stick into a computer; she wants to show me some photos which have been recently donated. I stare at the screen as it lights up with a sepia image of eight beaming Surrey Ladies competing for the 1917 long-distance swim from Raven's Ait.

The women stand in line on concrete blocks, apparently on the edge of the water, wearing one-piece costumes bearing the club badge. Second from the right is Ivy Hawke, her hands on her hips, also beaming. Another photo from the same date shows nine women in the process of jumping from a big barge, watched by uniformed soldiers. A big banner reads: THE SURREY LADIES SWIMMING CLUB ANNUAL SWIM. A third image shows Hawke being 'helped' out of the river after her swim, wearing a flowing white shift (as per modesty regulations), watched by people on a smaller Port of London boat. The day is cold; the male spectators are wearing coats, hats and scarves. Hawke was clearly an important member of the club; she's in every picture, including a group shot in which the women are fully clothed, with young girls in the front row. She's also seen posing on a boat with Hilda Coles; a caption on the back explains she was the 'bath superintendent'.

I'm hoping that Alison Young, who donated the images, might be related to one of the swimmers, but it turns out she's a collector who bought the photographs from a dealer at an antiques fair. She admits that, when it comes to swimming, 'I'm frightened to death of floating and cannot swim at all.'

However Rebecca Rouillard was so inspired by one of these photos that she decided to dig deeper, and she quickly became fascinated by Ivy Hawke. A swimmer herself, Rebecca had never imagined 'that women were swimming long-distance races in the Thames a hundred years ago'. She competed in her first open-water swim at the age of eleven, the Midmar Mile in South Africa, taking part every year for the next six years with her best time around twenty-four minutes. She stopped swimming competitively when she left school but a couple of years ago, and now living in England, she heard about the Human Race event from Hampton Court Bridge to Kingston Bridge. She joined the Kingston Royals Swimming Club and began to train. Then she realised her club had come into existence as the result of an amalgamation between the New Kingston men's club and the Surrey Ladies in 1980. This meant that Rebecca had another strong link to Ivy Hawke, and she set about finding out more.

Ivy was born on 12 April 1903, and lived in Surbiton, where her mother ran the Spread Eagle Coffee Tavern. She was fourteen when she won the 1917 Thames race, an annual long-distance swim, usually starting from Raven's Ait and in which the finish line varied, depending on who swam the furthest.

Members of the Surrey Ladies Swimming Club, the Thames' first club for women. Ivy Hawke, nicknamed the 'Smiling Swimmer', is second from left in the middle row.

She won a number of races from Raven's Ait to Kew Bridge, to Chiswick church and to Albert Bridge at Chelsea. The island was a popular place for other swimmers to begin as well; this was where, in 1888, Madame Darnley Mitchell, the 'accomplished swimming mistress of Kingston baths', had started her swim to Henley. It was also here, in July 1899, that Frederick Lane, amateur champion of Australia, made his first public appearance in England during a half-mile race against two Otter Club men. Lane 'led from start to finish'. The following year he became the first Australian to represent his country in swimming at the Olympic Games, winning two gold medals at the 1900 Paris Games – although he was actually part of the British team. Raven's Ait has changed over the years; it's been home to the Kingston Rowing College, and the Navy League's TS *Neptune*, the TS standing for training school. Today it's an 'exclusive island venue' used for weddings, business meetings and conferences.

After Hawke's swims from the Ait, she did what a lot of long-distance Thames swimmers did at the time: she set her sights on the Channel. The river was seen as an ideal place – perhaps the only place – to train for a swim between England and France that would cover at least twenty miles, and many earlier and future Channel champions started their careers in the Thames. Hawke failed on her first attempts, in 1922 and 1927, and then in 1928 she made it from France to Dover in nineteen hours and sixteen minutes, becoming the fifth woman and the third British woman ever to successfully swim the Channel. 'Miss Ivy Hawke, 23 year-old London Girl . . . conquers Channel,' reported Pathé News, which filmed the last leg of her triumph. She can be seen ploughing through the swell using a steady front crawl, the accompanying rowing boat lurching from side to side. At times the only part of her visible is her white hat, and at the end she's surrounded by cheering supporters, clearly shattered but wearing her trademark smile. No wonder she was nicknamed the 'Smiling Swimmer', with the press applauding her dogged endurance and the 'long, persistent, lonely fight' against the shifting currents of the Channel. 'I shall be all right tomorrow,' she asserted the day after her swim, 'and after that I shall continue to help my mother at home.' In 1929 she tried to swim from England to France but had to give up three miles from the end. The following year she was demonstrating her stroke at the opening of Surbiton Lagoon.

'Ivy has inspired me,' says Rebecca Rouillard, 'and made me grateful for my neoprene wetsuit and my fog-resistant swimming goggles.' She donned both when she took part in the Hampton Court to Kingston race, the first time she'd ever swum in the Thames. She found the water 'very clear and beautifully calm, it hardly seemed to be moving' and completed the course in one hour and twelve minutes, quicker than she'd anticipated – her family were still having breakfast and missed her finish – and she will 'definitely be back to do it again'. Rebecca came across Ivy

Hawke quite by chance. But Ivy's story spoke to her, and made her feel a connection with the past. When she competes now she's motivated by the women who swam before her and the legacy they left behind. Now that Rebecca knows Ivy Hawke's story, it won't be forgotten after all and perhaps the Surrey and the Kingston Ladies can at last take their rightful place in the history of British swimming.

During the early 1920s, meanwhile, a new form of river bathing for the inhabitants of Kingston was introduced when local man Samuel Emms bought property 'between High Street and the river' for a bathing station. This was again a pontoon, moored 'a few yards out in the stream', with an impressive 250 dressing cubicles on the bank. The site was for both men and women – mixed bathing was now being introduced at a number of Thames spots – with chutes supplied with mains water and diving boards. However, just as with the location of the 1880 pontoon, there was opposition, this time from the Free Church Council, and 'wordy battles' were fought through the pages of the local press. Some mocked that Emms had bought a white elephant, so on the day the bathing station opened he organised a parade through town led by a band – and an elephant. There is an Emms Passage in Kingston, possibly named after him.

The new bathing place was known as Boats and Cars, explains June Sampson, 'the idea being that it enabled people to arrive by car, park their vehicle then enjoy a boat trip or a swim in the Thames. It continued well into the 1930s.' For Jack Taylor, Media Office Manager at Kingston Council, the place was a favourite spot for his grandmother, Phyllis Broom, and her siblings from Broom Farm in Long Ditton. 'She wasn't a particularly keen swimmer, it was just what they did for recreation, like kids would go to an indoor pool now.' Jack has photographs of three of his grandmother's four siblings, two men and one woman, wearing one-piece costumes and sitting on a diving board in 1924, with Kingston Bridge in the

Phyllis Broom's siblings sitting on a diving board at Kingston's bathing place, known as Boats and Cars, in 1924.

background. Another from the same year shows people enjoying a water slide, which appears to be moored in the middle of the Thames, probably at Town End Pier where Queen's Promenade begins, 'where there is a slight kink in the river'.

The late novelist Leslie Thomas also enjoyed swimming near Kingston. He was born in 1931 and, after being orphaned at twelve, spent his adolescence at a Barnardo's home known as 'Dickies' in Kingston upon Thames. 'The river was like a bale of silk unwinding,' he later wrote, 'thick and smooth and quickly it ran like it always does when the water is warm. We swam for an hour or more until the river was darker and mistier, and running more into the sky every moment.' It's a peaceful interlude in Thomas' story of growing up in a children's home during the Second World War, as he floats happily on his back among the stumpy green islands. He also swam near Hampton Court Bridge in the River Mole, a tributary of the Thames, 'a deep and languid

A water slide moored in the River Thames at Kingston in the 1920s, probably at Town End Pier.

river, with fish in its olive cellars and with shadowy weeds running and folding like the long hair of girls'. Thomas and his friends fling themselves 'into the sweetness of the river' with not a care in the world, and laugh and play in the Thames, just as children have always done.

10

Teddington

'Miss Eileen Lee's Remarkable Effort. All Thames'
Records Eclipsed'

Surrey Comet, August 1915

Teddington Lock, a couple of miles downstream from Kingston and the point at which the Thames enters the London Borough of Richmond, marks the beginning of the tidal river. It's here that the Thames comes under the control of the Port of London Authority (PLA), as it has done since 1909. For swimmers a tidal river is an obvious challenge; swimming with the tide gives speed, swimming against it is incredibly difficult, and so timing is of the utmost importance. Sea levels rise and fall because of the gravitational forces of the moon, sun and the rotation of the earth, with tides highest around a full and new moon. The PLA provides tide tables, giving high and low water times, as well as water heights. But these are only forecasts, based on past measurements and the positions of the sun and moon in relation to the earth. What can't necessarily be predicted is the weather and wind, atmospheric pressure, and heavy rain in the Thames Valley can all affect tide times and heights.

Arriving at the start of the tidal Thames has been eventful for several noted endurance swimmers. For Lewis Pugh, after days spent swimming in a heatwave in 2006 with virtually no flow at all, 'I got to Teddington, the water cooled down, and heaven arrived. There are two high tides and two low tides every day, so every six hours the tide changes. If you're swimming from Teddington to London, it is *impossible* to swim against an incoming tide. Even kayaking is tough work when the incoming tide is at its fastest. So when the tide was coming in, I would climb out and sleep on the riverbank for the six hours. Then one hour after high tide, when the water started flowing out to sea again, I would jump in, and literally *fly* with the outgoing tide. Myself and Nick flew past buildings, quays, moored boats and under bridges. It was quite magnificent!' Likewise, when David Walliams arrived at Teddington, 'I really sped up. I had to wait a while but the flow is quicker. You get a bit outside London as well, if the river is narrow and if there's been rain, but it didn't help that much. At Teddington Lock I did accelerate.'

In Victorian times the lock was the site of two significant swimming events. In September 1865 the London Swimming Club organised a race at Teddington which the press described as 'who could swim the longest as well as furthest without touching anything and without taking any stimulant or refreshment'. This was for many years regarded as 'the longest and most famous swim in England' and the winner won the championship and a gold medal, valued at five pounds. Fifteen of the 'leading swimmers' of the day started from Teddington Lock; only two reached Barnes and the winner was a Mr Wood, who completed eight and a quarter miles with the tide in three hours sixteen minutes. The men ranged in age from fifteen into their forties and 'probably even older', all wearing 'slight bathing drawers'. One competitor from Coventry did well up to Mortlake, 'when the poor lad was handed in half dead'. Many 'struggled on until they were dead beat' and were hauled out of the water 'in a very exhausted condition'. Similar races, commented the press, 'are not likely to become popular'.

The following year three races were staged from Teddington Lock as part of Britain's first National Olympian Games. The National Olympian Association (NOA), the world's first national

Olympian association, was formed in 1865. One of its founders was Ernst Ravenstein, president of the London Swimming Club and former president of the German Gymnastics Society. The idea was to have a national, multi-sport event of 'manly exercises', held over three days in three different locations, with medals (rather than money) as prizes. At 6 p.m. on 31 July 1866, the opening event of the National Olympian Games began on the River Thames, with one-mile, half-mile and quarter-mile races starting from a barge moored a mile above the lock, all for 'gentlemen amateurs'. Heavy rain and wind meant some competitors dropped out; the three winners were all from London although there were entries from Southampton, Brighton and Liverpool. The NOA held another Olympian Games in Birmingham in 1867 and then a third in Shropshire in 1883, before winding up.

There appear to have been few major swims from Teddington in the following decades until, half a century later, Eileen Lee, whose father was the lock keeper, set a new world record. In July 1915, she had swum from Richmond to Tower Bridge, and then she repeated the course, only this time heading upstream. Then nineteen years old, she left Tower Bridge a little before 9 a.m. on 23 August and, using the 'right arm over stroke', swam until half past three, covering twenty-one and three-quarter miles in six hours and thirty-eight minutes. According to the *Surrey Comet* there were loud cheers from soldiers on Tower Wharf as she began her swim and cries of 'good luck'. At Westminster she received an ovation from wounded convalescing soldiers at St Thomas' Hospital, which she 'acknowledged with a wave of her arm'. Just before reaching Fulham Railway Bridge she 'took a few tablets of chocolate, laughingly inquiring if it was lunch time'. The paper described her 'graceful motion in the water, which she only slightly disturbs in swimming', adding that she had considerable power in her right arm, was an enthusiastic boxer and 'an expert with the foils', and intended to swim the Channel.

In August 1915, nineteen-year-old Eileen Lee (right) covered nearly twenty-two miles between Tower Bridge and Richmond and went on to set a world record in the Thames.

Eileen Lee's plan was to swim to Richmond and then return with the tide to Putney, but at Richmond the tide was 'still running' so she switched to a slow breaststroke and continued upriver. She paused in the water 'opposite the Pigeons' for six minutes where she 'partook of food' before continuing to Hammerton's Ferry at Marble Hill. There she waited for the tide to turn before beginning her return journey.

The *Thames Valley Times* reported that she was 'frequently cheered by different groups on the riverside at Richmond' but it was then announced she would finish at Kew Bridge. She had experienced 'much discomfort from the bright sun at Chiswick' and by Kew her eyes were so 'inflamed by the sun's rays' that she was advised to 'relinquish her object of going down river'. She also experienced a strong headwind and had to dodge bits of floating boxes. At Kew she was helped into a boat by her instructor, Walter

Brickett, the coach and trainer for the British swimming team during the early 1900s, having 'wound up with a good strong spurt' and walking along the landing stage 'without much sign of fatigue'.

Lee had only started swimming at the age of fifteen and the paper noted that, while many had completed long-distance swims, they had done so on tides, and 'no swimming of any importance has been recorded as starting from the lower reaches of the river and finishing up stream'. *The Sportsman* added that Lee's feat would 'stand as a record for some time'.

The *Daily Mirror* printed photographs of Brickett feeding her during the swim, at one point spooning food into her mouth and later offering her a piece of chocolate. A Gaumont newsreel of September that year opens with Lee swimming a speedy front crawl followed by a boat laden with people, Walter Brickett standing up at the back dressed all in white, furiously waving his arms to urge her on. Moments later she can be seen swimming equally fast in the other direction, now doing breaststroke and between two rowing boats. Then she's striding on to the dock, dressed and wrapped in a coat, arm in arm with Brickett and surrounded by beaming friends. The final shot shows her with a large towel wrapped round her head posing with Brickett, still talking animatedly, next to whom is her father, Teddington lock keeper Patrick Lee.

In June 1916, now described as the 'women's world record holder', she 'eclipsed all records made by men as to time', swimming twenty-three and a half miles in seven hours from the Naval College at Greenwich. Then, on 19 August, she topped that by showing 'wonderful endurance' and swimming a staggering thirty-six and a quarter miles from Teddington in ten hours seventeen minutes, thus setting a new world record for women. She started at Teddington at seven in the morning, diving from the stern of a boat in which sat her mother, 'in charge of the culinary department', as well as several London journalists ready to attest to the authenticity of the swim. Lee caught the ebb tide, reached

Wapping Pier after six hours, nine and a half minutes and returned 'on the flood' to Kew Bridge.

Conditions were said to be ideal, with the water between Putney and Mortlake so smooth it resembled a mirror on the downward part of the trip. For nearly three hours she maintained a 'perfectly even twenty-six strokes per minute'. Described as 'invariably cheerful' and regarded by Brickett as 'the most docile swimmer it would be possible to have charge of', at twenty-five miles she confessed to feeling 'a bit tired' but announced her determination to 'see it out'.

The tone of the press report is one of utter admiration: 'All records were being pulverized. The swimmer herself was in the happiest of mood.' She had beaten the previous record holder, 'an Austrian lady' who had swum twenty miles in ten hours. This was Madame Walburga von Isacescu (her name is spelt in a variety of ways), presumably in the Danube where, in 1902, she had swum for twelve hours between Melk and Vienna. Two years earlier she had become the first woman to 'attempt to rival Webb' by swimming the Channel. She was then thirty, of medium height and 'powerful physique'. But, twenty miles out of Calais, she was forced to give up.

Yet despite her being 'long distance lady champion of the world' in 1916, I can find very little on Eileen Lee but for a handful of newspaper clippings. What happened to this young woman who had only started swimming at the age of fifteen and a few years later covered more than thirty-six miles from Teddington, through London and back to Kew? Why does she disappear from the sporting pages after 1916? Was she perhaps a casualty of war? I had given up trying to find out more about her, when, one evening I received an email from someone I'd never heard of, Jill Morrison. The message window was blank and I was about to add it to the spam folder when something made me click on it. The email came from Seattle, Washington State, and began with the words, 'I am Eileen Lee's granddaughter.' Jill had read on the internet that I was writing a book on Thames swimming and wanted to put me in touch with her cousins Barbara Allan and Cathy Stroud who live in Hamilton, Ontario, and have researched the family's history, because 'I think Granny was quite the amazing woman and it still boggles my mind that she did what she did'.

Now, at last, I was to find out more about her grandmother's life. Eileen Lee was born in Sheffield on 27 October 1895, the second eldest of thirteen children. Her father, Patrick, was a naval officer who was awarded several medals during the course of his career, including a Silver Medal and Certificate from the Royal Humane Society in 1892 for heroism on HMS *Audacious*. He also served on HMS *Inconstant* where one of his shipmates was Prince Philip's grandfather, Prince Louis of Battenberg. Patrick had joined the Royal Navy on his fifteenth birthday, retiring after twenty-three years as chief petty officer. He qualified as a naval diver, and after leaving the navy worked for the River Thames Conservancy; he rejoined the navy in 1917 before reaching the rank of sergeant major in the army, serving until 1920.

When I contact Barbara Allan, she sends me two photos of Patrick Lee. In the first he looks dashing in his Royal Navy uniform, a row of medals on his jacket; in the second he appears decades older, a pipe in his mouth and a sou'wester on his head. 'Granny was having her portrait taken by a professional photographer (I don't remember why) and her father stopped by the photographer's studio to pick her up on his way home,' explains Barbara. 'As soon as he walked in the door of the studio, wearing his rain gear, the photographer yelled "DON'T MOVE" and took the photo of Patrick Lee. This photo then appeared on packages of Skipper Sardines!' Her great-grandfather also achieved local notoriety when, in 1910, while working as the assistant lock keeper at Teddington, he was 'summoned for detaining a parrot' that he was keeping in a cage outside his house at the lock and which apparently belonged to someone else.

Eileen's father Patrick Lee, pictured here in his Royal Naval uniform, was the lock keeper at Teddington.

His daughter Eileen, meanwhile, appears to have won her first race in 1912 and Barbara sends me a letter dated September 1913 in which her grandmother is offered 'our very hearty congratulations on your excellent swim at Liverpool the other day'. It's only when I look at the letter heading that I realise Eileen must have been a member of the Kingston Ladies Swimming Club. It is signed by Vera Offer, honorary secretary, sent with best wishes for Eileen's future success, noting that 'if the distance had been greater you would have done better still . . . you did credit to your club and instructors'.

As to why Eileen never attempted the Channel, Barbara believes 'financials were part of the decision, but the bigger obstacle was the war. It was deemed far too risky for all involved for her to be in the Channel for the length of time the swim would have taken when war ships including submarines were doing battle.' And the reason I couldn't find anything about her grandmother after her triumphant Thames swim in 1916 was because Eileen Lee moved to Canada. In 1919, along with her husband Maxwell Rowley Morrison, she left England and after several moves settled in Hamilton, Ontario. She was still famous enough to have been invited to meet the Prince of Wales, then travelling through Canada, at a drawing-room reception at 'the Armories' on 22 October 1919. But it appears that Eileen did not accept the invitation: 'maybe she didn't go since the reception was held on a Wednesday night from 10 p.m. to 12 a.m., so maybe a bit late for a mother?' suggests Jill.

But she continued her swimming career, and in the mid-1920s, now the mother of five children, she entered the annual Canadian National Exhibition swims in Lake Ontario which Jill describes as 'quite a gruelling swim. Granny did continue to have an amazing life. She taught swimming, ran a dance studio where one of her students, Frank Augustine, went on to become a principal dancer with the Canadian National Ballet, and in 1942 she started schools for the education of children with special needs in Hamilton. She also ran summer camps for special education kids and adults. Granny's youngest child and daughter was born mentally handicapped as a result of the doctor who came to the house to deliver the baby being drunk and the cord was wrapped around the neck, cutting off the oxygen supply during the birth. She had a personal interest in these children as a mother of one.

'Granny was a natural-born teacher,' adds Barbara, 'but her life was a hard one after marrying and having seven children.' It was made harder by the fact her husband, a graduate of Sandhurst, had been a victim of mustard gas during the war: 'the pain was excruciating for him and he turned to alcohol to numb the pain. Once his youngest child was born, he could no longer take the pressures and returned to England to seek compensation in the courts for the mustard gas. He died a few months before I was born.' Eileen Lee remained in Canada, however, with her seven children, eighteen grandchildren and four great-grandchildren. She died on 20 April 1976.

Her grandchildren always knew about her record-breaking swims, particularly the one from Teddington lasting ten hours. Two of her sisters, Delia and Doris, also swam the Thames and 'earned recognition in their own rights, but Granny's swim became the most famous of the Lee children as it set a world record,' says Barbara. 'She certainly could have taken gold at the Olympics given the opportunity.' Both her granddaughters, Jill and Cathy, were competitive swimmers, Cathy competing in Canada and the United States, winning 'many first-place ribbons and medals', while Jill changed direction and began instructing and examining children for the Red Cross and Royal Life Saving Society swimming programmes.

Barbara sends me a photo of her grandmother taken around 1915. She's standing on a beach with another young woman, both in bathing costumes as if about to start on a swim. Eileen has a regal bearing, her face full on to the viewer, while the top of the photo is pitted with holes from where it's been proudly pinned to Cathy's bulletin board for forty years.

In 1967 Barbara went on a family trip to England to visit relatives and it was then that she finally saw the site of her grandmother's famous swim. 'We stopped at Teddington and chatted with the current lock keeper who permitted me to actually work the same lock that Grandpa Lee did, located just across the river from their house. I was eleven years old, and the thought of turning that big wheel to open the lock was very intimidating to say the least! The lock keeper was quite surprised that he was chatting with a former lock keeper's granddaughter, one all the way from Canada, and offered to me, the eldest of five little girls there and standing shyly by my mum, the opportunity to work the lock. I really didn't want to, it looked so heavy, but the gentleman encouraged me and actually helped me get the wheel to start. I was right, it was sooo heavy! The entire time I was turning the wheel, only one thought was in my head, here I am, touching something that Grandpa Lee touched so many years ago and I will never forget doing this for the rest of my life!'

And what did she think of the River Thames? 'I thought it was very small at Teddington, as we had already seen it up in London, and I was amazed that this little lock was holding a river that became so big further upstream. The thought that Granny swam here was lovely, as in Teddington the river is very charming. But thinking of her swimming further upstream was not so pleasant as the river turned into a highway!'

The family have certainly treasured Eileen Lee's memory and sporting legacy. While they are disappointed to have lost letters from Noël Coward, born in Teddington in 1899 and a close friend of their grandmother's, they have a silver challenge cup from the Kingston Ladies' Club engraved with the words, 'Sunbury Lock Hampton Court Bridge to or below Molesey Lock or below Kingston Bridge for long distance swimming'. There's a list of names, dates and distances, beginning in 1905 with Claire Parlett, who swam to Richmond Lock, and ending with Eileen Lee swimming from Hampton Court to Hammersmith in 1912.

The family also has newspaper clippings, three medals (including one from a Crystal Palace fête in 1915), a set of their grandmother's dumbbells and a carved statue of Eileen Lee in wood and bronze, her hands held above her head in a diving position. But, best of all, Barbara tells me she has her grandmother's swimsuit and, when she asks if I'd like to see it, I email back YES! The next day she sends the picture and my first impression is that it looks so flimsy, this one-piece costume with capped sleeves and a Union Jack on the front. It's a hundred years old, faded to a dull grey, a little ragged below one arm, as if eaten by moths. I think of the Lycra costume I normally wear, and how heavy and waterlogged Eileen's must have become after hour upon hour swimming in the Thames. Was this the one she wore in August 1915 when she swam between Tower Bridge and Kew, struggling against a strong headwind, dodging pieces of floating boxes, her eyes so inflamed by the sun that she had to stop after nearly twenty-two miles? And did she wear it the following summer when the press reported 'all records were being pulverized'? Whether or not she did, 'Granny's swimming costume is a hoot!' says Barbara. 'How she swam in a suit with capped sleeves, buttons and legs that went down the thigh a bit just boggles the mind.' While the cloth is very thin, 'it's not too bad for something that had a lot of use, was greased, oiled and had who knows what else from the river on it,' adds Cathy, who keeps it in a towel in her dresser with her own costumes and swimming meet t-shirts.

Not only did Eileen Lee continue to swim in Canada, but she set about teaching others as well, at the school she founded in Hamilton in 1942. 'She wanted people to know how to swim so that they could save themselves,' says Barbara. 'These children never knew that they were being taught by a world champion. She was simply "Mrs Morrison". There may have been drownings in the river that she knew of as a child. With her father being a naval officer and diver, I'm sure swimming had something to do with that as well. One of Granny's sisters mentioned to us that, when they were small, Grandpa Lee just took them and threw them into the river and said "swim" so they did! Rather an odd thing to do but they did manage to figure it out. What a character! She rarely spoke of her swims as she considered it bragging, which appalled her. If she started bragging I'm sure all her siblings would have knocked it out of her in a hurry! We are so thrilled that not only Granny's story but the stories of so many who swam the river are finally being shared. The focus always seemed to be on the Channel swims and the river swims largely ignored.'

'Granny really never talked about her great feats,' says Cathy, 'in our family the deed was/is always more important than the glory. The British stiff upper lip, never complain, never explain, was always there to an extreme with her. She was very brave for swimming in a place that still, 100 years later, can cause gastro-intestinal issues. Maybe I am just putting my twenty-first-century values, ideas and knowledge on an era that didn't have the same, but it still wouldn't make me want to ever swim in the Thames! If she didn't want the accolades she shouldn't have swum a world record. She also has grandchildren who think the world should know how wonderful she was.'

11

Richmond

'Glide gently, thus for ever glide,
O Thames! that other bards may see,
As lovely visions by thy side
As now, fair river! come to me'

William Wordsworth, 'Lines written near Richmond', 1790

The town of Richmond, from where Eileen Lee set off to swim to Tower Bridge in 1915, is situated in London's most attractive borough, at least according to the town's website, and is among the wealthiest areas in the UK. Outside the railway station, however, as I walk past upmarket chain stores on my way to the local studies collection, I see a man on the pavement with a handwritten cardboard sign which reads 'Homeless'. I've come to see a scrapbook belonging to the Richmond Swimming Club, founded in 1883, and covering nearly fifty years of the history of Thames swimming. The collection is housed in the Old Town Hall, close to the riverside where the Thames glitters in the sun, the broad promenade overlooked by affluent buildings that rise up from a manicured lawn. The Thames runs through the borough for twenty-one miles and it was the beauty of the river here that inspired Wordsworth's 1790 poem, where 'in thy waters may be seen/ The image of a poet's heart'.

It's a sunny day and people are already lining up for boat rides near Richmond Bridge, completed in 1777 and once an ancient ferry site. Horace Walpole, writing to a friend a few years before the bridge was finished, complained, 'It has rained this whole month . . . the Thames is as broad as your Danube . . . The ferry-boat was turned round by the current, and carried to Isleworth.' Charles Dickens often stayed along this stretch of the river. In the summer of 1839 he rented Elm Cottage in nearby Petersham for four months, writing to the artist Daniel MacLise, 'Beard is hearty, new and thicker ropes have been put up at the tree . . . swimming feats from Petersham to Richmond Bridge have been achieved before breakfast, I myself have risen at 6 and plunged head foremost into the water to the astonishment and admiration of all beholders . . .' But while Dickens may have loved a swim, there were soon bathing regulations in place. In 1844 a letter writer to *The Times* objected, 'I have myself gone to Richmond for a river bath, but found numerous ill-natured announcements on boards, that I must be taken into custody . . . if I attempted it before so late an hour that would prevent my getting a conveyance to town the same evening.'

As with other Thames-side towns, there is little on swimming at the local museum, but for an electro-plated nickel silver cup engraved, 'Won by Tom Ward, 16th Sept. 1871, Swimming Match Richmond to Kew'. Unfortunately, explains curator Sue Barber, there are no details of the event and the man who donated the cup found it in a skip in the Isle of Wight.

The atmosphere inside the local studies collection is friendly and relaxed, the low-ceilinged attic room crowded with books and pamphlets. Archivist Felix Lancashire has the scrapbook ready for me, a large blue hardbound document including handbooks and annual reports, which together provide a potted history of the evolution of swimming in England. The book begins with an 1885 programme for the annual entertainments held by the club, which was amalgamated with the Kew Bridge Swimming Club, at the Richmond Baths. This was the headquarters of the club, and its president was the MP Thomas Skewes-Cox. A few years later the

Life Saving Society was demonstrating 'rescuing and resuscitating the Apparently Drowned', while club members were competing in a lighted candle race, attired in nightdress and nightcaps.

The Richmond Club also swam in the Thames. In 1895 fixtures included a half-mile handicap held in June, with the club using the 'dressing barge' belonging to the Surbiton Swimming Club, while three years later a quarter-mile river race was introduced. As with the Otter club, the venue for the river races changed over the years; the half-mile was sometimes held at Walton, and the quarter-mile at Petersham, Staines or Walton. In 1902, the Richmond Club's president was now a JP – he was knighted a few years later – and another river race was launched, a two-and-a-half-mile scratch race for the Holbein Shield, between Teddington and Richmond locks, 'on the ebb tide'.

The three river races soon acquired formal titles. The Majority Challenge Cup for the half-mile was inaugurated in 1903 to commemorate the club's 'coming of age', and the Wishart Challenge Cup started in 1907 for the quarter-mile at Walton.

Club members were clearly established swimmers. In 1906 they were competing in the 150 yards championship of London, where they practised 'the "crawl" stroke'. Two years later they had 'some of the fastest swimmers in the south' and one member, S. Parvin, reached the semi-finals of the 100 metres backstroke in the Olympic Games. But the number of people entering the river races was beginning to dwindle. In 1909 'inclement weather completely spoilt' the half-mile, while only six entered for the Holbein Shield. In 1911, again with bad weather, it was down to just three men.

I turn the page to find a letter written in 1915 explaining there were no fixtures arranged for the current year and no handbook had been published. And while I know what's coming, it's still a shock as I come to the club's report for the spring of that year. It makes bleak reading: gone is the usual page-long account of successes in swimming and water polo; instead there is a list of members who have joined His Majesty's Forces – as privates, lieutenants, troopers and gunners. Church bells begin to chime ominously outside the attic room as I turn to the next year's report. Now the men are missing, wounded, killed in action. Soon these young men, former champion swimmers, are invalided, gassed and prisoners of war, while some were awarded medals such as the Military Cross.

But while there were no fixtures because of the war, the club began to promote races at local schools and in 1916 there is the first mention of girls, with 'prizes for Boys and Girls Races' included in the list of expenditure. The next entry is for 1926 when its patrons are HRH the Duke of York and the Most Honourable the Marquis of Cambridge. The fortunes of the club had changed again, just as they did with other Thames clubs like those at Reading. Now there were a large number of junior members and the river races, still at Walton, were underway. But attendance wasn't as good as it had once been. In 1924 the races were 'deplorably supported' despite the 'considerable time and expense' they took to organise. In 1927, the year of the General Strike, there was still a 'poor number of entries' to the Thames races. The scrapbook ends in 1931, but the club still operates today at the Teddington Swimming Pool and since 2009 it has incorporated the Richmond Ladies Swimming Club. It describes itself as 'a friendly, non-competitive club', which, just like its Victorian forebears, offers 'a wide range of activities' with swimming sessions, snorkelling, synchronised swimming, water polo and water volleyball.

It wasn't just the Richmond Club that swam on the Thames. In September 1907 the *Daily Mirror* reported on 'the most important swimming race ever held in England', under the auspices of the 'Weekly Dispatch'. Thirty-three people swam fifteen and a half miles from Richmond Lock to Blackfriars in what became an 'annual through London swimming contest'. This was not promoted by the ASA, but drew swimmers 'from nearly every one of the Continental nations' and would continue until 1939. In the first year John Arthur Jarvis, the painter and paper hanger who would

Competitors line up for the start of the inaugural Richmond to Blackfriars race in 1907, 'the most important swimming race ever held in England'.

become English long-distance champion, won, followed by Dutch champion Pieter Lodewijk Ooms. Jarvis, then in his mid-thirties, had begun racing at sixteen, and had been the leading world middle- and long-distance swimming champion between 1898 and 1902, winning numerous 'world championships' at European events. At the 1900 Olympiad in Paris he won the 1,000 metres in the River Seine. But by the 1906 Olympic Games in Athens he was 'past his best', according to the *Oxford Dictionary of National Biography*, and his Richmond race was therefore 'perhaps his most satisfying and most publicized achievement'.

Just one woman took part in this race, and that was Lily Smith. The *Mirror* devoted its front page to a pictorial coverage of the event, showing Smith, appropriately 'wrapped in sackcloth' waiting for the race to start, Richmond Bridge packed with spectators and the Thames full of men thrashing about in the water. In 1908 Smith again took part, as a member of the Ladies Perseverance Club, at a time when many of the *Mirror*'s pictorial features were now focused on suffragettes being released from Holloway Prison. While the first

The British women's Olympic swimming team of 1912, their towelling robes on the poolside. From left to right: Bella Moore, Jennie Fletcher, Annie Spiers, Irene Steer. Chaperone Clara Jarvis, whose brother John Arthur Jarvis won the first Richmond to Blackfriars race, stands behind.

Woman's Suffrage Bill had been presented to the House of Commons back in 1832, the fight for the right to vote had now become militant. In 1907 the Women's Freedom League had been formed and the year of Smith's swim there was a mass suffragette rally in London, while the following year the first hunger strikes started.

The 1908 Richmond swimming race doesn't appear to have been segregated, although the winners were, as in this case Smith came second, with the 'lady' winner I.B. Armstrong of the Kingston Ladies Club. Overall, fifty-seven people started the race, only eighteen finished (of which, it appears, six were women), and Jarvis won the men's race, fighting off competitors from Holland, Belgium and France.

As with her successors Eileen Lee and Ivy Hawke, Smith was an established long-distance swimmer; that same year she swam sixteen miles in the Channel, and a photograph from around 1910 shows her next to Lee's trainer, Walter Brickett. She won the 'ladies half-mile

Lily Smith.

In 1912 'London's best known lady swimmer' Lily Smith set her sights on the Channel in order 'to put a stop forever to all this twaddle about the weaker sex'.

championship in the Thames' for three years from 1907 (the location isn't stated) and was also a noted water polo player. In 1911 she attempted a round trip of the Solent, but hit a submerged barrel on the way back and, such was the loss of blood, she had to stop.

By 1912, when Smith had set her sights once more on the Channel, she was 'London's best known lady swimmer'. The daughter of the superintendent of the City Fire Station and the Thames fire floats, she'd now swum twenty miles from Dover to Ramsgate. Nineteen twelve was the year women swimmers and divers first competed in the Olympics, and it also marked the launch of a window-smashing campaign by suffragettes in London's West End, leading to sentences of hard labour and solitary confinement for 'outrages' and 'acts of insubordination'. Smith was very clear about the political significance of her upcoming swim, although whether she was asked her views by the press or volunteered them isn't clear. 'I am going to swim the Channel in order to demonstrate that woman is the physical equal of men,' she said. 'I am going to put a stop forever to all this twaddle about the weaker sex. Yes, I am a firm believer in woman suffrage.'

This must have been a daring statement to make, for the idea of women's suffrage was threatening the very foundation of 'civilisation'. MPs had been warning for years that it simply wasn't fitting for women to enter the arena of politics or engage in public affairs; their proper sphere was the home. During debates in the all-male House of Commons in 1912 some said it was ridiculous to regard women as 'a sort of china doll in a sacred hearth', but others saw the vote as a badge of difference, a 'difference of masculine character and coercive power' which was necessary for the safeguarding of empire. The 'mental equilibrium of the female sex' was not as stable as that of the male; they had a tendency to hysteria, an argument that was seen to have full scientific backing. It was 'not cricket' for women to use force as the suffragettes were

In 1907 Lily Smith accompanied Jabez 'Jappy' Wolffe for four hours during his Channel swim. He tried the crossing twenty-two times.

doing: would we end up with 'masculine women'? If, as many
believed, men were superior mentally and physically, how startling
it must have been when Lily Smith entered the male sporting arena
– and actually swam alongside men in the River Thames from
Richmond to Blackfriars. But as with Eileen Lee, I can find very
little on her life, except two images, both from between 1910 and
1915. In one she stands with Brickett, while the other is a portrait
of a powerfully built, clear-eyed young woman with long flowing
hair, the top half of her costume covered entirely with medals.

Despite debates about women's mental and physical abilities,
the press were hopeful when it came to Smith's plan to swim the
Channel, pointing out that she had swum for over four hours with
Jabez Wolffe in his Channel attempt in 1907. In all Wolffe would
try, and fail, to cross the Channel twenty-two times, although he
did complete several marathon swims. He also coached a number
of successful Channel swimmers, but controversially disqualified

"Health & Strength" Series

"Jappy" Wolffe. Channel Swimmer.

Despite repeatedly failing to cross the Channel, Jabez Wolffe completed several
marathon swims, and was an accomplished walker, cyclist and rower.

American Gertrude Ederle on her first attempt when he ordered another swimmer to take her out of the water. Wolffe claimed she'd collapsed, which was disputed by several eyewitnesses, as well as Ederle herself. But in 1926 the 'Queen of the Waves' would become the first woman to swim across the Channel and the fastest person yet.

When it came to Lily Smith's attempt, the press believed 'there is no reason why a woman with her splendid physical endowments, grit and staying power' should not manage it. Her diet during training included plenty of cream and meat; while in the water she ate dry toast and sponge cake. She was 'a magnificent specimen of English womanhood' who already had 'between 70 and 80 medals'. The fact that American swimmer Rose Pitonoff was also about to try the Channel may have had something to do with the tone of the reports, with the *New York Times* promising an 'Anglo-American contest of a novel kind'. But, sadly, Smith was forced to abandon the Channel after six hours, and gave up again the following year in a state of collapse when her near 'lifeless form' had to be pulled on to the accompanying boat. By 1914 she was topping the bill, along with her sisters, at theatrical aquatics displays. Six years later a Pathé clip shows her swimming with two others in the sea; she's then seen sitting on the steps of a beach house or bathing machine, laughing, before striding down the steps and across a pebbled shore to the water. What happened to her after that I have no idea, because, like so many other champion Thames women, she just disappears. Pitonoff also failed in her 1912 Channel attempt, but did accomplish 'a fine performance in the Thames' when she swam sixteen miles from Richmond to below Tower Bridge.

In August 1910, meanwhile, the winners of the annual through London 'swimming Derby' from Richmond now received £100 and a gold cup. Forty-nine people started the race, and this time fourteen of them were women. Among these, and of particular interest to the American press, was sixteen-year-old Elsie Aykroyd (sometimes spelled as Akroyd), 'the New England lady amateur, who by a fine burst of speed at the start led the field in the early part of the contest'. She was the first to pass Hammersmith Bridge but 'lacked stamina' and by halfway was 'hopelessly out of the race'. This was a disappointment to the *New York Times*, who'd been eagerly following Aykroyd's progress, promising she was 'expected to prove more or less of a sensation to the Britons'. She had been swimming 'almost since she was able to walk' and after arriving in England she 'broke the time record' for eight miles between Barnes Bridge and Chelsea Bridge. Other American newspapers called her the 'sixteen-year-old mermaid' and the 'best girl swimmer this country, if not the world, has ever produced'. She was the first woman to complete the Revere Beach–Nahant Beach swim in Massachusetts, greeted by 150,000 enthusiasts, using the 'space-devouring underhand Australian stroke'. Her motto was 'Do or Die!', which she shouted out at the beginning of each swim. The problem with the fifteen-mile course from Richmond, however, was cramp; 'at the start she was kicked in the stomach but she did not feel any effect until later'. But the following year Aykroyd won the Boston Light Swim, from Charlestown Bridge to Boston Light, competing against three professional male swimmers. She was the only one to finish the nine-mile race, fighting strong tides for over seven hours.

While Richmond was a spot for some seriously competitive races it was also, like other Thames towns, a place for fun. Pathé News made two films during the First World War believed to have been shot at Richmond. In one, titled 'The Heat Wave, London children solve the problem of how to stay cool', a mass of children jump off a narrow pier into the Thames. They appear all to be boys, most of them naked, as they dive-bomb, topple and fall into the water, which quickly becomes a soup of splashing bodies. Another film shows the 'London Scottish' crossing the Thames during a route march. Three men are helped out of their kilts, then dive off a punt in shorts and

In 1929 a temporary lido was built on the Thames at Richmond with a raft, slide and diving board.

costumes, watched by women in a nearby rowing boat as they swim across the river. After the war a temporary lido was built on the Thames; a postcard from the 1920s shows it near Richmond Bridge, a structure similar to the floating pontoon at Kingston in the same period, with a large raft for bathers, both men and women, steps down to the water, a slide and a diving board.

Some sixty years later Richmond was again the starting point for a memorable swim when Kevin Murphy covered forty-two miles through the centre of London, all the way to Gravesend. Today Kevin is known as 'King of the Channel', having completed thirty-four Channel crossings – more than any other man. He is also the honorary secretary of the Channel Swimming & Piloting Federation and president of the International Marathon Swimming Hall of Fame.

In 1970 Kevin had become the first Briton to complete a double Channel crossing. The year of his Thames swim he had already made two double and six single Channel crossings. 'I had never swum in the Thames before,' he explains today, 'but I had a habit of doing long swims early in the season as training for the Channel. My plan was to do a three-way swim in July and we were looking for a sponsor, and in June the sea is cold whereas rivers are warming up. It was quite cold, though, it was a horrible wet day, with diabolical conditions.' He was then thirty-one and working as assistant news editor at the London *Evening News*. 'The Thames was on my doorstep; I was living in Harrow, and working on Fleet Street. I dreamed it up because I thought it was a good challenge. I chose Richmond because that is the last point where there is a lock and I wanted a continuous swim, while Gravesend is as far as you can get before it becomes an estuary. There was a lot of difficulty arranging permission. The person helping me and training me at the time was Will Smith; he was a tugboat skipper at Gravesend and through him I met Don Able. Able was my pilot and he was a Thames waterman and very helpful. We had to get permission from the PLA, and I ended on their jetty at Gravesend. Smith knew the right people and got their permission, I think because it was a time when the Thames was a lot cleaner and the PLA thought it was a good idea to prove it. I don't remember people saying the Thames was dirty, but I would have ignored them anyway. It tasted slightly muddy, it wasn't too bad, although when I got to Gravesend it became brackish and salty.'

Kevin started at three o'clock on the morning of 14 June 1980. In pouring rain he swam three miles against the last of the incoming tide, then picked up the tide and shot through central London, passing Big Ben at 7.40 a.m. He reached Gravesend, having swum front crawl the entire way, in seventeen hours twenty-five minutes, three hours earlier than he'd estimated. And was he wearing a wetsuit? 'Wetsuits are for wimps,' he laughs, 'I just had trunks, goggles and a hat. Endurance swims you start at one end and you don't stop until you get out at the other, you don't do it in stages wearing a wetsuit. A wetsuit is a rubber ring.' The Thames is on a par with the Channel, he says, perhaps even more difficult because most of his Channel swims are around fifteen hours, and the logistics of a Thames swim are considerable. He ate and drank 'whatever was handed to me, it would be high-carb drinks now, back then it was probably a biscuit and a cup of coffee', and followed Channel rules that forbade him to touch anything. 'Marathon Man Murphy swims his way to record,' trumpeted the *Evening News*, reporting that he was 'nearly run down by a cargo ship on the Woolwich–Gravesend leg as he swerved to avoid another vessel', but he 'will be back at his desk tomorrow'. So would he do the Thames again? 'I'm a little past it now,' says the sixty-five-year-old, 'I have lots of injuries. My shoulders are buggered. But I'm still going to do another Channel swim. The recent by-law stopping people from swimming through London is a great shame. I set a record and there's no point setting a record if no one can beat it.'

But five years later Channel champion Alison Streeter – who has swum the Channel forty-six times, more than anyone else in the world – did beat Kevin's record, in fourteen hours twenty-eight minutes. She was also the first recorded endurance swimmer in the Thames to raise money for charity. Born in 1964, Alison's first Channel crossing was made two days after her eighteenth birthday. Today she has retired from swimming (her shoulders are 'shot to pieces'), and won't give interviews. But her mother, Freda Streeter, describes her Thames triumph: 'in 1985 Alison was raising money to swim from Ireland to Scotland but the weather was atrocious and she didn't do it, so she did the Thames from Richmond to Gravesend. The PLA said the swim couldn't be done, and not by a woman. We found a Thames waterman who knew every inch of the Thames. But there were difficulties, like the wind in the lower Thames before Gravesend. I was on the big boat and a friend was on a dinghy that was at the mercy of the wind, it blew him away from her and under a pier. The tide was so fast he was in danger of being swept away.' Alison also 'fell over a shopping trolley, she was in the shallows because the tide was so strong, and she caught her foot on a submerged trolley'.

It was Freda who taught her daughter to swim. 'She was a bad asthmatic and by the age of seven she'd never managed a week at school. What could we try? We were told rowing, swimming or singing. Well, singing was out of the question and I couldn't send a seven-year-old to row, but she could swim and swimming kept the asthma at bay. She said one day she'd like to try the Channel and we just laughed. When she was twelve on came the news about the youngest girl to have swum the Channel and she said, "that's one record I can't have".'

But Alison went on to break many records of her own and is the first and only woman to have swum the Channel three ways non-stop, in 1990. The press, always alert to a woman's physical appearance, described her as '5ft 4in and stocky with it, Streeter is built for battling the waves'. A currency trader, she was known to field phone calls from her employers during Channel crossings, saying, 'it gives me something to think about'. Ninety per cent of an endurance swim is down to mental strength, she explained, and the remaining 10 per cent is physical.

Freda says her daughter was not aware of the tradition of women swimming in the Thames: 'Alison didn't know their history, women's swims have been wiped out.' They might once have filled the sporting pages of the national press, but at some point the chain that linked her to Lily Smith, Eileen Lee and Ivy Hawke was broken, so when Alison set a Thames record in 1985 she didn't know about the women who had come before her or the way she was building on their legacy.

As for swimming in Richmond today, the local newspaper carries the usual warnings and reports of fatalities. In August 2001 a licensed river 'waterman' pulled a man from the Thames at around 1 a.m. 'I have worked on the river for 25 years,' he told the press, 'and I have seen a number of bodies pulled from the river. This guy didn't have long to go.' But locals such as TV personality and author Bamber Gascoigne still enjoy river swimming. His first time in the Thames was during his schooldays at Eton in the late 1940s: 'it was a tributary, a sluggish backwater, and a normal place for the boys to swim. There were lots of weeds and an unpleasant beastly feel, and it was rather dangerous, two boys got polio so it wasn't done after that.' Bamber moved to Richmond about thirty years ago and one day he saw Fred Hauptfuhrer, London bureau chief for *People* magazine, 'who lives in a magnificent house by the river', swimming. 'The Thames was still pretty dirty,' he says, 'but we thought if an American can do it surely we can too.' So on a hot day he took the plunge.

The seventy-eight-year-old still swims today and says there has been 'a massive change in the Thames, there used to be nothing in the water but eels and nothing on the surface but mallards, now there are herons in the trees and crested grebes on the banks. I don't do the macho Christmas Day swim, I wait until it's hot.' The furthest he's swum is half a mile upstream and back: 'you very much feel the current on the way back, swimming at high tide is the nicest. Once a seal popped up next to me, and looked at one with some curiosity, it spent a week in Richmond where there was easy fishing and then it got bored and swam off.'

According to the Teddington lifeboat service, since 2002 they have only been 'turned down twice' when setting out to rescue someone, once when there was a report of 'a man in distress in the water at Richmond. The man was Bamber Gascoigne, a regular swimmer in the river, who assured the police that he was OK.' Bamber doesn't recall this incident, but says 'the PLA police boat know us and give us a wave'. He often swims with his wife,

Christina, and a group of around ten friends at Richmond and Twickenham: 'swimming is a noticeable activity, so we cross the river and swim the other side, it's an informal thing, if it's a hot day and high tide in ten minutes then we will have a swim. A few years ago there was a motor boat, with an open roof, and around ten extremely drunk young ladies on board, one recognised me and asked if I was me and I said I was. I asked if they were a hen party and they said if they gave me a glass of champagne would I toast the bride? So I trod water and toasted her and on they went.'

He says swimmers do have to be careful of boats around Richmond: 'it is busy. I wear my specs so I can see. Once I saw a sculler and I shouted, "swimmer ahead!" and he stopped at once. It can be dangerous and we discourage people from swimming if they don't know about the river. On Saturday nights people are drunk and they jump in and their mates cheer them on, then the tide carries them and the state they are in they want to get back to where they started instead of crossing the river. Some years ago three people died in different parts of the Thames and the headline in one of the newspapers was "Killer River". A week later I was there swimming and a police officer called out, "are you coming in, sir?" I said, "yes, soon, officer", and I swam on a bit longer. As I got out the police officer said, "are you aware, sir, that this is a killer river?" Well, I told him it wasn't and we had a chat and we left the best of friends.'

'Killer river' or not, the Thames at Richmond has long been beloved of swimmers, from Dickens' joyful head-first plunge in 1839 to the formation of the town's swimming club in 1883, from record breakers John Arthur Jarvis and Lily Smith at the turn of the century to Kevin Murphy and Alison Streeter's endurance swims in the 1980s. Now that I'm about two-thirds of the way through my journey downstream, having travelled some 150 miles from the source in Gloucestershire to Richmond, I'm wondering how many other forgotten champions I have still to find as I catch the train to nearby Kew, a place I often went to as a child, but never as an adult, on the hunt for Thames swimmers.

12

Kew–Chiswick

'On the way to Kew,
By the river old and gray,
Where in the Long Ago
We laughed and loitered so'
William Ernest Henley (1849–1903),
'On the Way to Kew'

The district of Kew was the starting point for one of the most famous swimming championships on the River Thames, a five-mile course to Putney which first ran from here in 1890 and, except for the interruption of the First World War, continued until 1939. When I arrive at Kew Road Bridge the scene is disappointing; from street level it looks more like a motorway, but as I start to walk across the bridge I see a brown, silty beach at the far end providing easy access to the water. I think of a report I read from 1882, when a woman and her two-year-old child were spotted here and when a passer-by commented that it was 'cold for the child to be out', the woman replied, 'it will be colder soon'. Two bodies were later found tied together with a handkerchief and apron, with the child bound to her mother's waist.

The Thames has always been a place of tragedy and death, whether deliberate or accidental, and Kew is no exception. It was incidents like these, and particularly the plight of unmarried mothers, that inspired Jerome K. Jerome to a more sombre passage in his otherwise comical *Three Men in a Boat*, when the three friends discover the dead body of a woman, lying 'very lightly on the water'. She had 'loved and been deceived . . . left to fight the world alone, with the millstone of her shame around her neck'. After keeping herself and her child 'in miserably paid drudgery' she eventually drowned herself and the river 'hushed away the pain'.

But Kew plays a happier role in the history of Thames swimming as the setting for the five-mile long-distance championship. This initially began in 1877 and was known as the 'Lords and Commons race' because the cup was subscribed for by members of both Houses of Parliament. The original course was from Putney to Westminster Bridge or vice versa, then it was changed from Putney to Charing Cross. In 1879 the race was handed over to the Metropolitan Swimming Association, and was later run by its successor, the Amateur Swimming Association (ASA). In August 1890, 'owing to the dirty state of the river', the ASA decided to move it to Kew. The course ran from Kew Railway Bridge, half a mile downstream from where I'm standing, to Putney Pier. Sixteen swimmers competed that first year, with eleven finishing and qualifying for 'standard certificates for swimming the journey within 10 minutes of the winner'. By 1897 'colonials and foreigners' were taking part; in 1899 the winner received a sixty-guinea challenge cup and the race began from the 'Anglia Boat-house at Kew'. Only three men entered that year and just one managed to finish because the water was so cold.

Other races were held at Kew as well. In 1891 clubs affiliated to the 'City of London Swimming Association' had held their annual 1,000 yards swim from 'Maynard's Boat House to the Ibis Club House'. The following year the Zephyr Swimming Club, 'one of the best known amateur organisations in the metropolis', had their annual mile handicap with nineteen people swimming from 'Kew-bridge' to the 'Ship at Mortlake', while the ASA held a 1,000 yards race from 'Kew-bridge' to the 'Ibis Boat-house'.

Kew was also the starting point for a memorable long-distance swim by seventeen-year-old Annie Luker when, in August 1892, she set off for Greenwich intending to swim eighteen and a half miles to 'establish claim to the female championship of the world'. By London Bridge, the press reported, she was showing signs of tiring but she 'struggled on with the utmost gameness', refusing to leave the water. However, after nearly five hours and having covered sixteen miles, with 'no refreshment at all', she was helped out of the river and on to the accompanying boat, exhausted. Apart from Madame Mitchell swimming from Kingston to Henley in 1888, this is the earliest long-distance Thames swim by a woman I've yet found, and, as usual, further information is thin on the ground. Annie was born Hagar Ann Luker in 1870, in the Thames-side market town of Abingdon, one of eight children whose father, John Pearson Luker, was a swimming professor who was said to have trained Captain Webb for his Channel swim. While she appears to have started her career as a river swimmer, she went on to become a famous high diver. In January 1894 she was appearing at the Royal Aquarium, diving 'from the mid-air platform into the shallow tank used by the male divers', took part in an aquatic entertainment at Earls Court, and in May that year performed a 'sensational dive' from London Bridge.

A reporter from the *Pall Mall Gazette* described her as a 'quiet, innocent-looking' little figure, with 'timid dark diving eyes; the sort of girl one would expect to scream at a black beetle'. Yet she was thrilling London on a nightly basis diving 70 feet into the Aquarium tank, sometimes sharing the billing with a boxing kangaroo and a talking horse. Her debut had certainly been dramatic; the feat had already been performed by a number of men when a member of the audience stood up to declare that a woman could do it. Annie Luker duly made her perilous plunge and 'the effect was electrical'. She had wanted her husband – 'I'm married, you know' – to make the challenge but 'he was too nervous' so a friend took his place. Her husband, however, couldn't overcome his fears: 'he never comes to see me, he couldn't stand it. We live close by, and he waits for me at home.' In 1895 she was described as Champion Lady Diver, still at the Royal Aquarium, where she continued to dive until 1900, and she was now appearing in the press as part of an endorsement for Ellimans Muscle Rub Lotion. She also worked as 'swimming instructress' at the Caledonian Road Baths in London.

Meanwhile, the long-distance amateur championship from Kew was still going strong, and in 1905 *The Times* reported on 'certainly the best race ever seen'. John Arthur Jarvis had held the title for seven years but this time he met his match in the form of B.B. Kieran, the Australian amateur champion, and D. Billington, who'd won the mile amateur championship a few weeks earlier at Highgate Pond on Hampstead Heath. Jarvis made a 'plucky effort', but was overtaken by both men, with Billington the eventual winner. In 1914 the race was won by H.C. Hatfield, but it was then put on hold during the war, resuming in 1920 with 'very few competitors'. In 1925 it attracted twenty-seven of the 'world's best swimmers' and was won by Paulo Radmilovic, also the winner in 1907. Radmilovic, born in Cardiff in 1886, had a glittering career, representing Great Britain in five Olympic Games, twice as captain of the winning water polo team.

The Kew to Putney race for men continued until the outbreak of the Second World War, while at some point a separate race for women was introduced. In 1921 the 'ladies' long distance swimming championship' from Kew to Putney was won by eighteen-year-old P. Scott from Cardiff. Twenty-two women took part and all completed the course.

In 1923 the winner was Hilda James, already a swimming superstar who had won a silver medal at the 1920 Olympics in Antwerp as a member of the British 4x100 metres relay team. When the Americans took gold with their speedy style, sixteen-year-old Hilda asked them to teach her their novel stroke and then introduced the American crawl to the UK, making her a 'pioneer of modern freestyle,' explains Ian McAllister, her grandson and biographer.

Born in 1904 in Garston, Liverpool, Hilda's religious upbringing meant she was not allowed to do RE at school and so as an unusual alternative she was taken for swimming lessons at the local baths. Although at first she hated her hand-knitted costume and didn't fancy cold water, after dodging lessons by hiding in the changing cubicle she was encouraged into the pool. Bill Howcroft, a respected swimming race official, soon spotted her star qualities and started to coach her; Hilda James then began competing at ASA championships and took two surprise gold medals at the Olympic Tests in 1919. This was despite having left school at thirteen to help her mother and sick brother, and now working full-time as a shop assistant. After the 1920 Olympics in Antwerp, swimming

Women launch themselves off from a boat at the start of the long-distance race from Kew to Putney in 1923. The winner was Hilda James (far left and closest to the camera) who three years earlier had won a silver medal at the Olympics.

in a roped-off canal basin in cold, dirty water, she became known as 'the English Comet', dominating ASA competitions in the early 1920s, officially breaking six world records, and unofficially, because of time-keeping problems, breaking many more. She was invited to the 1922 Women's Swimming Association of New York American Summer Tour, held to raise awareness of swimming as a sport and hobby for women, and used the Atlantic crossing to trial a new role as Cunard Club swimmer on RMS *Aquitania*.

Then, in July 1923, she won the long-distance Thames race, followed the next month by the eight-kilometre Seine long-distance championships, in choppy water full of sewage. But then triumph turned to crushing disappointment. Her mother insisted on accompanying her to the 1924 Olympics. When the Olympic Committee told her there was already a chaperone and that she would have to go at her own expense, she refused to let her daughter go. Hilda was under twenty-one and a minor: there was nothing she could do but bow to her parents' wishes. That year, however, she won the Thames championship again, before leaving the world of amateur swimming to join Cunard officially as the first celebrity crewmember.

By now she had 'broken and lowered English records at almost every yards distance available,' explains Ian. A Gaumont clip from 1927 shows her swimming freestyle like a tornado through the water, followed by breaststroke, backstroke, trick swimming and dives. His grandmother retired 'to keep house, have a child, and return to live with her parents again', although in the mid-1960s she would teach Ian and his brother to swim. Then, in 1982, at the age of seventy-six and now with a pacemaker, she brought the house down at Guinea Gap Baths in Merseyside with an impromptu swimming display during a memorial gala for another well-known open-water swimmer, Ernie Warrington.

While Ian always knew about his grandmother's swimming career, and used to beg for information about her trophies, he

A 1925 publicity photo of swimming superstar Hilda James in her role as Cunard 'cruise hostess' aboard RMS *Carinthia*.

only began his research in earnest when his own son was born and 'it became a mission to leave a record of his interesting great-grandmother' to go with all the memorabilia. 'I think she did the Thames because it was on the circuit and coach Howcroft would have put her up to it,' says Ian. 'She was a sprint swimmer really and more used to a pool but it was an ASA championship race; and if you put her in water she would swim.'

Ian himself swam up to school level, while 'my son is a brilliant swimmer, he's a volunteer lifeguard at Bournemouth and he's built like an eel'. Yet although he has many medals, trophies and archive pictures, he doesn't have any of his grandmother's blue silk swimming costumes: 'she cut one down and made it into a swimsuit for my brother's bear!' Thanks to her adoring grandson's thirty years of research, Hilda James is better known than many of her contemporaries and to Ian's delight she was recently nominated for inclusion in the International Swimming Hall of Fame.

Joyce Cooper winner of the 1931 Women's Long Distance Swimming Championship from Mortlake to Putney, one of several long-distance Thames races for women.

In 1939, meanwhile, the Thames women's race from Kew to Putney was won by Ruth Langer, an eighteen-year-old Austrian refugee. Also a noted swimmer, three years earlier Langer had refused to take part in the Olympic Games in Berlin, later explaining, 'being Jewish, it was unthinkable to compete in the Games in Nazi Germany, where my people were being persecuted'.

As I walk back across Kew Bridge I'm wondering why, with all this illustrious river racing history, I haven't found any reports of people swimming around Kew any more and, unlike at Henley, Marlow, Maidenhead, Windsor and Hampton Court, there are no mass-participation events either. I head down to the Thames Path, stop at the Kew Pier ticket office and ask the man inside if he ever sees people swimming. 'Not with all the sewage they pump in,' he says, pointing just past the bridge. I'm later told that in the summer of 2013 a man leapt into the Thames from a pub at Kew Road Bridge for a dare, and swam across the river and back before winning a prize of a pint of beer.

Downstream in the neighbouring district of Chiswick, however, people still swim on a regular basis. In the 1920s there were open-air baths here where 'brilliant weather attracts parties of bathers,' explained Pathé News which filmed men and women splashing around together, while dozens clamber up diving boards and hurl themselves off. Today Chiswick is the location of the Great River Swim, held annually from Chiswick Pier and until recently organised in conjunction with a local restaurant, Pissarro. It started in 2002 and is in aid of Chiswick Sea Cadets, who provide activities such as 'Throw the Rope', 'Fishing for Ducks' and face painting, reminiscent of riverside carnivals of yesteryear.

Steve Newell, the swim's founder, explains, 'I'd been doing Iron Man triathlons but I'd retired by then having done twelve years of that. I was talking to friends at the Pissarro one day. I played golf with some of them and we'd been toying with the idea of hitting a golf ball across the Thames when one said, "I bet you couldn't swim across", and I said of course I could. I tried it out one summer's day at high tide, from Chiswick Pier to the Surrey bank, which is about 200 yards. My wife was there watching just in case. I had no doubts about my ability to do it, but there is a lifeboat station next door so help was at hand in an emergency. It was my first time to swim in the Thames, although I'd fallen out of boats before, when it was not that pleasant but not so bad.'

Just as would later happen at Henley and Maidenhead, when Steve advertised a Thames swim others joined in. 'I let the PLA and river police know and they came and watched. But we found it was fraught with difficulties. If you swim right on high tide there is no current, but at low tide there would be no water. And you are crossing what I call the shipping lane and that can be difficult.' So the second year they swam parallel to the bank; 'there is a quiet area near the pier. We did about 600 metres. I borrowed a sizeable buoy from the Human Race people and at low tide I went out and fixed it to the seabed.'

The first year fifteen people took part, the next year numbers dropped, because of weather, and only six people entered. 'There had been a thunderstorm and the sewers were overflowing. There had been a general alert to canoe and row clubs not to go on the river. So we almost didn't do it.' But then Steve says he got a better understanding of the river and in 2004 'we went up to one kilometre, to a green navigational pole at the upstream end of Chiswick Eyot, to the island and back. You start by swimming into the tide knowing it will turn in a few minutes, then you keep close to the riverbank as there is less current at the edge. It's a slightly unfair race because if you're fast then you get to the turnaround point and the tide is still coming in so you get a good push back. But for a weaker swimmer you get halfway and then you're swimming against high tide.'

However, he says, 'people just like to swim the Thames and especially the tidal Thames because it's a challenge'. A lot of people come from the Serpentine Swimming Club in Hyde Park: 'where they swim it's flat and calm and there's no current and they fancy a change of scenery'. Wetsuits are not required, although 'the PLA say we have to have insurance, it is a little more costly without a wetsuit rule'. From 2010 the swim was extended to a full mile to include a clockwise circumnavigation of Chiswick Eyot. In 2012, sixty people took part; the most they've ever had is 120.

Unusually, Steve was well aware of the swimmers who have come before him even before he launched the Chiswick event. 'I was introduced on one occasion to a quite elderly gentleman and he had a postcard photograph of his aunt who'd won the race from Richmond Lock to Blackfriars in 1911.' Steve is also part of a group who swim in the Thames roughly every fortnight, from the

Black Lion pub in Hammersmith, half an hour before high tide, to Chiswick Pier. 'On a sunny evening it's idyllic, there are nice houses to look at, and with a strong tide and a good stroke you can do it in a quarter of an hour, or you take in the scenery and it takes twenty-five minutes.' Again many come from the Serpentine Club, most not wearing wetsuits. There is no entry fee and it's run on a voluntary basis. Steve supplies a dinghy and a friend rows it. On one recent evening they had eleven swimmers, with only one in a wetsuit, and the water was 13 degrees. Rod Newing, who regularly takes part, explains, 'it is a very scenic and historic part of the Thames'. Steve says the PLA seem 'unconcerned about the Hammersmith swim, they say they want to work with me not against me. It's only when there are a hundred people that they want to warn ships and river clubs. They don't close the river but they send out a warning.' However, some rowing clubs disapprove: 'they feel the upstream river belongs to them. They've done well, in the Olympics and everything, and they feel they own the river. But they don't like operating at high tide.' The PLA insists on public liability insurance in exchange for a notice to mariners and, while this used to be costly, he says the insurance situation has improved. With more organised open-water swims, partly on the back of the triathlon boom, 'insurance companies are now better able to judge the risks and costs have started to fall to an affordable level'.

As elsewhere on the Thames, there are accidents at Chiswick involving unorganised, careless or drunk swimmers. In August 2003 the owner of a courier company dived into the river at around 9 p.m. to save a drowning man who had 'drunk one too many' and was struggling against the high tide. 'This kind of thing can be dangerous,' said a spokesperson from Chiswick's RNLI lifeboat, 'people don't understand how strong the river can be.' The lifeboat had already been called out 'over 170 times' that year and had recovered forty-eight people from the river.

Such warnings aren't new and seem to have increased in the

past forty years, initially as we were first encouraged to move away from the river and into indoor pools and now, with the closure of so many pools and lidos, as we make our way back to the Thames. In the early 1980s youngsters in Chiswick were said to be risking their lives by swimming during a hot spell. One resident said, 'I have lived here for eighteen years and it is only since the Chiswick swimming baths closed that children have been coming here in larger numbers. You can't stop them wanting to swim. It is very worrying. They haven't a clue about the tides. They just launch themselves into the water and then panic when they are quickly carried off.' Sewage can also be a problem. In the summer of 2004 torrential downpours led to the river's worst pollution incident in twenty years, with blocked sewerage pipes and Thames Water pumping up to one million tons of raw sewage into the river to prevent it from spilling into homes and streets.

Jason Finch, former director of the Thames Explorer Trust, an educational charity based in Chiswick, stresses the general cleanliness of the Thames, but also warns of the dangers of swimming. The Trust work with around 18,000 schoolchildren a year, taking them on to the foreshore at ten sites in London and helping them learn about geography, wildlife and history. 'You'd be amazed,' he says, 'at the number of children who live in London yet never go to the Thames . . . or who come and see the Thames at, say, Docklands and think it's the sea. A lot of our work is really helping people realise how wonderful the Thames is. It is the cleanest river flowing through any world city and has a hundred and twenty-five different species of fish. Sometimes at Chiswick it feels like we're overrun with geese, cormorants, swans and herons.'

But as for swimming, the Thames is much wider than people think: 'at Chiswick it's 144 metres wide but when we ask visiting school groups how wide they think it is, most guess 50 metres or less! The current is much stronger than people realise as well; it's not helped by the fact that the Thames is much narrower than it

Chiswick is the location of the Great River Swim, which began in 2002 and is held annually from Chiswick Pier.

was originally, because of artificially built riverside embankments, so the same amount of water flows deeper and faster than it ever did when the river was "natural".'

He says it's no wonder that two of the busiest RNLI stations are on the Thames, at Embankment and Chiswick, and are among only a handful nationally that have a full-time crew rather than volunteers; such is the demand for their services. 'The other aspect that makes Thames swimming dangerous,' says Jason, 'is the amount of river traffic – you could be hit by a boat!', whether they be rowers around Chiswick, river ferries and taxis in central and eastern London, or freight ports further east. But when it comes to the Thames foreshore, today it's a relatively empty landscape. 'You have us doing our educational work, dog walkers and sunbathers and sometimes the modern mudlarks at work. If you were to go back historically in many places it was an amazingly busy place. Really the foreshore has only become empty since the end of the Second World War.'

But there were plenty of people around on 7 April 2012 when Australian Trenton Oldfield decided to demonstrate against government cuts by disrupting the 158th University Boat Race between Oxford and Cambridge. Footage filmed from the riverbank shows both boats heading towards Chiswick Pier, with several motor boats behind, and then a lone swimmer appears. The rowers pass on either side of Trenton; incredibly, he isn't hit, and as he ducks under the blades they stop, to cries of 'you idiot!' and 'get out of the water!' He is then yanked out and thrown on to a boat, to loud applause, and is jeered as he's arrested and led away.

Trenton had apparently entered the water about five minutes earlier, and waited for the boats to arrive. The race was eventually won by Cambridge. During the subsequent court case he was found to have acted dangerously and 'displayed prejudice in sabotaging the event which he regarded as elitist'. He argued that the race was 'a symbol of a lot of issues in Britain around class. Seventy per cent of government pushing through very significant cuts are Oxford or Cambridge graduates.' He was jailed for six months for causing a public nuisance. Trenton's stunt received widespread coverage, but record-breaking river swimmer Andy Nation feels 'he is not a credit to swimming in the Thames' because 'like a naughty child he just did it to get attention'.

13

Putney

'Swimming [is] the best sport in the world for women'
Annette Kellerman, 1918

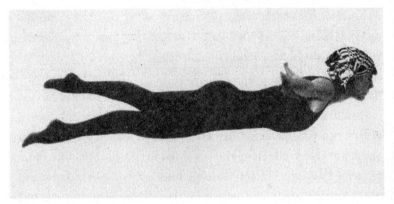

Annette Kellerman is one of the few women champions still internationally known today. Here she demonstrates the breaststroke.

Putney Bridge in west London is a significant spot in the history of Thames swimming for several reasons. It was here, for example, that in 1905 Australian Annette Kellerman began a swim that would launch her international career, while today people are no longer allowed to swim downstream from Putney to the Thames Barrier without a licence from the PLA. I approach from the Putney side of the bridge, down the high street from the station, where I can see the fifteenth-century tower of St Mary's church just on the riverside. At the other end of the bridge is All Saints' church, and according to local lore the two sisters who 'founded' the churches lived on opposite sides of the river. When they visited each other they gave instructions, either 'Full home, waterman' or 'Put nigh', and thus the two towns earned their names – Fulham and Putney.

But this is no quaint river crossing and, as with Kew Bridge, travelling across the Thames here is more like walking beside a motorway. Traffic thunders along the A219, and there are so many buses, vans and cars that it's a relief to pause for a moment and rest my eyes on the water below. The Thames is wide, with patches of shore along the banks, but it also feels like a river in a city; I've long left the countryside behind.

At the Fulham end of the bridge I walk down steps to Bishop's Park. The noise of the traffic is suddenly silenced and all I can hear are birds. The recently renovated park has its roots in Victorian times and its facilities now include an 'urban beach' for children to play on, although not on the river itself. I stop in the sculpture garden in front of a statue of two figures in stone. They seem to be embracing; perhaps it's a love story. Then I bend down to read the plaque beneath it where I can just make out a single word: GRIEF. Suddenly the sky thickens with clouds and when I look behind me the water beneath Putney Bridge has been thrown into threatening dark shadow. I think of Mary Wollstonecraft, the feminist philosopher and writer best known for *A Vindication of the Rights of Woman*, who in 1795 threw herself into the river here. In April of that year she had returned to England from a trip to Scandinavia to learn that her lover and the father of her child, Captain Gilbert Imlay, had moved in with another woman. One November night in heavy rain she jumped from Putney Bridge – some reports say she rented a boat and rowed over to Putney after finding Battersea Bridge too crowded. Incredibly, she was pulled out of the water alive and taken to a doctor. Wollstonecraft had left Imlay a letter, written 'on my knees', imploring him to send their daughter to Paris. 'When you receive this, my burning head will be cold . . . I shall plunge into the Thames where there is the least chance of my being snatched from the death I seek.' Wollstonecraft survived, returned to her writing career and two years later married William Godwin, dying as a result of childbirth in 1797. How desperate she must have been, and how ideal the Thames would have seemed as a place to end it all for someone who couldn't swim.

But as is often the case in the story of the river, this was also the setting of joyful occasions and in the nineteenth century Putney was the starting point for several races between champion men. In August 1869 the first ever amateur mile race in the Thames, from Putney to Hammersmith, was won by Tom Morris in twenty-seven minutes eighteen seconds. The long-distance amateur championship also began (or ended) at Putney, before the course was changed to Kew. In July 1877 the inaugural winner was Horace Davenport from the Ilex Club who swam from Putney to Westminster in just over one hour thirteen minutes. Davenport was 'the finest long distance amateur swimmer that England has ever seen', according to *The Badminton Library* of 1893; he played an important role in the ASA and one of his later feats was swimming from Southsea in Portsmouth to Ryde in the Isle of Wight, and back.

Other races for men were held at Putney in Victorian times. In 1874 there was a two-mile swimming championship to Hammersmith, won by E.T. Jones from Leeds, 'champion swimmer of the world', who had recently won the mile championship in the Serpentine. Two years later Jones again raced the same Thames course and won, this time against another famed swimmer, J.B. Johnson, for a cup 'instituted by the Serpentine Club, which represents the championship of England' with a 'hundred pound aside bet'. The press reported thousands assembled on the towpath and bridge, and the 'scene on the river was quite unprecedented'. In 1895 Professor G. Peat, 'well-known high diver', decided to dive from Putney Bridge and swim to Hammersmith, where he also dived off the bridge, 'for a wager and a medal'.

But for me it is Annette Kellerman's swim from Putney that is most memorable, for she is one of the few women champions from the past still internationally known and honoured today. Born in 1886 in Sydney, New South Wales, her father was Australian and her mother 'one of Paris's greatest pianists'. As a child she had 'a very distressing' leg condition, probably rickets, and wore leg braces until she was seven. Once the braces were off, and following medical advice, she started swimming. By the age of sixteen she was the 100 metres world record holder. She then set a women's world record for the mile in thirty-two minutes twenty-nine seconds, a time she later lowered to twenty-eight minutes, and her first long-distance swim was ten miles in Melbourne's Yarra River. She also gave exhibitions of swimming and diving at the Melbourne baths, and swam with fish in a glass tank at the Exhibition Aquarium. Then, with her father, Frederick, she set sail for England to try and 'swim back the family fortune', lost in the Depression of the 1890s.

During the long voyage from Australia she paced the decks to keep fit, often walking as much as ten miles. But London, she later wrote, was the 'bitterest disappointment' of her life and the streets 'as still as the dead'. Father and daughter rented rooms in Gower Street and approached local swimming clubs, but according to her biographer Emily Gibson 'there was no chance of Annette performing as a professional in a country where an amateur was seen as superior'. However, the British press had already reported that Kellerman was here to swim the Channel and 'she will probably do some record breaking while in England'. Soon she was giving an exhibition of fast swimming at an indoor bath, the press explaining she 'hails from the land of the Cornstalk' ('cornstalks' was a term sometimes used to describe 'the first generation of non-indigenous inhabitants' born in Australia), with a debut that included the 'standing-sitting-standing honeypot' or 'cannonball' dive. Kellerman demonstrated the then popular trudgeon style (similar to front crawl) at Westminster Baths, as well as swimming 'a length on her side with her hands tied behind her back' and some fancy diving, 'giving the Australian "Cooee" just before disappearing'.

'Try swimming, old chap.' Montague Holbein, who in 1899 covered forty-three miles from Blackwall to Gravesend and back, the longest Thames swim ever recorded at the time.

But with their money running out, father and daughter moved to King's Cross, where Kellerman stayed in a windowless attic room. Then Frederick came up with the idea for a publicity stunt: his daughter would swim the Thames. After all, what better place could there be for Annette to make a name for herself than England's most famous river? The *Auckland Star* reported that she had taken up residence near Kew and 'is in active training for her proposed attempt to break the records of Montague Holbein, Fred Bownes and Matthew Webb in the matter of long distance swims in the Thames'. No mention is made of any women's records Kellerman may have wanted to beat, as if those who came before her never existed; or perhaps it was just seen as more dramatic and newsworthy for a woman to attempt to break a record set by a man.

On 25 July 1899, Montague Holbein had swum from Blackwall two miles past Gravesend and back, covering forty-three miles in the longest Thames swim ever recorded at the time. He began at Blackwall Pier, 'went down river on a strong ebb' and then turned with the tide after Gravesend and 'came back on the flood to Blackwall'. Although he didn't manage to reach the pier 'owing to the tide failing him', he left the water 'quite fit and strong' after swimming for just over twelve hours. He used a slow but powerful stroke, described as 'half-side, half-back'.

Born around 1862 in the Thames-side town of Twickenham, Holbein was a cotton 'warehouseman' and had already achieved 'practically world-wide fame' for 'some marvellous feats on a bicycle'. He was also a cross-country runner and distance walker. A man of 'exceptional physique and power' according to the press, 'he made one of the finest distance riders English cycling ever produced'. He broke a number of records and in 1891 came second place in the first Bordeaux–Paris bike race.

But a cycling accident, which fractured his leg and left him lame, forced him to retire and, as with Annette Kellerman, doctors advised him to turn his attention to swimming. 'When I recovered, my leg was very stiff,' he later wrote. 'My doctor said to me: "try swimming, old chap; it may benefit the limb." I took his advice, and to my great surprise became so fond of the water that the idea struck me to break records in it as well as on land. I have never gone in for quick swimming, staying being more to my liking.'

Holbein definitely had staying power. In 1908 he would manage an incredible fifty miles in the Thames, without leaving the water. Again he began and ended at Blackwall, finishing the swim in just over thirteen hours, and 'anybody seeing him climb the ladder lowered from the tug in attendance would never have dreamed that he was returning from a fifty mile swim in rough water'.

Holbein also became noted for his attempts to swim the Channel. In 1901 he was pulled out four miles from Dover, his eyes so damaged by the salt water that he couldn't see for four days. The following year he wore a mask made of 'sticker's plaster' with glass, but this attempt failed – 'I was completely blind, and in considerable agony' – as did the next. In 1914 he wrote a book entitled *Swimming*, whose opening words were: 'Everyone ought to know how to swim. We are a nation of sailors . . . and yet swimming is an art, even to-day, which is strangely neglected.' Unusually for a champion who made his name in the Victorian age, Holbein was still swimming in his later years. In August 1936, at the age of seventy-four, he covered eighteen miles from Richmond Lock to London Bridge. Images from the time show him preparing for the swim, being greased down ready to start his journey, his white handlebar moustache as bright as his swimming cap. He died in 1944.

Fred Bownes, meanwhile, the Australian press explained, had swum just over twenty miles from Blackwall to Gravesend (no date is given), while Webb had managed forty miles in the Thames in

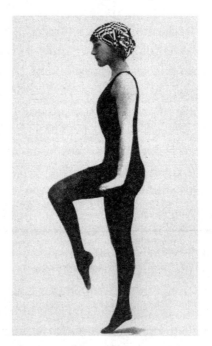

'I shall never forget that swim through the flotsam and jetsam of London': Annette Kellerman demonstrates how to tread water.

1878. It was the records of these two men, as well as of Holbein, that Annette Kellerman apparently intended to beat, although exactly how isn't clear considering her route was far shorter than either Holbein or Webb's.

On 30 June 1905 her father hired a boat and a boatman and, on a diet of mainly bread and milk, she dived into the Thames at Putney. 'It was an awful trip,' she later wrote. 'I shall never forget that swim through the flotsam and jetsam of London, dodging tugs and swallowing what seemed like pints of oil from the greasy surface of the river.' As she got to Blackwall 'three and a half hours later', the press had arrived in time to see her getting out, covered in grease. 'I was absolutely starving, and there was nothing to eat. Lunch had been forgotten. The wharf-keeper's "tea" of bread and cheese had just been brought, and he generously gave it to me. Never before had food tasted like these hunks of bread and cheese which I devoured, sitting on the wharf in my bathing costume.'

While Kellerman is one of the few women from the early 1900s whose name hasn't been erased from sporting history, details of her swims – their lengths and exact dates – are contradictory. According to the Annette Kellerman Aquatic Centre and her biographer, she swam twenty-six miles in five hours; the Sport Australia Hall of Fame puts it at sixteen miles. But British and Australian newspapers of the time reported it was thirteen and a quarter miles, which she completed in three hours, fifty-four minutes and sixteen seconds. If it was thirteen miles (and Kellerman's own reference to the swim lasting under four hours suggests it was) then it was by no means a record for a woman in the Thames. Annie Luker, for example, had swum fifteen miles in 1892. But even then the *Brisbane Courier* found it hard to accept. 'The record for the mile is 23min 16 4/5 sec, standing to the credit of B.B. Kieran, and the figures as cabled give Miss Kellerman an average much under record time. If the figures are correct, it is obvious that Miss Kellerman must have had the assistance of tide.'

In the UK, the *Daily Mirror* saw an ideal opportunity for publicity and decided to sponsor her Channel swim, inaccurately said never to have been attempted before by a woman. The only person to have successfully made it across unaided was Captain Matthew Webb and that had been thirty years earlier. The paper paid her expenses and a fee, and in return had exclusive coverage. It offered her eight guineas a week to swim along the coast in preparation and for the next two months she swam from Dover to Margate, averaging forty-five miles a week. She was also sponsored by Cadbury's Bournville Cocoa, which she drank regularly during her trial swims although it made her sick.

In July 1905 she 'beat all records for the swim from Dover to Ramsgate', covering around eighteen miles in four hours twenty minutes, beating a time set by Jabez Wolffe by ten minutes. The course had only ever been completed by three men, including Captain Webb. The *Dover Express* devoted some space to her successes so far, describing her as 5 foot 7 and weighing 12 stone. Another paper insisted that her training performances were 'accompanied by weird Maori yells, which greatly heightened the excitement'. A few years later a group of 'Maori Girls' would swim fifteen miles in the Thames from Richmond, telling the press 'we are almost an amphibious race' and dismissing the distance as 'child's play'.

In August 1905 a group of seven swimmers began their Channel attempt – among them Kellerman, Holbein, Wolffe and Thomas Burgess (who in 1911 would become the second person to succeed after Webb) – starting from different spots. Kellerman set off from Dover, covered all over with porpoise oil and with her goggles 'glued on'. The men were allowed to swim naked, 'but I was compelled to put on a tiny bathing suit' which left her armpits chafed raw. Did she really intend to swim the Channel naked? It seems an incredible thing to do, considering the amount of publicity surrounding the event and the fact that Edwardian 'ladies' were still expected to be covered from top to toe at all times, even on the beach.

Thomas Burgess was one of seven swimmers, including Annette Kellerman, who in August 1905 attempted to swim the Channel. In 1911 he became the second person to succeed after Captain Matthew Webb.

Kellerman lasted six hours, and although she had to give up on this attempt because of rough seas and seasickness, as well as two further attempts, it stood as a women's record for many years. 'I had the endurance but not the brute strength,' she wrote in 1919. 'I think no woman has this combination; that's why I say that none of my sex will ever accomplish that particular stunt.' But then, of course, in 1926 Gertrude Ederle became the first sportswoman to cross the Channel. She wore silk trunks and 'a narrow brassiere' (which she removed once she got going), making her possibly the first sportswoman to swim in what would eventually become the bikini. Kellerman later said she favoured women over men when it came to long distances 'because we have more patience', and challenged any man in the world to swim against her at any distance over ten miles.

One British paper praised Kellerman's 'powers of physical endurance of mean order, and for a mere girl in the first bloom of womanhood to battle with the waves for six hours is little short of marvellous'. She quickly became a celebrity, and was invited to swim for the Prince of Wales (later George V). But she wasn't allowed to appear with bare limbs, so she sewed a long pair of stockings on to her suit, thus inventing a prototype of her one-piece costume that would revolutionise the world of swimming for women. Despite her failed Channel attempt, Kellerman then set off for France where in September the same year she competed against seventeen men racing down the Seine, finishing joint third with Burgess, and watched by half a million spectators. She also beat the Austrian swimmer 'Baroness Isa Cescu' in a twenty-two-mile Danube River Race from Tulln to Vienna. This was presumably Madame Walburga von Isacescu, whose record Eileen Lee would break in 1916.

Kellerman was as well known for her swims as for what she wore. Aside from wanting to swim the Channel naked, and being made to cover up before appearing in front of the Prince of Wales, in 1907, while about to do a three-mile swim, she was arrested on a Boston beach for wearing her one-piece costume – at a time when most women were still wearing corsets, sleeves and a hat. She was charged with public indecency in what may well have been a cleverly orchestrated publicity stunt. During her court appearance she said it was more criminal for women to have to wear so many clothes in the water; they would never learn to swim and they had a greater chance of drowning. The judge allowed her to wear her suit, if she kept it hidden under a robe until the moment she got into the water. She went on to design the famed 'Annette Kellerman black one-piece suit', the first modern swimming costume for women.

Kellerman's legacy is incredibly important: she was a record holder, made impassioned arguments about clothing that restricted women's movement, and her career illustrates how 'the fairer sex' could find physical freedom as well as international recognition through sport. The Thames was central to this story; it was where women displayed their stamina and endurance, both physical and mental. Kellerman wasn't an outspoken champion of women's rights in the same way as her successor, Lily Smith. 'I am not in favour of women's trying to ape men in athletic affairs. I am glad this sort of new woman is dying out,' she wrote in 1918, but she did devote an entire chapter of her autobiography to an examination of the position of women in a male arena.

Swimming, she believed, was 'a woman's sport' because men had so many other sports 'where women make a poor showing' or weren't allowed to compete. 'I am not trying to shut men out of swimming,' she wrote. 'There is enough water in the world for all of us.' But women were more graceful than men, had almost as much strength, and could nearly equal them in terms of distance. Men swimmers, she noted, had 'physiques more nearly resembling those of women' and she found Jabez Wolffe 'pretty fat for athletic work'. Swimming she concluded 'will make the thin women fat and the fat women thin'.

Swimming was also the only sport in which women were 'catching up' with men; in long-distance swimming women's world records came within 10 per cent of equalling men, while in running it was 73 per cent and in 'strength' events it was 60 per cent. In addition, women had more 'fatty tissue' which meant they stayed warmer, could more easily float and were less liable to get cramp.

But the topic Kellerman was most passionate about was clothing and her book includes numerous images of her wearing 'suitable tights' for exhibiting diving, an 'ideal bathing suit' for public beaches 'where swimming tights are not permitted', a jersey swimming cap for going to and from the water, and a fashionable silk bandanna worn over a rubber bathing cap. Women, she explained, needed to exercise their knees, which walking in skirts prevented, and attempting to drag loose-flowing cloth garments through water was 'like having the Biblical mill-stone around one's neck'. There was no more reason that a woman should wear heavy, awkward bathing suits than there 'is that you should wear lead chains'.

After retiring from long-distance swimming, Kellerman toured theatres across Europe and the United States starring in aquatic acts as the Australian Mermaid and Diving Venus. She is said to have pioneered water ballet, today's synchronised swimming, although she once wrote that 'this trained seal stuff gets on one's nerves'. In 1908 a Harvard academic, who had apparently examined the physiques of 10,000 women, declared she 'embodies all the physical attributes that most of us demand in The Perfect Woman'. Kellerman told reporters, 'I'm perfectly healthy, that's all.'

She revisited England a number of times, giving free lectures for women in 1913 and appearing in shows in the late 1920s where she was billed as the 'leading exponent of physical education and wonder woman of the water'. In 1912 the *Cheltenham Looker-on*, in a feature called 'women's chit-chat', described her as 'an authority of physical culture' who 'holds that swimming is the best of all exercise for girls'. Attitudes to women swimming were certainly changing; there were more swimming baths, some allowing mixed bathing, seaside resorts had dropped the Victorian regulations and 'finally, the old, ugly cumbersome bathing dresses have been discarded' and 'any woman can now wear without inviting remark the tight fitting stockingette style dress, most convenient for swimming'.

Kellerman went on to become a Hollywood film star, one of the main reasons she's still remembered today, with all the accompanying glamour, publicity shots and international audience. She starred in *Neptune's Daughter* in 1914, where she set a 'world high diving record' of 28 metres, and performed her own stunts, including leaping into a pool of crocodiles. In *A Daughter of the Gods* she appeared in many scenes naked and although she later insisted she was wearing 'very thin tights', this was made much of in the film's pre-publicity.

Kellerman's athletic achievements, like those of Annie Luker, Lily Smith, Ivy Hawke and Eileen Lee, led to a shift in public attitudes towards women. If we could swim as fast and as long as men, and perform equally perilous dives, if we could easily rise to the challenge of the Thames or the Channel, then maybe we weren't the 'weaker sex' after all. Perhaps we could even cope with having the vote. 'Those who contend that woman is too weak physically to contend with a man at the voting booth and therefore should be denied the franchise should go to see Annette Kellerman in *A Daughter of the Gods*,' declared the *New York Times Journal*. 'If votes were obtained by physical or mental courage,' echoed the *Boston Post*, 'Miss Kellerman would demand a million of them.'

In 1918 she wrote a bestselling book, *Physical Beauty and How to Keep It*, and travelled the United States lecturing on health and fitness. In 1952 her life story was turned into a film, *Million Dollar Mermaid*, starring swimmer-turned-actress Esther Williams. In 1974 Kellerman was inducted into the International Swimming Hall of Fame, the same year of her death at the age of eighty-nine.

Kellerman's 1905 swim in the Thames from Putney wasn't an isolated event in terms of women's swimming, although it's usually treated that way today. Although she doesn't appear to have made any mention of those who came before her, and she must have known about them, she was building on a tradition that went back to Victorian times. Today the memorabilia that survives from her career is extensive – film posters, colour postcards, press shots, adverts for Black Jack liquorice, cigarette cards, along with her own books, a biography and a picture book for children. Yet when she is written about now it is as if what she did in the Thames and elsewhere was unique and had never been done before or afterwards. Kellerman, we are led to believe, was the exception.

Eighteen-year-old Agnes Nicks surveys the Thames opposite the Houses of
Parliament in 1928. She became known as a cold water expert.

She wasn't the only woman to choose Putney as a place to begin
a swim. In March 1931 it was the turn of a cold-water expert,
twenty-one-year-old Agnes Nicks, who attempted to swim the
university boat race course from Putney to Mortlake in water that
was 35 degrees and to 'break the standing cold water record' held
by Dorothy Wiggin of California. But she was taken out 'in a state
of exhaustion', put aboard a boat and 'conveyed to a riverside house,
and there put to bed, and surrounded by hot water bottles'. A few
months later Nicks was back. In October she became the 'amateur
long distance record holder' by completing a ten-mile swim from
Putney to Tower Bridge in two hours to 'inaugurate her "cold water
season"'. She then dashed off in a taxi to Holborn Baths 'to wash
away the oil and petrol of the Thames'.

In November Pathé News filmed 'Miss Nicks swimming in the
Thames near the Houses of Parliament'. The caption reads: 'October,

November or December weather means nothing to Miss Nicks – she begins just when most other Eves leave off.' Nicks does a rapid front crawl, alongside a male swimmer described as her trainer, and accompanied by a small boat. She appears to be arriving at Westminster Bridge and then at Tower Bridge where her trainer helps her staggering out of the water and looking near to collapse. Did Nicks know of Kellerman's swim in the Thames twenty-six years earlier? She would certainly have been familiar with her through her films, and the press covered Nicks' swim much as they had done her predecessor's. 'And still they speak about the weaker sex!' reads a second Pathé caption, driving home the fact that women might now have the vote but that didn't mean we were men's equals. The clip ends with Nicks sitting on a pebbled shore, rubbing her hands and then clutching a towel to her face. Repeatedly described as 'a London typist', she appears to have been a member of the Excelsior Club of Highgate, which means she would have swum at the Kenwood Ladies' Pond on Hampstead Heath, a favourite venue for year-round swimmers – as it still is today.

In the 1930s, meanwhile, swimmers had a new facility at Putney where a 'beach' was established at Putney Embankment, which continued into the 1940s. Photos show a sloping stone embankment busy with sunbathers, bikes, prams and dogs, while children paddle in the Thames. Perhaps like schoolchildren at Chiswick forty years later they were attracted to the river because there was no longer an indoor swimming pool at Putney; the baths which had opened in 1886 had closed, and there would be no indoor provision for swimmers until 1968.

Today, on the Putney Pier side of the Thames, is the stone that marks the place where the university boat race starts; it first began in 1829 from Henley, but there's nothing to commemorate any of the swimming races held here. While the Wandsworth Heritage Service has archives about local swimming baths there is 'very little if anything about swimming in the Thames,' explains Heritage

Officer Ruth MacLeod. Why is there nothing to commemorate Horace Davenport's swim in 1877, Annette Kellerman's in 1905 and Agnes Nicks' in the 1930s? Where are the monuments, statues and plaques to our swimmers? Sometimes during this journey down the Thames it seems that all we have left are 'No Swimming' signs.

But in 2011 there was good news for Putney bathers when local newspapers declared commuter 'swim lanes' were 'to be created in the River Thames for fit commuters following the success of the capital's "Boris bikes"'. Dredging would begin soon, to ensure the lanes were open in time for the summer. Each lane would be roped off to prevent pleasure boats and debris floating in front of swimmers, while sprinkler systems would operate during peak hours to keep the water clean. The first lane to open would run from Putney Bridge to Westminster, and swimmers would be charged a non-refundable deposit of £1.50 for towel hire. The only problem was, the article appeared on April Fool's Day.

In reality, as from July 2012 it is now illegal to swim downstream from Putney without a licence from the PLA. So it's unlikely anyone will ever be able to officially replicate Annette Kellerman's debut British river swim, as she made her way through the flotsam and jetsam of London swallowing pints of oil and emerging three and a half hours later to sit on the wharf at Blackwall to ravenously eat her lunch.

14

The Port of London Authority

'A person must not without the prior permission of the PLA, given in writing, and in accordance with such conditions as the PLA may attach to any such permission: swim (with or without a flotation device) in the Thames anywhere between Crossness and Putney Bridge'

2012 by-law

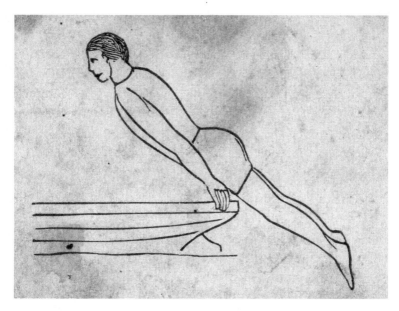

Instructions from Professor Bocock on the best way for a swimmer to leave and enter a boat.

The by-law that governs swimming from Putney down to the Thames Barrier was introduced in 2012, but well before this there had been heated discussions between the PLA and those intent on swimming through central London. In 2005, for example, Andy Nation originally planned to swim from the source to Southend but was told to stop at Teddington. 'Out of courtesy I had told the PLA about my swim and they said, no, I couldn't swim through London,' he explains. 'I got out the book of Thames by-laws and said, "can you tell me where it says I can't swim through London?" They said, "we can't but we can make it very difficult for you", and they did.' Andy says the charity he was raising money for asked him just to do the non-tidal Thames, after being approached by the PLA.

The following year, when Lewis Pugh similarly intended to swim from source to sea, 'he rang me up about his swim and asked what I'd done about the PLA. I said I'd wanted to give them the finger but because of the pressure they put on the charity I'd had to get out at Teddington. The PLA are scared of their own shadow. They control the water and they think they can stop any activity. It's not in the spirit of what adventure and pushing the boundaries of human endeavour is about. As long as you do it responsibly and safely then they should do everything they can do to assist you.'

Lewis Pugh, meanwhile, says he was told that under no circumstances could he swim beyond Teddington during his 2006 journey along the length of the Thames, as it was too dangerous. 'When I met with the PLA I explained that I'd safely swum in significantly more dangerous parts of the world including the Arctic and Antarctica. The PLA said if I attempted it a number of things were going to happen. One, a ship could try to avoid me and run aground, two, it could hit me, three, there were strong currents which would pull me under. They said, even if I made it, it would encourage people less able than me to do it and they would drown. I explained I wouldn't be swimming anywhere near any shipping, I'd be swimming along the edge of the river and I would have a safety boat next to me. They would not budge. To me they were being silly and not even considering the merits of the case.'

Lewis then walked out of the PLA's office, 'determined to go to the source and start to swim. There was an important principle, which I felt strongly about. To me this was a human rights issue. Surely rivers are natural resources. They are part of our common heritage; it's not right to say to people you can only use the river if you own a boat, but not if you don't. Every Briton should be entitled to swim down our rivers to our heart's content – providing we do so safely. Throughout the swim I received calls and emails from the PLA saying they would arrest me if I swam past Teddington. I ignored them. There was no specific law preventing me from swimming down the tidal section of the Thames. However, I began to worry about the issue as I neared London. They would surely have a residual Common Law right to pull me out, if I was deemed a danger, and being a maritime lawyer if I got arrested it wouldn't look good for either side.' Lewis says he then had a phone call from Downing Street: 'the Prime Minister said "please get out at Westminster and come and chat with me. I want to discuss climate change with you."' But he dismisses the idea of currents that can suck a swimmer under: 'it's nonsense. I didn't experience that at all. It was fast, though, down to Chelsea it was super-fast, I was flying. I doubt the PLA will grant permission to anyone to swim the tidal section of the Thames now they have legislated on the issue. Sadly, I was the first, and, it would seem, the last person to swim the full length of the Thames.'

Other long-distance swimmers, however, have more sympathy with the PLA. In 2010 American adventurer Charlie Wittmack also wanted to swim through the capital as part of his world's longest triathlon. But he had to get out at Lambeth Bridge and run through the capital before re-entering the water downriver of the Thames Barrier. 'I met with the PLA and had a really interesting conversation,' he remembers. 'I had friends attuned to the legal issues and when I went to meet the PLA I knew there was no law that was prohibiting me from swimming through central London and down to the east barrier. So I met with them essentially to get their blessing, and then I learnt just what a dangerous place it was to swim.

'As an adventurer and extreme athlete I'm always careful that people need to do the proper training and preparation. Most things I do like Everest, others aren't going to do; it's not on their doorstep. But the Thames runs through the heart of one of the most populated cities in the world. In the legal world we refer to those type of things as an "attractive nuisance"; people might see me and might want to take on the same challenge. The decision was mine, I got out at Lambeth, the BBC was there and we tried to use the coverage to discourage people from the central London section because it's too dangerous, so there were media stories that even the most experienced adventurers wouldn't do it.

'It's a complicated issue and I would defer to the experts at the port authority. We discussed that the new regulation was coming and wasn't yet in effect, and in a sense it created an opportunity for me to be the last person to swim the entire length, and I was excited about that, to do a challenge that would thereafter become impossible. The PLA were frustrated; they knew it was dangerous and they didn't have the legal authority to prevent it. That's an unusual situation to be in! The new regulations are probably good; any regulations that protect life and health are good and important. And, after all, there are other challenges to do in the world.'

The next year, when David Walliams set off on his Thames journey the original idea was once again to swim through London, but he agreed to leave the water at Westminster Bridge. 'The PLA didn't want us to do it at all,' he recalls, 'they said people would emulate me. Every year there are fatalities, people drown. It's a hard one to deal with. People *might* do that and they might not, it could even put people off because they saw me on TV.' David says the new by-law is 'sensible; to get in the Thames in central London is crazy, it's dangerous and there's lots of traffic. I had a team and everyone knew I was doing it but, even then, I was hit by rowers. People are not expecting to see you there. The PLA's job is to protect people, they are answerable to the government and the Mayor and no one wants fatalities. But we were raising two and a half million pounds and hopefully saving people's lives. I'd have liked to continue to the Thames Barrier and ultimately to the sea but at the barrier there's nowhere to stop, the charity was concerned about having a media event, and at the Houses of Parliament you had a crowd and good shots. The PLA said I had to get out and to get back in would have killed the momentum. In Sport Relief challenges there's always a risk, people have died swimming the Channel, or climbing Kilimanjaro. It was hard to walk away because someone might copy me, and actually I haven't met anyone who's said, "that looked nice". They're more likely to say, "I can't imagine how you did that."'

The 2012 by-law was 'confirmed' by the Department for Transport, after 'extensive consultation' and advice from the RNLI, the Maritime Coastguard Agency and the police, that 'attempting to swim in the River is dangerous and should not be undertaken'. The PLA argued that not only had swimming in central London not

'Swimming in the Thames is akin to rambling on the M25. A hazardous undertaking.' A 2012 by-law prevents people from swimming between Putney and the Thames Barrier without a licence from the PLA.

been allowed for years, but the by-law was in the interests of other river users, 'as a boat having to stop suddenly or swerve to avoid a swimmer could put the boat and/or its passengers at risk of injury . . . passenger services are a growing part of the commuter and tourist travel network in London and freight services keep thousands of lorries off London's roads'. It was at pains to point out that the by-law would not prevent 'a David Walliams-type charity swim', but was designed to 'balance the interests of all river users in the use of our great river. To be clear: we have not "banned" swimming over the 95 miles of river that we cover. From Teddington Lock to Putney and from Crossness to the North Sea there are no explicit requirements, bar people using their common sense.'

But many people reacted furiously to the by-law. On internet forums some said it was a result of Trenton Oldfield's disruption of the boat race a few months earlier, others that the PLA was 'another nanny among the thousands blighting the daily life of Britain'. One commentator said if you had to apply for a licence before swimming it 'removed any spontaneity' and was therefore a de facto ban; another wondered whether the licence issued was waterproof so that it could be produced when asked for.

The by-law still remains controversial and so, when Martin Garside, corporate affairs manager at the PLA, offers to take me out on a patrol boat to illustrate why it's not a good idea to swim through central London, I leap at the chance. It's a cool November afternoon when we meet at a coffee shop near Tower Pier, along with Steve Rushbrook, PLA deputy harbour master for the tidal Thames in the London area. He's been with the PLA for twenty years, while his father used to work on a Thames salvage boat. Martin has a printout he wants me to see, a list of incidents from January to October this year. So far there have been 153 'confirmed persons' in the river – either dead or rescued – and 34 'possible persons'. There have been 23 swimmers in difficulties, 19 people cut off by the tide and 18 people in the mud. There have also been 230 incidents of people threatening to jump into the Thames. Police helicopters have been called out 71 times, the RNLI lifeboats 747 times. In total, 2,330 people have been saved or assisted, and 35 have died.

I'm shocked by the figures, as Martin intends me to be, especially the fact that an average of thirty-five to forty-five people die in the Thames in central London every year, and the latest statistics only go up to October. 'Christmas is coming; people will have drunk too much,' says Martin. 'These figures show the range of all human behaviour, from a man trying to impress his girlfriend, to drunken acts of bravado, to endurance swimmers. People inadvertently fall in while walking a dog, there are attempted suicides. A classic is to try and swim across when drunk. It's a dangerous place. The Thames is not a theme park or adventure playground.'

A few months ago Martin went to the funeral for a young man who died at Gravesend; 'one second he was there and then the other second he was gone. He was strong and fit and he had gone to help people in trouble. There are some frustrations with us; people think we're faceless bureaucrats, but Steve lives and breathes the river, as his father did. We love the river, too, but a body is found once a week. We help recover them, we meet the families, we are in a different place from those who want to swim.'

'Every day we get the coastguard report,' adds Steve, 'overall we've seen a steady rise in the figures. Swimmers are a summer phenomenon; you don't see them in the first part of the year, and then it increases.' Martin says half a dozen people now contact them every year, saying they want to swim the Thames and are doing it for charity. 'They are very vague. We ask, "what charity are you doing it for?" They say, "I don't know."'

Martin has brought me a book commemorating the PLA's century of service from 1909 to 2009, its jurisdiction now running ninety-five miles from Teddington to the outer Thames Estuary. It helped rebuild the Port of London after the Second World War, made the river safer and cleaner, and 'reconciled the diverse ways in which the tidal Thames is used'. Out of habit I turn to the index and look up 'Swimming'. There is a single reference in the 230-page book: the PLA's swimming club's annual open-air gala at the Millwall Cutting at the West India Dock in the early 1930s, watched by 4,000 people. A page on sport on the river doesn't mention any swimming, but explains the PLA has overseen the annual university boat race since the Authority was created, and is now involved with coordinating fifty major events.

Martin says that while the Teddington to Putney stretch is OK for swimmers, below Putney, where the channel is narrower, there are issues of tide, transport and bridges. 'If a swimmer meets with a boat, the swimmer will come off worse. They say it's about their freedom to do this, but what would a skipper with a vessel of two hundred people on board do? Mow them down? But he's human; he would swerve to avoid them. So does he crash into a bridge, or into another vessel? This is what we asked David Walliams: "what would a boat do?"' The PLA would have preferred David to leave the water at Vauxhall, which they say would have been a safer option, and when he wanted to swim to the barrier there were 'tense negotiations'. The PLA presented him with the hazards and there was a debate between ending at Vauxhall and Westminster. As for potentially falling ill from swimming in the Thames, 'he said he'd be inoculated, but against what? I'm not a doctor but I can't see how you can be inoculated against an intestinal parasite.'

Random wild swimmers are reckless, says Martin, and while the circumstances are different, the river overwhelms them very quickly. 'It's not about us stifling individuality; it's a busy highway. If someone swam from Putney or Hammersmith, we'd want to be advised. If it's in central London, then no.' Swimming across the river, he explains, is more difficult than swimming along it. 'We have given a licence to swim beyond Putney; people can do Putney to Vauxhall if it's risk-assessed. A swim involves a lot of management, and some cost. The burden is on them to do the risk

The Port of London Authority's control centre overseeing the river at Woolwich. An average of thirty-five to forty-five people die in the river in central London every year.

assessment, but then the by-law is there to protect them. The "b" word I would use is balance, not ban.'

When I comment that some experienced Thames swimmers dispute the dangers of eddies and underflows, he laughs in disbelief. 'Those who don't believe they exist, we would gladly take them out and show them.' And with that we pay for our coffee and head back to Tower Pier for a boat ride.

Before I get on board the PLA patrol boat I'm given a life jacket, which has a canister inside. 'It will inflate if you fall in,' says Martin, 'if you do, don't try to swim, just wait to be rescued.' I step a little gingerly on to the boat and walk to the front where there is a man at the wheel. 'Bob,' says Martin introducing us, 'this is Caitlin. She's doing a book about swimming the Thames.' Bob Bradley, PLA marine river inspector, doesn't look round. He just gives a heavy sigh. 'Stick to swimming pools,' he mutters.

We set off upstream towards London Bridge, while Martin gestures repeatedly out of the window: 'the tide is going out now, so we're going against it. Look at the current around those buoys.' He wants me to understand what would happen to a swimmer in these waters: 'if you come up against a barge or something you go straight under. You could hold on to a tyre, but not for long. You could get hold of a grab chain', a series of chains looped across the walls and put up after the *Marchioness* disaster, 'and hang on the side, but you won't last long and you will be being dragged through the water.'

The sinking of the *Marchioness* was one of the worst river disasters in modern times. In the early hours of 20 August 1989, the 90-ton pleasure cruiser was run down by the 2,000-ton dredger *Bowbelle*, near Cannon Street Railway Bridge. The *Marchioness* sank in less than a minute and fifty-one of the 131 people on board, most of them attending a birthday party, drowned. The causes were said to be poor visibility, both vessels using the centre of the river and lookouts not being given clear instructions. As a result of the tragedy, safety on the Thames was tightened up, new regulations came into place and in 2002 the first lifeboat service was established, a dedicated Search and Rescue service for the tidal River Thames, with four lifeboat stations, at Gravesend, Tower Pier, Chiswick Pier and Teddington.

'Look at the waves there,' says Martin, pointing to the shore on the left. He explains that the Thames carries 70 per cent of British inland waterways traffic and this is 'category C water', which means there can be waves at least a metre high. He gestures to a young man standing at the back of our boat; 'if we threw him in now, with a life jacket on, he would drift down the river'. He then points out more evidence of the tidal flow beneath London Bridge, where water swirls around the pillars; 'anyone who tells you there aren't eddies and whirlpools . . . you would be sucked under,' he assures me. 'If we dropped an orange in here and came back for it in five minutes, it would be gone and carried under.' I look again at the force of the water between the pillars; anyone actually in that spot would be blasted around, and Martin says when someone disappears here, their body isn't found for four days.

Bob, who has worked for the PLA since the 1960s, has been onsite within five minutes of a report of a person or body in the water and couldn't find anyone. He was off duty during the *Marchioness* disaster, but was at the scene within forty minutes and found no one there either. Many survived the impact, he says, but died in the river. The PLA now have rafts that can be inflated quickly to hold up to sixty people. So far the only time they've used them was to try and save a whale.

Bob turns the boat around and we head downstream. I ask Steve what this scene would have looked like in Victorian times. 'They had wharves and lighter boats twenty-four/seven, they had all sorts of boats, but they wouldn't have had the piers. The Thames is narrower here now, so the tidal stream is faster, and it's more enclosed. It was more common to be on the river then. But they wouldn't have had as many passenger boats.'

Bob stops the engine; we're going with the tide now and we're moving fast as we reach Wapping police station. 'I don't want to be macabre,' says Martin, 'but this is where the bodies go.' He points at a pier with a little shuttered boathouse. 'If we got a report of a body right now,' he says as we turn and head back to the Tower, 'we'd go and find it.' I think of Andy Nation and Lewis Pugh, both of whom argue that as long as we do it safely we should be allowed to swim in what is a free public resource. But, on the other hand, I wouldn't want to have Martin's job and to have to explain to inexperienced swimmers why this stretch of the Thames can be treacherous, or to be the one on call when a swimmer dies.

Steve would prefer no swimming all the way from Putney to the Thames Barrier: 'it's dangerous, however strong a swimmer you are.' Yet what about all the old Thames swimmers, those like Horace Davenport, who won the first long-distance amateur championships in 1877 from Putney to Westminster; Annie Luker, who in 1892 swam from Kew to Greenwich; and Montague Holbein, who managed forty-three miles from Blackwall to Gravesend in 1899? There they were racing in the filthy waterway, surrounded by hundreds of boats and watched by thousands of spectators, and there was no law to stop them. I haven't even got started on all those who came after them – Annette Kellerman, John Arthur Jarvis, Lily Smith and Eileen Lee – when Martin turns away from surveying the river out of the patrol boat's window and asks: 'The Victorian era? Wasn't human life cheaper then?'

15

Battersea–Lambeth

'I seek not to wander by Tyber or Arno,
Or castle-crown'd rivers in far Germanie;
To me, Oh, far dearer,
And brighter, and clearer,
The Thames as it rimples at fair Battersea'

Excerpt from a song published in
Bentley's Miscellany, 1839

Some three miles downstream from Putney, on the south side of the river and heading towards central London, is the inner city district of Battersea. While the recent by-law means people can't in theory swim around here, it was a popular place for bathers and racers from at least the 1600s. Back then, when the river was generally considered clean, Charles II and his brother James enjoyed many an evening dip 'to bathe themselves' around Battersea, Putney and Nine Elms. King Charles was certainly a river lover, with 'a propensity for swimming in the Thames at 5.00am at all seasons,' writes his biographer Antonia Fraser, plunging into its freezing waters while 'his courtiers shivered on the bank'. He was also said to have established contests on the Thames, when it was common for members of the aristocracy to sponsor working men to swim for a wager.

Swimming and 'foot races' became fashionable in England during his reign, explains *The Badminton Library*, and when Colonel Blood was arrested in 1672 for stealing the Crown Jewels at the Tower he confessed he 'had engaged' to shoot His Majesty as he went to swim in the Thames above Battersea. However, as Colonel Blood was about to take aim, 'the awe of majesty paralyzed his hand' and he changed his mind.

One of the earliest Thames races reported by the press took place at Battersea, some 150 years later, when in August 1826 'a party of printers took an aquatic excursion up the river' in order to decide a wager 'between them and a gentleman of some sporting celebrity'. The course was from Battersea Bridge to Blackfriars, four and a half miles with the tide without stopping, which another swimmer had successfully managed a few weeks earlier for a twenty-guinea bet. In this case a Mr Jolley, 'champion of the Typos', managed the swim in one hour thirty-five minutes, accompanied by pleasure boats and a band that played 'See, the Conquering Hero Comes!' as he got to Blackfriars – a tune that it would become standard practice to play for future long-distance Thames swimmers. The tide must have added to Jolley's speed considerably, as he appears to have been doing a mile in twenty-three minutes, while he 'only turned himself on his back for 40 yards' twice during the whole time.

It's a bleak morning in early May and everything looks dull when I get off a bus at Battersea Bridge. I'm intending to walk a little way upstream from here to try and find the site of a swimming match held in 1838. The road, the pavements and even the sky are grey, while ahead of me the row of Victorian street lamps that line the bridge look suitably gloomy.

The original bridge was a wooden construction, completed in 1771, and by Victorian times it was the scene of many boating accidents. In one incident in the 1870s three young men were rowing upriver and when one stood up under the bridge to haul in his oar the boat capsized. The bridge was crowded with pedestrians and the cries for help soon reached the Thames Police. All three men survived; as usual, none of them could swim.

The job of the Thames Police, formed in 1798 and described

as England's oldest police force, was to protect property in the ships, barges and wharves within London, to 'keep the river clear of reputed thieves and suspected persons' and to rescue those in trouble. The Victorian press often reported on 'terrible discoveries in the Thames', such as the day the police found a 'set of lungs' floating under Battersea Bridge, and twelve hours later another set at the railway pier. In 1873 the Thames Police saved 32 people from drowning, and 'prevented' six suicides. In total there were 150 deaths in the Thames that year, four times the number there are today: 25 were suicides, 79 were accidentally drowned, 4 were from accidents. In the remaining forty-two cases it wasn't clear how the person came to be in the river and they were therefore classed as 'found drowned'.

As I leave Battersea Bridge and walk right along the river I pass a series of moored houseboats and a sign warning 'Private Property'. Between the boats and the road there is a beach of sorts, its surface a slimy green; a group of ducks huddle on a pile of twigs, bottles and plastic bags. I'm heading to Cremorne Gardens where one of the first recorded swimming races on the Thames was held, between pupils of the recently formed National Swimming Society 'and others' for silver cups and snuff boxes during an exhibition match from Cremorne House Stadium to Battersea and back to Chelsea.

In 1831 Cremorne House, the former residence of Lord and Lady Cremorne, had been bought by Charles Random, also known as Baron De Berenger. He turned part of it into a sports club and his plans for 'The Stadium' or 'British National Arena' included a six-day Olympic Games, with one day devoted to 'feats in swimming and other aquatic exertions'. The twenty-four-acre site would be a place for 'manly and defensive exercises, equestrian, chivalric and aquatic games and skilful and amusing pastimes'. The art of swimming, wrote Random, was 'so much neglected, although so truly an important acquirement to persons in all spheres of life'. Lessons would be offered, 'aided by novel contrivances', but only early in the morning in order not to offend 'decency', as presumably

A balloon ascent at Cremorne Gardens depicted by Walter Greaves in 1872. The twelve-acre pleasure gardens opened in the 1840s, before this it was the site of a sports stadium, which boasted a school of natation and where races were held across the Thames.

the pupils were naked. There was a 4-foot-deep ornamental lake, which would serve as a School of Natation for young beginners, and 'The Honourable the Thames Navigation Committee' had recently granted 'the *extraordinary* privilege to the Proprietor of the Stadium, of constructing a floating swimming school of *large* dimensions, with permission to moor the same in the river'.

This certainly sounds an organised way of promoting the art of swimming. As with the opening event of the first National Olympian Games at Teddington Lock in 1866, the Thames was seen as the ideal spot for some 'manly exercise' in a city that was now home to numerous sporting clubs, societies and associations. During the 1838 race, the two heats 'started with the discharge of artillery', then at half past three swimmers wearing different coloured jockey caps and flannel drawers ran out of tents on the riverbank and 'plunged into the bosom of father Thames'. It appears to have become a regular event. In 1840 the *Morning*

Herald announced, 'SPORTING NOVELTIES. A SWIMMING RACE twice across the Thames by AQUATIC JOCKEYS will take place at Cremorne house, King's Road, THIS DAY'. *The Town* ran a colourful description of the scene: 'Upon entering the grounds, we observed a number of faces familiar to us, amongst which were the Duke of Dorset, the most noble the Marquis of Waterford, Lord Waldegrave, Count D'Orsay . . . "Here come the jocks!" saluted our ears . . . We turned round and beheld a file of stark naked adults, marching round the grounds, in order to show themselves' before diving into the Thames. A moment later and 'a multitude were unrobed. The Duke of Dorset was the first to fall into the line. His Grace's skin had a shrivelled, yet very glossy appearance.'

Despite aristocratic enthusiasts eager to prove themselves in the Thames, Random's grand plans were not to be and a few years later the Stadium closed. Cremorne then became one of several pleasure gardens along this stretch of the river, offering concerts, fireworks, balloon ascents and galas. The Thames was now a place for entertainment and carnival, as it would be a little later on the upper river. The artist James Whistler moved to Lindsey Row in Chelsea in 1863 and his windows faced the Thames which he painted over forty years, whether the exposed piers of Battersea Bridge at low tide or fireworks at Cremorne Gardens. But for bathers in this area the river could be dangerous. In the summer of 1857 a sixteen-year-old boy died while bathing near Cremorne Gardens when he fell into 'one of the mud-holes' with which 'the river is intersected'.

A bright blue sign announces I've arrived at the Gardens, a tiny park with cobbled stones and benches. On the right is a set of big black gates, ornately decorated with flashes of gold, which open on to a small patch of grass. I walk towards the river, to a pier and iron railings. In front of me is a large red 'No Swimming' sign. The shore below is covered in pebbles and rocks; water has collected in a big dirty puddle. I knock on the door of the park keeper's office and ask if this used to be the Victorian pleasure gardens. *'Pleasure* gardens?' replies the park keeper. 'I've no idea.' He comes outside and looks around. 'Although someone once told me their great-great-grandfather used to come here and there was a wire across the river and they used to walk across it.' And does he ever see anyone swimming here now? 'No,' he says, 'though we did see David Walliams go past. We were saying, "is it him or is it a seal?"' Aside from naked races in Victorian times and the swimming school outlined by Random, Battersea was also the location for a proposed floating bath, a precursor to various pontoons along the Thames such as the one at Kingston in 1882. 'The want of proper accommodation for bathers and swimmers in the Thames has long been felt,' explained the press. But now a limited company had been formed, with a capital of £60,000, 'for the purpose of constructing floating baths on rivers and lakes, with filtered water of uniform depth and temperature'. This would begin with 'a covered and well-ventilated iron bath, to be placed in the Thames off Battersea Park'. *Lloyd's Weekly* reported in 1870 that there would be a 60x40 feet bath, but it's not clear if this ever happened because it wasn't until 1875 that the 'first floating bath' on the Thames was announced and that was at Charing Cross, off the Embankment, while the following year another was proposed near Albert Bridge.

There is little in the way of any modern swims or races recorded at Battersea, although in the early 1950s local children often enjoyed jumping from the bridge. One remembers 'street urchins, myself included, jumping from the first arch' into the river. They then 'swam to the adjoining steps, ran along the warm pavements back on to the bridge, and jumped off again'. Bridge jumping appears to have been quite common in the 1950s. Londoner Alan Smith told his children he had been the youngest person ever to dive off Hammersmith Bridge, upstream from here, in 1952. 'He was fifteen years old and he was in a diving squad of some kind,' says his daughter Stephanie, and when he died the family scattered his ashes on the river he loved so much that he always called it 'Old Father Thames'.

Bridge jumping was once quite common in central London; as late as the 1950s local children enjoyed jumping from Battersea Bridge. Here two divers leap off the Embankment near Westminster Bridge in May 1934.

More recently, Battersea was where politician John Prescott set off for a swim in 1983 to protest against the government policy of dumping nuclear waste at sea. He'd agreed to take part in a National Union of Seamen and Greenpeace demonstration to attract attention to the issue. His mission was to swim two miles from Battersea Bridge to the House of Commons in 'frogman's gear' with a mask, oxygen and wetsuit. John liked the notion of a long swim – 'it reminded me of Chairman Mao swimming down the Yangtze' – but didn't fancy the water: 'one gulp of the Thames and you'd be a goner'. Appearing on *TV-am* shortly before his swim, he said he hoped it would be 'over quick'. His plan was to wait until the tide had gone out 'with the rest of the crap' and then set off. A congratulatory telegram from comedian Spike Milligan advised him to have a typhoid shot.

Originally, John wanted to climb out of the water at the Palace of Westminster, go up the steps on to the House of Commons terrace and deliver a petition to Prime Minister Margaret Thatcher at No. 10. But he wasn't allowed to land at the House and was told the steps couldn't be used 'for a political purpose'. He argued that if he was refused landing rights he might be in danger, quite apart from the danger he might already be in from the polluted river. It was finally agreed he could arrive at the steps, but couldn't walk up them to Parliament. Instead he'd step into a boat and then move off again.

John completed the swim in 'about an hour' on a freezing cold December day, accompanied by demonstrators in boats. He climbed out at the steps of Parliament, got in a boat and went to a landing stage at Westminster Bridge where he walked to Downing Street, still in his swimming gear. Greenpeace demonstrators 'had been planning to use me as a Trojan horse,' he later wrote, 'to get into the Palace of Westminster', by following him up the steps. A few weeks later, they took another route by climbing the clock tower of Big Ben.

The only other swim at Battersea to have received any coverage in recent years was that of a five-metre-long Northern bottlenose whale. It was spotted on 19 January 2006, having swum through the Thames Barrier, the first time the species had been seen in the Thames since records began in 1913. The following day it was seen at Battersea and then, near Albert Bridge, it was captured and lifted into a barge, but died before it could be returned to the sea.

The tradition of swimming around Battersea seems to have been lost in recent decades and while it was once a place of manly exercise and amusing pastimes with a school of natation for beginners, there are no plans to introduce swimming events as has happened further upstream. Perhaps the river here is perceived as just too dirty and crowded, quite apart from the 'No Swimming' sign and the 2012 'ban'.

I leave Cremorne Gardens and walk back along the Thames on my way to Chelsea and then Lambeth bridges. The sun is coming out and Battersea Bridge looks more inviting now; a cherry tree is heavy with blossom, golden inlays on the side of the bridge glisten and soon I come to Albert Bridge with its silver towers and pink-panelled sides, its unusual colour scheme chosen in order to make it more visible to ships during heavy fog. There are plenty of boats moored in the middle of the river, while on the roadside are regular danger signs warning of strong currents. On the opposite side is Battersea Park, once the proposed site of a floating bath.

When I get to Chelsea Bridge, nearly a mile downstream, the entrance is blocked by builders and a small forklift truck; on the southern side loom the chimneys of Battersea Power Station. The original bridge opened in 1858, with four cast-iron towers topped with lamps that were to be lit only when Queen Victoria was staying in London. Long before the bridge was built, in the mid-1600s, Sir Dudley North, civil servant and economist, was known for his swims around here. He was an intrepid swimmer and a 'master of the Thames' who could 'live in the water an afternoon with such ease as others walk upon land'. He would leave his clothes on the shore, run naked 'almost as high as Chelsea' for the 'pleasure of swimming down to his clothes before tide of flood', gliding along with the current like an arrow, dodging anchors, 'broken piles and great stones'.

Chelsea was also where two well-known eighteenth-century figures chose to swim. 'I am cruel thirsty this hot weather,' wrote Jonathan Swift to his friend Esther Johnson in June 1711, 'I am just this minute going to swim.' He presumably went naked, as he had someone 'hold my night gown, shirt, and slippers' and borrowed a napkin from his landlady 'for a cap'. He assured Johnson, 'There's no danger, don't be frighted. I have been swimming this half hour and more; and when I was coming out I dived, to make my head and all through wet, like a cold bath; but as I dived, the napkin fell off and is lost, and I have that to pay for.' He also had trouble with 'the great stones' which were so sharp that as he came out of the Thames he could hardly set his feet on them. The next night it was back for a dip again, but with 'much vexation . . . for I was every moment disturbed by boats, rot them . . . the only comfort I proposed here in hot weather is gone; for this is no jesting with these boats after 'tis dark . . . I dived to dip my head, and held my cap with both my hands, for fear of losing it. – Pox take the boats! Amen.'

Benjamin Franklin, who would become one of the 'founding fathers' of the United States of America, also swam at Chelsea. During a stay in England in 1726 he showed off his swimming skills on a Thames excursion with friends: 'At the request of the company, I stripped and leaped in the river, and swam from near Chelsea to Blackfriars (3½ miles) performing on the way many feats of activity, both upon and under water, that surprised and pleased those to whom they were novelties.' One report has him demonstrating overarm, breaststroke, backstroke and then overarm again as people, clearly surprised and impressed in a city where few could swim, stopped to watch.

Franklin, who grew up near the sea in Boston, had been swimming since a child and had 'been ever delighted with this exercise'. While in England he taught two friends to swim in the Thames and, before returning to America, he considered opening a swimming school, much like Random a hundred years later. In 1968 Franklin was inducted into the International Swimming Hall of Fame, which describes him as 'one of our first marathon and ornamental "synchronized" swimmers'.

So, well before Eton College had its seven bathing places along the river, Sir Dudley North was running naked along the Thames near Chelsea in order to swim back to his clothes, Jonathan Swift was taking a dip to escape the heat and Benjamin Franklin was showing off and inspiring others with his skills. The tradition of Thames swimming appears to be even older within the city than it is in the clear reaches of the upper river.

By Victorian times Franklin's skills would have seemed a little less remarkable, although life saving was still in its infancy and the Royal Humane Society frequently handed out medals for those brave enough to try and save another's life. In 1882 Bram Stoker of subsequent *Dracula* fame, then in his mid-thirties, was awarded a bronze medal for attempting to save a man in the Thames. On 14 September, at about six in the evening near Chelsea, a man aged between sixty and seventy and presumed to be a soldier, jumped into the river from the steamboat *Twilight*. Stoker, who was on the same boat, travelling to London Bridge and perhaps on his way to the Lyceum Theatre where he was acting manager, threw off his coat and jumped overboard. After 'grappling' with the man for five minutes, both were hauled back on to the boat and Stoker carried the man to 27 Cheyne Walk where his brother, Dr George Stoker, was unable to revive him. Bram was rewarded for his 'gallant attempt' and went on to create several fictional characters who would successfully rescue people from drowning.

By now there was an opportunity for more people to swim in the Thames, around a mile downstream from Chelsea Bridge, near Vauxhall Bridge. These were Pimlico floating baths, established by the Floating Swimming Bath Company, with plans showing a glorious front elevation like a huge conservatory. The Board of Trade approved the idea towards the end of 1873 and the bath would be moored off Grosvenor Road, at the end of Ranelagh Road. However, press reports say the 260x47-foot pool was erected opposite Pimlico Pier.

It's not easy, walking parallel with the Thames along Grosvenor Road today, to find where the baths might have been. At the end of St George's Square Garden there is still a pier, then comes Pimlico Gardens and the Westminster Boating Base. But past this there is no access to the river – which is blocked by a petrol station, flats and office buildings. I stand on tiptoe at the end of Claverton Road and peer over the stone wall at the choppy waters of the Thames.

The sound of traffic behind me on Grosvenor Road is never-ending, while on the river there is nothing moving at all. Where would the floating bath have been, was it ever built and, if so, did people use it?

I walk on to Vauxhall Bridge, the first cast-iron bridge over the Thames, where the air is noisy with the clanging of builders' cranes. Below street level the bridge is colourful, a riot of orange, red and blue, with large bronze figures gazing out over the water. It was here in the mid-1800s that there were charges of 'indecent' bathing upsetting steamboat passengers and where a clown called Mr Barry set sail in a washtub pulled by geese all the way to Westminster Bridge.

I head next to Lambeth Bridge, around three-quarters of a mile downstream and the 'ugliest ever built' according to *Dickens's Dictionary of the Thames*, where Lord Byron enjoyed a lengthy swim in 1807. On 11 August, the nineteen-year-old wrote to Elizabeth Pigot that he was about to set off for the Highlands. He would hire a boat and visit the Hebrides and then, if the weather were good, set sail to Iceland. 'Last week I swam in the Thames from Lambeth through the 2 Bridges Westminster & Blackfriars, a distance including the different turns & tacks made on the way, of 3 miles!! You see I am in excellent training in case of a squall at Sea.' Byron must have swum more than once in the Thames, for the poet James Leigh Hunt remembered first seeing him in the river sometime around 1809: 'There used to be a bathing-machine stationed on the eastern side of Westminster Bridge; and I had been bathing, and was standing on this machine adjusting my clothes, when I noticed a respectable-looking manly person, who was eyeing something at a distance.' This was Mr Jackson, a prize fighter, waiting for his pupil, Byron, who was swimming against somebody 'for a wager'.

If Byron sounded boastful in his letter to Pigot, he would soon have reason to be and today his epic swims are almost as enduring as his poetry. Three years after his swim from Lambeth he crossed the Hellespont, on his second attempt, inspired by the Greek myth of Hero and Leander, covering four miles in one hour ten minutes. Leander drowned one evening while swimming across the Hellespont to visit his lover, Hero, a journey he made every night. He 'swum for love, as I for glory,' wrote Byron in 'Written After Swimming from Sestos to Abydos'.

Later he swam from the Lido in Venice 'right to the end of the Grand Canal, including its whole length'. Byron was inducted as an Honour Swimmer by the International Marathon Swimming Hall of Fame in 1982 and is considered one of the earliest pioneers of open-water swimming. The 1828 *Book of the Society of Psychrolutes* at Eton contains a calendar with notable dates in the history of swimming, including the birth of Lord Byron, 'the first poet and first swimmer of his age'. Born with a contracted Achilles tendon, 'Swimming gave him some of the most exhilarating moments of his life,' writes Charles Sprawson, 'though he always wore trousers to conceal his disfigurement. Only in swimming could he experience complete freedom of movement, the principal to which he devoted his life.'

I stand on Lambeth Bridge, no longer the 'ugliest ever built' but today painted bright red in parts, the same colour as the seats in the House of Lords. Downstream the view is impressive, with the towers of Westminster Abbey and the Houses of Parliament, and I think about the waterway below me and the stories it carries with it. This really is, as former MP John Burns declared in 1929, 'liquid history'; where naked aquatic jockeys, poets and politicians all stripped off to immerse themselves. When Benjamin Franklin took to the river in 1726 he would hardly have had the option of an indoor pool, and nor did Byron in the early 1800s, aside from a couple of London 'Pleasure Baths'. But even if warm indoor baths had been readily available, both would still no doubt have preferred the glorious wild openness of the River Thames.

16

Westminster

'Ne'er saw I, never felt, a calm so deep!
The river glideth at his own sweet will:
Dear God! the very houses seem asleep;
And all that mighty heart is lying still!'
William Wordsworth, 'Composed upon
Westminster Bridge', 1802

Westminster Bridge is one of the most recognisable spots in London, towered over by Big Ben and the Houses of Parliament and long romanticised by painters and poets. 'What sight in the world can be finer,' asked George Henry Birch in his 1903 study of the Thames, 'than that from the bridge at Westminster as we stand close to the statue of that Boadicea who in the far-gone days burnt this Roman City of Londinium?'

The original bridge was opened in 1750; today's version is a modest looking construction painted pale green, the same colour as the seating in the House of Commons. The steps leading up to the bridge are packed, people photograph themselves on their iPads in the shadow of Boadicea in her war chariot, the still impressive bronze monument designed by Thomas Thornycroft and placed here in 1902. Big Ben chimes midday; a city cruiser churns up the river water like dirty snow, there's the slap of a police boat speeding under the bridge. Westminster Pier is similarly heaving; tourists buy ice creams and queue up for boat rides; pavement shops sell

Union Jack umbrellas and postcards, while from somewhere up on the bridge comes the sound of a lone bagpiper.

Back in Birch's day the scene was a more sombre one, 'the wherries and boats which used to ply on [the Thames] have long gone. The steamboats, with their crowded decks, have gone also. Nothing is stirring on the tideway but a wretched tug, which hoots from time to time like some horrid monster in distress.' The deserted river was no longer a popular highway, but a 'receptacle for filth' – as it had been for decades. A satirical etching by William Heath in 1828 showed just how concerned people already were about the state of the water, as a woman hurls down her teacup in horror when she sees monsters swimming in a magnified drop of Thames water. This was the year that a Commission on the London Water Supply reported on its investigation into the city's drinking water, but it wasn't until much later that a proper sewage system was installed. In the boiling hot summer of 1858 such was the stench that MPs in the Houses of Parliament were driven from parts of the building that overlooked the river. The curtains of the Commons were soaked in chloride of lime in an attempt to ward off the overpowering smell, and a Bill was rushed through to raise money for a new sewer scheme, designed by noted engineer Sir Joseph Bazalgette, and to build the Embankment. Both would have a significant impact on the river, the sewer making it cleaner and the Embankment making the Thames far narrower and its water therefore faster flowing.

The work wasn't completed until 1875, and in the meantime Captain Matthew Webb chose Westminster for a swim in order to show he was capable of swimming the Channel, an idea then dismissed as ludicrous. Webb, born in Shropshire in 1848, had grown up a seeker of adventure, daydreaming of one day performing 'a great feat or act of heroism'. He learned to swim when he was eight in a 'pond, or the River Severn, which ran near our house'. At the age of twelve he joined the merchant navy to fulfil a childhood longing for the sea and in 1873 received the Stanhope

In 1874 Captain Matthew Webb swam six miles from Westminster Bridge in order to show he was capable of conquering the Channel, using a 'slow, methodical, but perfect, breaststroke'.

Gold Medal from the Royal Humane Society for trying to save a sailor who had fallen overboard. When in 1873 Webb read about J.B. Johnson's failed attempt to swim the Channel he was inspired to try it himself. So he did what so many long-distance swimmers did after him: he swam in the Thames.

On 22 September 1874 Webb went out on a boat from Westminster Bridge with swimming professor Frederick Beckwith and journalist Robert Watson. He 'plunged immediately under the arch' of the bridge and ended at the Regent's Canal Dock, covering nearly six miles in one hour twenty minutes. 'We grew tired of watching Webb's slow, methodical, but perfect, breaststroke, and magnificent sweep of his ponderous legs,' remembered Watson. Webb then made his 'first public swim' on 3 July 1875 from Blackwall Pier to Gravesend, twenty miles 'of course with the tide'. It was this Thames swim that 'greatly encouraged me in making the attempt to swim across the Channel' and so off he went to Dover to start 'practising'. On 24 August, on his second attempt, Webb swam from Dover to Calais in twenty-one hours forty-five minutes. He was the hero of the hour, the first person to swim the Channel without using any aids, and the toast of the nation.

Of all Thames champions, Captain Matthew Webb remains the most famous today, although it's his Channel swim he's remembered for. Webb completed other feats in the Thames, performed in the United States in tank shows, and in London at the Royal Westminster Aquarium, and took part in stunts, including a six-day swim at the Lambeth Baths. And all the time he was trying to come up with something – anything – that could surpass what he'd already done by crossing the Channel. In July 1883 he thought he'd found a new way to earn a fortune, but died while trying to swim through the whirlpool rapids on the Niagara River below Niagara Falls. His object, wrote Watson, 'was not suicide but money and imperishable fame'. Today there is a memorial to Webb at Dover, and in his birthplace of Dawley where there is also a road and a school named after him.

Shortly before Webb's Channel triumph, meanwhile, his rival Captain Boyton also set off from Westminster to swim the Thames. A couple of months earlier, in May 1875, he had already crossed the Channel and become an international celebrity – although unlike Webb he did it wearing a rubber life-saving suit. While Webb is included in the International Swimming Hall of Fame as an Honour Swimmer, Boyton is listed as an Honour Pioneer Contributor.

On 20 July 1875 Boyton left Westminster, clad in his famous suit, and walked down the House of Commons stairs, 'loudly cheered' by people on the bridge and where three special steamers with a 'distinguished company' accompanied him. Boyton paddled his way to Vauxhall Bridge within fourteen minutes and, as he reached Chelsea Suspension Bridge, received a 'salute from the pier guns'. After three miles he had a rest, then got on to a boat and returned to the water at Hammersmith before arriving triumphant at Richmond.

Boyton was born in 1848, although it's disputed if this was in Ireland or the United States, and was known as 'the Fearless Frogman'. A 'showman and adventurer', he was a dedicated advocate of a suit invented by C.S. Merriman as a life-saving device for steamship passengers. The pair of rubber pants and shirt were held tight at the waist, while tubes could be used to inflate air pockets inside. Wearers remained dry and could float on their back, using a paddle to propel themselves feet first. This was one of many swimming aids and devices at the time, and in the coming decades inventors would patent a whole array of air bladders, buoys and floats, webbed gloves and winged boots, most of which were 'crude and utterly illogical', according to *The Badminton Library*.

Boyton swam up and down several rivers in the USA and Europe to publicise the suit and often, as was the case in the Thames, invited journalists to accompany him. He later toured with his own aquatic circus, opened an amusement park in Chicago and then one on Coney Island. Unlike all the failed Victorian swimming aids, the International Swimming Hall of Fame reports that a 'similar suit' is today used by the United States Navy and Coast Guard for sea rescue operations.

There were some other unusual swims from Westminster as well. In August 1878 a lieutenant in the Hungarian army decided to swim to Greenwich on a horse named Sultan. He was accompanied by a steamer carrying representatives of the Austrian, Spanish, Persian and Chinese embassies. However, the horse, perhaps unsurprisingly, didn't like the cheering and after five miles the swim was abandoned because Sultan was 'suffering from nervousness'. The lieutenant had recently patented a saddle with which to cross rivers on horseback and was clearly eager to demonstrate this, but he'd pledged to the Society for the Prevention of Cruelty Towards Animals that he would stop if the horse were unhappy.

Ten years later Westminster was again the scene of a novel swim when Jules Paul Victor Gautier set off for Greenwich, the first this daring exhibitionist would make with his feet and hands bound with rope. Gautier was born in 1856 and by his early twenties was taking part in amateur swimming races. He was a pianoforte

'The daring professor'. Jules Paul Victor Gautier, who swam the Thames with his hands and feet tied.

maker by trade, and in 1880 he first appeared in the press not for his swimming but because of his temper. One evening a man named Harry Scarborough was about to enter a pub in Camden Town when he thought he felt Gautier's hand in his pocket and accused him of being a thief. Gautier, furious at the allegation, waited until Scarborough came out of the pub and 'wanted to fight him' until he was stopped by a police constable. Scarborough then boarded an omnibus; Gautier got on, too, but was pushed off by the conductor. So then Gautier, in single-minded fury, ran alongside the bus until Scarborough got off and went to a police station. Some twenty minutes later, as Scarborough was 'proceeding in the direction of his home', he was set upon by Gautier, who exclaimed, 'I have got you now', attacked him and kicked him, breaking his leg. Gautier was later arrested. He pleaded mistaken identity, but the jury found him guilty, although they recommended mercy 'on account of the provocation which he had received in being falsely accused'. Gautier was sentenced to three months' hard labour.

A little over a year later he was back to swimming, taking part with four other men, all noted champions, in 'the mile professional championship' at the Welsh Harp in Hendon where he came last. He was described as 'late of France' and in the 1881 census he puts it as his birthplace. In reality, Gautier had been born in Islington, but for the time being he appeared happy to maintain the myth. By the end of that year an aquatic gala was held at the North London Baths 'for the benefit of Jules Gautier, the champion of France' and a few years later he was at the Lambeth Baths competing in the 'Professional Swimming Association's Handicaps races', making two finals but each time coming fifth.

He took part in events at the Royal Aquarium, where he was described as 'coming from Paris', and worked as a swimming instructor or 'professor' to the North London Swimming Club. Then, on 16 September 1888, at the age of thirty-one, Gautier tried his hand at something a little different, swimming three and a half miles in the Thames with his wrists and feet tied. 'Our old enemies the French are at us again,' reported *The Licensed Victuallers' Mirror*, 'This time Waterloo went the other way. For the "fight was fit" within a stone's throw of Waterloo on the South Western. It was a bloodless victory. Professor Jules Gautier represented France on the occasion . . . He is the Champion Long Distance Swimmer of that gallant and impulsive nation. He essayed the apparently impossible task of swimming from Westminster Bridge to Greenwich with his hands and feet tied on Sunday.'

The Victorians, and later the Edwardians, loved public feats of skill and endurance, the more bizarre, dramatic and potentially fatal the better, whether at fairs, music halls, seaside piers, agricultural halls or aquariums. Competing for a challenge and a wager were admirable things to do, while swimming as an organised event, with rules on everything from distances to clothing, was still in its infancy. When Jules Gautier set off from Westminster, extreme endurance events were all the rage, especially pedestrianism (competitive and often long-distance walking) which in some cases lasted six days straight. So it's no surprise that a 'dense concourse' assembled on the Embankment to witness 'the daring Professor' who had 'challenged all comers to try the feat with him. But all comers were no comers.' Amid cheers from the crowds on land and in boats, and as Big Ben struck a quarter to one, Gautier jumped from a skiff and 'took to the water like a duck'. Followed by 'an interested mob' on boats and protected by 'a vigilant river police' he reached Cherry Garden Pier 'as fresh as he started. An enthusiastic demonstration awaited him here, and he expressed a wish to go on to Greenwich. As, however, he had beaten the record his friends did not consider this advisable. So he reluctantly left the water – the hero of the hour.'

Gautier, noted *The Licensed Victuallers' Mirror*, was a 'native of Normandy. He is 5ft 4½ inches in height. And he weighs ten stone. A wiry man who strips well. And though he has not a very powerful physique, looks capable of any amount of endurance. He has shown us Londoners how to perform a feat not long since deemed as impossible. A feat too which has its uses. For it demonstrates the perfect facility with which an accomplished swimmer can make his way through the water, no matter how heavily handicapped. Gautier swims with a side stroke, bringing his bound hands around in a semi-circle. It looks clumsy and awkward of course. But it is wonderful the pace the Professor can get on. He is a bold and skilful swimmer. And a modest and unassuming man. Good Luck To Him.' Gautier completed the three-and-a-half-mile course in fifty-five minutes.

'The long-distance swimming champion of France, Jules Gautier, has done rather a neat thing in natation,' commented another paper. 'We don't admire big feet, as a rule, but Jules can certainly stand on his feat for bigness. Our good old national prejudice compels us to add, however, that, strange as it may appear, the "tied" was actually in his favour. Vive la France!' The following year Gautier was appearing at a swimming exhibition at Clacton-on-Sea, where he was said to be 'the champion of the world for speed', born at Caen in Normandy but coming to England at the age of four. His trick swimming (popular in the period at indoor and outdoor venues and performed by both men and women) now included 'smoking, singing, and writing; peeling, sucking, and eating an orange in the water, turning somersaults, the spinning wheel etc.'. He was still instructor to the London Swimming Club, and now to the Cholmeley School as well – the private boys' school otherwise known as Highgate School.

The same year Gautier held an 'annual costume entertainment' at the Islington Baths and then in 1890 it was back to the Thames. 'Shortly after four o'clock yesterday afternoon a man was seen to mount the parapet of London Bridge, near Fresh Wharf, and plunge into the stream. He was attired in a tight fitting bathing costume, and as he took the dive it was seen that his hands were bound together, as also were his legs just above the ankle. It afterwards transpired that the man's name was Jules Gautier, the champion French swimmer.' In 1891 he issued a challenge to swim against 'any man in the world from Dover to Victoria Pier, Folkestone, with hands and feet tied, and allow them thirty yards start. This is not all. Gautier further undertakes to dive one hundred feet with hands and feet tied, and to take a clean header from the height of fifty feet with arms bound behind and feet tied. Jules, you see, is ready to face the foe. Is the foe forthcoming?' The answer was presumably, no.

Gautier continued to take part in swimming entertainments and then in 1892 decided to try the Channel. But first he swam from Folkestone to Dover with his hands and feet chained, though some reports said he was taken out of the water about a mile from Dover. Soon after he dived 71 feet from a platform on Folkestone Pier with 'his hands fastened behind him' and his feet chained together. But the Channel attempt seems to have been abandoned because of the coldness of the water. In 1893 he was performing 'sensational high dives' at Captain Boyton's World's Water Show at Earls Court, billed as 'champion Scientific High Diver and Trick Swimmer of the World'. The same year he tried to swim from Dungeness Lighthouse in Kent to Folkestone but was forced to give up.

In 1894 he began giving free swimming lessons to Islington 'pauper children'. 'The real value of a philanthropic measure of this kind is to be found in the fact that many of these children will probably enter callings which will expose them in a special degree to the risk of drowning,' commented *The Illustrated Police News* admiringly. 'Sailor and dock and waterside labourers of all kinds may be mentioned as a class to whom a knowledge of swimming would appear to be essential; and yet how few workers of this description take the trouble to learn the art?' The paper noted that 'not ten per cent of the merchant seamen' knew how to swim, while in the navy 'the men are compelled to learn, and very unwilling pupils many of them are too'.

Gautier continued to appear as a 'speciality artist' in vaudeville, dived from piers with his hands and feet manacled, and at the age of forty-two performed with one of his sons at New Lambeth Baths; he also wrote a book, *Learning to Swim*. Then, once again, it was back to the Thames, this time for a swim from Putney Bridge to Tower Bridge still with his hands and feet tied. Only now the issue of his nationality had been cleared up. A New Zealand paper reported that 'Gautier was born in England, although both his parents belong to Normandy'.

In July 1904 Gautier dived from a boat just above Putney Bridge; 'he adopted a peculiar stroke, his clasped hands being drawn swiftly downward, while his bound legs performed a fin-like twitch', and when he got to Tower Bridge he 'performed a series of evolutions and somersaults' in the water. In 1907, at by now fifty, he swam nine miles from Richmond to Putney, announced he would again try the Channel, and the next year covered nearly sixteen miles from Blackfriars to Richmond. Then, in 1909, he added a new twist: still swimming manacled, only this time 'he swam the university boat race course from Putney to Mortlake, towing a boat licensed to carry eight persons'. Gautier was tied to the boat with a rope, and won a wager of £100. In 1910 he again swam from Putney Bridge to Mortlake for a wager of £200. But then in 1919, at the age of sixty-two, Gautier's incredible career came to an end when he died from pneumonia. Whether this was related to his swimming exploits isn't known.

However, as in the case of Eileen Lee, his skills appear to have been passed on through the family, as I discover when I contact a Gautier family history website trying to find out more about the daredevil manacled swimmer. The response I receive is from none other than Jules Gautier's great-grandson, Brian, a retired civil servant at the Ministry of Defence, who has done extensive research into his famous forebear. The bad news is that he's leaving tomorrow for a two-month trip around Europe in his motor home. I worry we'll lose touch and I'll never get the chance to speak to a real life relative of a Victorian swimming hero, but then a few months later he gives me his number. 'My great-grandfather Jules had a pianoforte factory in London,' he explains. 'Someone once did a family tree, which I found in family papers after my grandma died, and I used that as a starting point. I did know about Jules, because as a child I read the *Lion* comic and every week it had a page of feats. One week it was Jules Gautier who had swum nine miles in the Thames with his hands and feet manacled. I assumed he was related because he had the same name as my father, but my dad was faintly embarrassed by the whole thing. That was when I was small, but I always remembered it.'

Brian had also seen a photograph of Jules Gautier on the bow of a boat, with his three sons, Jules, Albert and Victor, but although the image belonged in the family papers somewhere along the line it disappeared. And why does he think Jules pretended to be French? 'I think he just wanted to be someone he wasn't, he went to prison and my theory is he came out and pretended to be someone else, although he didn't change his name. I got the impression he felt offended being accused of being a thief and he tried to put it right but not in the right way. He wanted to put prison behind him in some way and it sounds more glamorous, to be French. His dad was born in France and came to England in 1850.' How does he think Jules managed to swim when he was bound at the wrists and ankles? 'I think it was a bit like doing butterfly, with a wriggle and a flick. I've had it described to me like that, pushing both hands down and scooping forward. And he waited for the tide so that would have helped. With the tow boat he was upping the ante.'

Brian's father's father, Albert, followed in Jules' footsteps. In around 1922 Albert moved from Islington to the coastal Yorkshire town of Bridlington, where Brian was born. 'He ran the baths in town, and taught local school children to swim. I never met him, he died a couple of years before I was born, but he was well known in town and people often say they were taught by him, including my wife's mother.' Albert was also an escapologist who did demonstrations off the pier, with his feet tied, and Brian started researching him as well. 'The local paper had a load of stuff; he was a bit of a self-publicist, although he doesn't seem to have mentioned his own dad, Jules. Albert had big crowds at his pier shows; it was the heyday of seaside holidays, and my dad had to go round with a hat to collect money, which is maybe why he was embarrassed.' As for Brian: 'I'm a fairly good swimmer but not competitive, but my grandson who is fifteen has just become Devon junior champion.' Louis Jules Gautier is 'well aware of the family tradition'; he recently won a scholarship to Kelly College in Devon, which has produced numerous international swimmers and Olympians. 'He's just been to a Geneva International Swim Meet with a team of thirty-three swimmers from Kelly who finished second overall out of fifty clubs attending,' says his proud grandfather. 'Watch this space.'

If it wasn't for the way Brian painstakingly researched and put together a family tree, collating dozens of newspaper reports and photographs, it's doubtful we would ever have known so much about Jules Gautier. Just as with Eileen Lee's granddaughters and Hilda James' grandson, he has kept the legacy alive. When I finish chatting to Brian and put down the phone I'm left wondering how many other people are out there with a champion swimmer in the family, just waiting for the right opportunity to celebrate them.

Long before Jules Gautier was making a name for himself in the Thames, meanwhile, plenty of others were swimming around Westminster as well, but their motive was simply enjoyment. The boys of Westminster School often swam in the river. 'It was possible until the forties of the last century to enjoy a dip without going far from Westminster Bridge,' wrote John Carleton in his 1965 history of the school. But tides and currents meant it wasn't the safest pastime. The Annual Register for August 1781 notes, 'Drowned, as he was bathing in the Thames, the 2nd son of Sir Charles Cox, Bart., an amiable and most promising youth of Westminster School.'

The usual place for pupils to bathe was off Millbank, a well-established bathing spot by the early 1800s. When in 1809 a Mr Crunden was arrested in Brighton for undressing himself on the beach before a swim, the defence noted that at Millbank where 'the Westminster boys have from time immemorial been accustomed to bathe' they did so 'as fully as much exposed to public view as the East Cliff at Brighton'. But then canvas screens were put up around the school's bathing place, just as they were at Eton and later at other Thames-side spots, thanks to headmaster Dr Edmund Goodenough. An entry from the *Town Boy Ledger* reads: 'In order that the fellows might bathe without losing their clothes and being otherwise molested as formerly occurred a canvas of 30 yds. long and 6 or 7 high was this year 1825 placed at Milbank at Dr Goodenough's expense.' 'Do bear in mind that the word "molested" had slightly different associations in the nineteenth century,' comments Elizabeth Wells, the school's Archivist and Records Manager; back then it would have meant to pester or annoy. Part of the river at Millbank was marked out for the boys, who were 'attended by a waterman', again just like the schoolboys at Eton. 'Much to the credit of the more modern masters of Westminster School, bathing, which was only winked at formerly, is now allowed under precautionary arrangements, to ensure perfect safety,' wrote R.B. Peake in 1841 in *Memoirs of the Colman Family*. The boys still bathed here until the late 1840s but then increasing pollution meant school bathing was transferred to the Lambeth Baths and later to a floating bath at Charing Cross. However, people continued to swim around Westminster. 'The Thames is altogether such a wonderful affair,' wrote Henry James in 1905. 'From Westminster to the sea . . . in its recreative character it is absolutely unique. I know of no other classic stream that is so splashed about for the mere fun of it.'

In Victorian times swimmers chose Westminster as the place to carry out exhibitions of things never done before, whether Boyton in his suit, the lieutenant on his horse, or Gautier, the manacled man. Today even swimming within the city is seen as a major, and dangerous, accomplishment, and no school would take its pupils to swim in the Thames in central London. Health & Safety and fears of pollution would never allow it, yet when the Westminster boys swam Bazalgette's new sewage system was still a pipedream.

At the beginning of the twentieth century the Thames still remained one of the greatest possible challenges for sporting swimmers, and was sometimes more ferocious than the Channel. On 18 July 1927 Mercedes Gleitze set off from Westminster to train for a Channel crossing, having already made several failed attempts. Her plan was to swim a staggering 120 miles from Westminster Bridge, down the Thames and around Beachy Head, to Folkestone, a feat unheard of for either woman or man. It was a journey that would take her twelve days and establish her as a pioneer when it came to Thames swimming. In 1890 Easton's attempt to swim for six days from Oxford had ended in failure on the fourth day; now here was a woman easily completing a swim that lasted three times longer, with around forty miles of it in the Thames.

Mercedes Gleitze being greased up before a swim. In 1923 she set a record for a ten-hour, forty-five-minute swim in the Thames between Putney and Silvertown.

Born in Brighton in 1900, Gleitze learned to swim by the age of ten and on 5 August 1923 she had set a British women's record for a ten-hour, forty-five-minute swim in the Thames, covering twenty-seven miles between Putney and Silvertown. This was her second attempt; she'd already tried the course a week earlier. Four years later 'the London typist', as the press repeatedly called her, set off from Westminster just before 6 a.m., accompanied by a motor launch whose skipper was a Mr Garman. But while she started with the tide the river became rough, she was swept off course and drawn under a group of barges, where she disappeared. 'The suction was terrible,' she later told reporters, 'the Channel was not nearly so treacherous as this.' She was trapped at a spot known as Church Hole off Wapping, said to be notorious for currents. 'I was sucked down rapidly and all manner of thoughts rushed through my brain. I felt myself going down and down. I rapidly became resigned, and thought all was over. I wondered how long it would be before I was to enter another world. When I came to the surface in a few moments I quickly became myself again. Thereafter I was accompanied down the Thames by relays of Thames police.'

Press coverage of the swim was minimal in terms of details, such as where and when she began and ended each day, instead focusing on this 'marvellous escape from death by drowning'. Gleitze had 'come up by a miracle' reappearing feet first and then floating motionless downstream before recovering, and local 'longshoremen' refused to believe it was possible. She continued her swim in a series of ten stages, swimming for six hours a day depending on tides, and taking only liquid food for the first two days before turning to solids. She arrived at Folkestone on the evening of 29 July, two days later than she'd planned, having been delayed by rough weather. Here she displayed her right arm 'pitted with bright red spots', presumably from jellyfish, between Canvey Island and Whitstable.

Then, less than three months later, on 7 October 1927, and on her eighth attempt, Gleitze finally crossed the Channel from France to England in fifteen hours fifteen minutes, making history as the first British woman to successfully complete the crossing. 'Thank God, I am conscious,' she declared, before collapsing on the shore in dense fog. Since Webb's 1875 swim, nine other people had managed the Channel, including three British men and two American women. 'Girl Conquers Channel,' announced the national press, Mercedes Gleitze was now 'the most amazing girl in England'.

However, some papers raised questions. The *Dover Express* noted that 'there was no one ashore to witness the landing' and that local motor boats 'report that the visibility was not so bad as was stated'. 'Miss Gleitze can have only one regret,' said Sidney T. Hirst, Hon. Secretary of the Amateur Swimming Club, 'and that is her oversight in not having on board any Press representatives and officials from the recognised swimming body.' But the *News of the World* gave her £500 for her 'plucky swim', and she immediately signed a contract 'to appear at a London theatre' where she would be paid £100 for 'a short speech', her fees then going 'to the London destitute'. Gleitze told one reporter, 'when a woman sets her mind on doing a thing it just has to be done'. But, perhaps conscious of repeated comments as to whether a record-breaking woman could be still feminine, when asked if she smoked, she replied, 'certainly not, I don't agree with the principle of women smoking, just as I don't believe in bobbed hair'. The paper then assured its readers that her own hair 'looks very womanly'.

But unfortunately for Gleitze, four days later another swimmer, Dr Dorothy Cochrane Logan, a Harley Street physician and professional swimmer who swam under the name of Mona McLennan, set a new Channel record for women, with thirteen hours ten minutes. Only she didn't: rather, she admitted, she'd done part of the course in a boat and had been paid £1,000 by the

Mercedes Gleitze (centre) was the first British woman to swim across the Channel, but she found the Thames more 'treacherous'. Norman Derham, the champion Southend swimmer, is behind her.

News of the World to claim a record swim. She said she was just showing why Channel records needed to be independently verified, but now Gleitze's swim was in severe doubt as well, to which her response was, 'All right, I'll do it again.' Like Lily Smith and Elsie Aykroyd who came before her and Ivy Hawke who came after, she exhibited the same sort of matter-of-fact determination. There had been previous bogus Channel claims. A Mrs Hamilton had 'spent the night' in a friend's motor boat in Dover harbour rather than swimming; another had been towed across by her accompanying boat. Gleitze told the press she had never suspected Logan of lying: 'what I have not got in my favour is the fact that no one saw me land' (apart from those on the accompanying boat), and she agreed there needed to be a governing body for Channel swimming.

On 21 October, Gleitze set off on her 'Vindication Swim' in order to 'restore the prestige of British women Channel swimmers in the eyes of the world'. As a result of the advance publicity, Rolex, which the year before had patented the first waterproof wristwatch, the Oyster, asked her to wear their prototype in exchange for a testimonial afterwards. This time she had the backing of a British businessman, Summers Brown, who had volunteered to finance the venture. And so, exactly two weeks after her first successful crossing, she entered the water once again at Cap Gris Nez. But after over ten hours, in water sometimes as cold as 50 degrees, she slipped in and out of consciousness, and seven miles from the end the medical officers accompanying her decided the swim should be abandoned. After protests from her to 'let me go on', those on the boat threw a twisted towel over her head and under her arms, and she was forcibly pulled on board.

The watch, which she actually wore round her neck, was still keeping good time and Rolex were quick to place a front-page advert in the *Daily Mail* with a picture of Gleitze, who became seen as a 'poster girl' for swimming. There was much coverage of her 'splendid failure', she had a 'wildly enthusiastic' welcome in London where she was besieged by autograph hunters and 'an excited woman admirer broke through the throng at Charing Cross and kissed her'. Gleitze announced she was not going back to being a typist but would become a professional long-distance swimmer and 'take up social-welfare work'.

By now she had signed a statutory declaration that her 7 October Channel swim was 'a bona-fide one', in the presence of the Commissioner for Oaths and a representative of the *Daily Mirror*. The declaration was also signed by her trainer, and on 1 November 1927 the swim was duly entered into the record book of the recently formed Channel Swimming Association, founded in order to authenticate swimmers' claims to have swum the English Channel and to verify crossing times. Mercedes Gleitze's record as the first British woman to swim the English Channel was now official.

And so began years of worldwide endurance swims. In December that year she set off to swim the Strait of Gibraltar. The following April, after five failed attempts, she finally succeeded in crossing the Strait, watched by 'hundreds of women', becoming the first person ever to swim the eight-mile course, in twelve hours

'The most amazing girl in England': Mercedes Gleitze.

fifty minutes. She also returned to the Thames and in December 1928, in water that was 36 degrees, swam from Tottenham Bridge to London Bridge on Boxing Day. The press reported 'six other girls refused to enter the water because of the wintery conditions'. That same month she was photographed barefoot working in a Manchester cotton mill where she'd been employed for ten days under an assumed name 'studying industrial conditions'. It's unlikely no one would have recognised 'England's heroine of the day' and the press, of course, were there to photograph her. But industrial conditions were close to her heart and she later used her earnings to set up the Mercedes Gleitze Home for Destitute Men and Women in Leicester in 1933, which survived until the Second World War.

In 1929 she swam thirty-nine miles in the Thames in twelve hours, which must have been a record for a woman (no one had yet beaten Holbein's fifty-mile continuous swim of 1908) and completed many endurance swims at indoor pools. During a forty-and-a-half-hour swim at Dundee Corporation Baths police had to 'deal with an attempt to rush one of the doorways' after 'thousands were unable to get admission'. Gleitze travelled extensively in Europe, the United States, Australia, New Zealand and South Africa, completing fifty-one marathon swims, nearly half of which took at least twenty-six hours. For many of these she was accompanied by music playing on a wind-up gramophone. Gleitze retired from swimming in 1933, after a failed attempt to cross the Channel from England to France, and withdrew completely from public life. She later became ill and eventually housebound, refusing to give interviews and shunning any further publicity, until her death in 1981.

Mercedes Gleitze is unusual when it comes to the story of Thames champions because, unlike other women, apart from Annette Kellerman, she is still honoured today. But until recently, just as with Webb, this was because of her Channel rather than her river swims. In 1969 she was inducted into the International Marathon Swimming Hall of Fame (IMSHOF), although it's not clear if she was ever aware of this, and many press photos of her still exist, partly because she was so photogenic. Here she is standing on a beach, her legs being rubbed with grease, sitting on the floor doing warm-up exercises and, oddly, wearing dainty heeled shoes, or preparing to dive into the Lambeth Baths. Unlike Ivy Hawke 'the smiling swimmer', or Lily Smith, resplendently covered in medals, Gleitze often looks a little shy in these posed shots. But images of her during her Channel swim tell another story, of sheer exhaustion and triumph, and her story was suitably included in *The Girls' Book of Heroines*.

Her legacy in terms of Thames swimming, however, has yet to be properly recognised. The fact that she swam 120 miles from Westminster to Folkestone in 1927 means she was the one who paved the way for the men who came after, such as Andy Nation, Lewis Pugh, Charlie Wittmack and David Walliams. When it

Lewis Pugh swims past the Houses of Parliament during his journey along the length of the Thames in 2006. Westminster has been the site of daring swimming feats since Victorian times.

comes to long-distance swims lasting days, it was a woman who got there first.

Now at last Mercedes Gleitze is being celebrated as a pioneering open-water swimmer. In October 2013, at the Global Open Water Swimming Conference held in Ireland, she was enshrined into the IMSHOF as an Honour Pioneer Open Water Swimmer. This was followed in September 2014 by another enshrinement held in Scotland, this time into the International Swimming Hall of Fame (ISHOF) as an Honour Open Water Pioneer Swimmer. In addition, a documentary, *Mercedes: The Spirit of a New Age*, has been made about Gleitze's swimming career by Northern Ireland producer Clare Delargy, and a feature film is underway. Mercedes' daughter, Doloranda Pember, meanwhile, has just finished writing a fully illustrated chronicle of her mother's swimming career.

I meet Doloranda at Tate Britain, a fifteen-minute walk upstream from Westminster Bridge, where I've suggested we chat in the gallery's restaurant because it first opened, although not to the general public, in 1927, the year of her mother's record-breaking Thames swim. The Rex Whistler Restaurant was once considered 'The Most Amusing Room in Europe', thanks to its specially commissioned mural, *The Expedition in Pursuit of Rare Meats*.

Doloranda is already seated when I arrive and I recognise her at once; she has the same delicate features as her mother. Behind her Whistler's mural covers every wall of the basement room, in hues of green and blue with many a watery scene. Not long after it was completed the mural was under 2 feet of water as a result of the massive Thames flood of 1928, but it survived and has recently been cleaned. Doloranda has come by coach from her home in Gloucestershire and she's brought some examples from her mother's extensive archives. There's a clink of cutlery and a chink of wine glasses from the lunch party at the table next to us, a waiter brings a tray of freshly baked rolls, then she begins to show me some of her mother's treasures.

Mercedes Gleitze left over 2,000 documents, including letters, newspaper cuttings, photographs, witness statements and swimming logs in boxes in the attic, and Doloranda has spent several years charting every single swim. 'Although she seldom spoke to us in detail about her achievements, because she left all these documents I've been able to record her career accurately in the biography I've just written. We had no idea how famous she'd been in her day. Now and again she might mention something but she kept her memories to herself, she was just a mother to three children and a housewife. She made herself invisible when she retired into domesticity and became totally reclusive. That's why she isn't as well known today as, say, Gertrude Ederle, but I'm about to put that right.'

Doloranda brings out one of the red exercise books her mother bought from Woolworths, its thick pages crammed with press reports. 'She glued them all in, and when she ran out of glue because of war shortages, she sewed them in.' Next she shows me posters announcing indoor swims, press photos from the Channel swim, a copy of the Channel Swimming Association's verification of the crossing, and several pages listing all her mother's endurance and open-water swims from 1923 to 1933. The collection is particularly important because when Gleitze returned home to her flat in Pimlico after her successful Channel swim in October 1927 it was to find that a leather travelling case presented to her by the Amateur Swimming Club had been stolen from her bedroom. The case contained 'swimming articles, programmes, and a number of press photographs of the last few years' and although there was money in the room, only the case was taken.

We talk about her mother's Channel swim and Doloranda explains that a journalist who had been invited to accompany the crossing cancelled at the last moment. As a result of this, Gleitze would never again undertake a swim without it being properly documented, and as just one example Doloranda shows me the original documents attesting to the fact she swam the Strait of

Gibraltar, page after page, in both Spanish and English, listing the names of every single spectator. But despite all these records, 'the thinnest file I've got is on the Thames swims', and, like me, she's been frustrated trying to find out more details.

We finish our lunch and leave the Tate, walking along Millbank before crossing the road to the Thames. We sit on a bench in Victoria Tower Garden South, the wall that separates us from the river dappled in shadow from overhanging trees. The water today is as green as Whistler's mural. The afternoon is sticky and muggy, we're disturbed by planes overhead and motorbikes on the road behind us, and I have to listen carefully to hear Doloranda as she tells me the story of her mother and the Thames.

'What do you think this was like,' I ask, 'when Mercedes swam here?' 'The Thames won't have changed, or most of the bridges,' she says, 'but the London Eye,' she lifts an arm to point across the river, 'that's new. And the water in the Thames in the 1920s would have been much more polluted, there would have been dead animals and other obnoxious deposits for a swimmer to contend with.' But this didn't deter Mercedes. 'Most women still led restricted lives at that time,' says Doloranda. However her mother 'was one of the new women of that era, and was determined to follow her dream', which in this case meant swimming the Channel.

'American swimmers who came to try their luck were heavily sponsored by newspapers; they had the money and came here and trained full-time. British women didn't have any funding. My mother had to earn a living; she was a working girl, she had rent to pay and limited holidays. She had little chance to train in the sea, and suddenly she had an idea one day, maybe she could use the Thames to train in at weekends. She lived in Pimlico and worked as a shorthand typist for a shipping company in Westminster, where her fluency in English and German was an asset. It was one of the new white-collar office jobs being offered to women, and better than domestic service. In the holidays she went to

Folkestone to train, but at the weekends the Thames offered her similar conditions to the Channel because of its tidal flow. She walked along the Embankment every day to and from work and that's what gave her the idea. It was not her original ambition to swim the Thames but she saw it as an opportunity. Swimming the English Channel was such a target, especially for a woman, because at that time no woman had ever done it.'

I say I'm amazed her mother could just get in and swim. 'She couldn't,' explains Doloranda, 'she got a licence from the Port of London Authority.' I stare at her, astounded that the PLA granted Mercedes permission to swim in the filthy, crowded river in the middle of London. 'She applied for a licence to swim on Sundays and they gave it to her. I find that incredible. The PLA didn't raise any objections about health and safety; they didn't say "no, it's too polluted". Mercedes just saw this body of water as somewhere to train. She used her initiative! Her motivation was to break records and make money for her planned charity, these were her parallel aims. On her walk to work she witnessed the unemployed, all the destitute people on the streets and under the bridges; this was during the years leading up to the Great Depression.'

I wonder if Mercedes worked in an office overlooking the river, and I ask where she swam from on these training weekends. Did she dive in from a beach or leap off a bridge? Did she hire a boat? 'I don't know,' says Doloranda, 'there are gaps in my knowledge.' Another gap is the 120-mile swim, and I ask where her mother would have spent each night. 'I suspect she would have got B&B accommodation at each of the landing places en route to Folkestone. It would have been the most practical thing to do. Unfortunately in her archives there are very few details of the actual swim – just about the start and the finish. However, I did find one press report that said she swam the tide out after that "near death" incident and landed at Erith at the end of the first stage. Lack of detailed information on this swim also frustrated me. I know the *Daily Mail* covered it because I have a letter she wrote to them asking for copies of the photographs they took of the swim.'

As for her liquid diet, Mr Garman, the boat skipper, would have handed her mugs of tea, coffee and hot milk, and when she turned to solids her menu while swimming normally consisted of egg and bacon, 'which must have been difficult to eat in the water!', ham sandwiches, fried fish, 'a raw egg drink that was supposed to be nutritious' – Doloranda pulls a face – 'Bovril, Ovaltine, grapes, and on one or two occasions roast duck'. I ask if her mother was aware of the swimmers who had come before her, the women who also broke records in the Thames going back to Victorian times, and she says she doesn't know and that the press reports in her mother's archives don't mention them.

For Doloranda, her years spent charting Mercedes' swims have been enlightening. It has given her the chance to learn about her mother's outstanding career – the details of which as a child she knew very little. Doloranda and her siblings all loved to swim, 'but none of us had her ambition'. She has only swum once in the Thames herself, at Maidenhead sixty-five years ago with friends, when she remembers getting tangled up in reeds. And today she no longer swims in public pools, because 'I've become sensitised to chlorine'.

Doloranda is immensely proud of the way Mercedes managed her own career and the fact that her 'endurance swims in corporation pools gave city-dwelling people, especially women and girls, the opportunity to see a woman do physical things'. As for the charity her mother established, 'although enemy action during the war destroyed the Charitable Homes, her Trust Fund is still active today and is being used to help people in poverty. The revenue from my book will go to Mum's charity.'

17

Charing Cross–Blackfriars

'Here at Hungerford Bridge floating swimming-baths are in the
course of erection . . . [they] will be open for bathers of either sex'
Walter Thornbury, *Old and New London*, 1873

It's a sunny morning in May and the riverside at Charing Cross
Bridge, around half a mile downstream from Westminster
Bridge, is crowded with luxury cruisers, boats with restaurants
and nightclubs on board, tourist coaches and open-top sightseeing
buses. It's a good spot for visitors to London, with the steel railway
bridge leading over the Thames to the Festival Hall, and nearby
the London Eye glinting like a silver beaded bracelet. But in
Victorian times this was a bleak place. In the 1820s ten-year-old
Charles Dickens worked close by at Hungerford Stairs, opposite the
entrance of today's Embankment Tube station, as a 'shop drudge'
at a blacking warehouse on six shillings a week. Dickens later
described it to his biographer John Forster as 'a crazy, tumble-down
old house, abutting of course on the river, and swarming with rats'.
He was based in the counting house on the first floor, overlooking
the Thames, where his job was to 'cover the pots of paste-blacking'
with paper. 'No words,' he said, 'can express the secret agony of
my soul' as his 'early hopes of growing up to be a learned and
distinguished man crushed in my breast'. He uses much the same
words to describe the young David Copperfield's experiences at the
fictional Murdstone and Grinby's Thames-side warehouse.

While Dickens would later enjoy swims at Richmond, his early experiences of the river explains why the Thames was such a lurking presence in many of his novels, a deadly sewer lined by festering mudbanks where in the opening chapter of *Our Mutual Friend* a boatman pushes off into the slime and ooze looking for corpses to rob.

But for others it could be a place of safety and pleasure. 'Here at Hungerford Bridge,' wrote Victorian author Walter Thornbury, 'floating swimming-baths are in the course of erection. These baths, which are planned on an extensive scale, containing many thousand gallons of filtered water, will be open for bathers of either sex. Experiments have been made which have established beyond all doubt that the Thames water can be easily and effectually filtered. When filtered it is found to contain a very large proportion of sea-water; in fact, we have heard it said that at high tide it is almost entirely sea-water, clear and green, as at Ramsgate or Margate. But this statement we are inclined to question.'

The idea with the floating bath was to give people a clean, secure place to swim. It was 'perhaps the most rational means yet decided for diminishing the number of deaths from drowning while bathing in the river, which invariably accompany a hot season,' reported the press. However, Thames water 'though improving, is not exactly the fluid in which bathers with delicate stomachs would care to disport themselves'. In September 1874 the Medical Officer of Health inspected 2,083 vessels on the Thames; ninety-three 'sick sailors had been found afloat', while of nineteen samples of drinking water taken from the boats, seven were 'unfit for human consumption'.

The designs for the bath were prepared in 1870 and the Thames Conservancy Board approached for mooring permission. London wasn't the only city to have floating baths; others did, too, such as Liverpool, where in 1816 a bath in the form of a ship opened at George's Pierhead on the Mersey. There were floating baths on other rivers as well, such as the Dee and the Clyde, while there were six at different places along the Severn, some lasting into the early 1900s. Within London, in 1819 the Royal Waterloo Bath, built inside a ship's timber hull, had been anchored off Waterloo Bridge. Historian Ian Gordon has identified seventeen floating baths in Great Britain, most built between 1870 and 1880, and cheaper and quicker than building a swimming pool on land. The tradition elsewhere in Europe went back even further, with floating baths, *bains flottants* or *Flussbader*, in Paris, Frankfurt and Vienna in the 1760s. These were more like barges for those interested in the 'beneficial medicinal effects' of cold-water bathing.

The plan for the Charing Cross bath involved a pontoon, with the bath in the hollow centre. It would be 6 feet deep in the middle

The Charing Cross floating baths as depicted in *The Illustrated Sporting and Dramatic News* in August 1875, shortly after they opened. The aim of the 'super structure of iron and glass' was to give bathers a safe, clean place to swim.

and at night would be 'emptied and swabbed ready for the next day'. The temperature would be 72 degrees. There were dressing boxes for 150 people, it would open for fourteen hours at a time, and its expected capacity was an impressive 2,500 people a day. In August 1874 the *London Standard* explained that the new floating bath was at the 'point of completion'. Certain hours would be 'set apart for ladies' and staff, both men and women professional swimmers, would be on hand to give lessons. In the evening the London Swimming Club would give lessons for free. In winter 'a stream of hot water' would pass through the bath to regulate the temperature. It must have been very warm; the following year the temperature was regularly raised to around 80 degrees Fahrenheit – no wonder it was called 'Hot Baths on the Thames'.

The *Penny Illustrated Paper*, however, was sceptical. 'It remains to be seen how far our comfort will be increased by the forthcoming opening of the floating bath to the west of Hungerford Bridge. At first sight it is certainly not perfect. Why is it covered at the top with glass? Why does not the water run through it, as is the case with each of the floating baths on the Seine?' Instead it 'appears to be nothing better than a covered tank'. In 1875 it was moored into position and opened in July that year, around the same time as the new sewer system was completed. Built by the Floating Swimming Bath Company, the 'super structure of iron and glass' was 153x25 feet. At one end was the filtering apparatus while at the other was a refreshment room. The *Birmingham Daily Post* assured its readers that it was 'larger and in every respect superior' to baths on the Seine. While the tidal stream was 'thick and yellow with mud and refuse' the water in the bath would be clear. Images in the press showed men diving off one of two arched girders, lounging by the poolside dressing boxes and swimming around an ornamental fountain.

The river water was passed through a filtering apparatus, which still allowed it 'to retain its natural salts and soft refreshing qualities'. There were also attempts to 'free the bathing water from the tint pervading it,' reported the *Illustrated London News*, but 'in effecting this decolorisation, the water would become less pleasant to bathe in'.

In 1876, the year porpoises were spotted in the area, the bath averaged 700 people a day, far fewer than anticipated. One issue may have been cost; a floating bath – at one shilling a swim – was more expensive than public indoor pools. In December that year the Charing Cross bath was turned into a Glaciarium. The public had 'shown that they fully appreciated swimming in the Thames in summer, but the winter months found the floating structure empty'. But trying to freeze the water with 'two ice machines' so people could skate proved difficult, as the 'extensive area of glass roof . . . greatly raises the temperature of the internal atmosphere'. Still, *The Times* reported 'ice two inches thick' had been formed and 'was skated upon, in the first instance, by two ladies'. It still continued as a bath, however, and was chosen as the site for aquatic displays. On 31 July 1879 one T. Ingram dived 65 feet into the water, which appears to have been a London 'plunging' record at the time.

In 1885 the South Eastern Railway Company apparently wanted to demolish the Charing Cross floating pontoon, but had offered it to the City Corporation 'for use of boys at the City of London School'. So did pupils use the floating baths? 'The short answer is no,' says the school's archivist Terry Heard. In the early 1880s the school moved from Milk Street to the Victoria Embankment and before the new building was finished a group of boys paid a visit, one describing what he saw: 'At the east end [of the basement floor near the Embankment] is a large iron grating, guarding a mysterious and winding cavern. On the occasion of our visit the gate was open, and I walked through, and was surprised to find myself suddenly on the bank of the Thames. I fancy this subway was used to bring building materials by water, but there were interesting rumours that it was intended for access to swimming baths, which it was suggested might be floated down the river from Charing Cross.' The floating bath was to be moored alongside the long narrow wharf opposite the school, with dressing boxes provided, and one of two tunnels leading from the school would be used as access.

In June 1881 the Court of Common Council of the City of London had received a letter from 'Admiral Sir George Elliott, KCB' asking for 'the formation of an approach from the Thames Embankment across the Wharf in front of the New City of London School to a Floating Swimming Bath'. This was 'to be placed in the Thames at the North-west end of Blackfriars Bridge'. It took the City Lands Committee nearly a year to recommend that the request be turned down, with the plan finally being abandoned in 1885. A decade later and the City of London School had its first organised swimming team, perhaps taking advantage of a swimming pool in the nearby St Bride's Institute. The school's own 'fine swimming pool' opened in 1937.

According to some reports, after a sale by auction failed to meet the asking price the bath was 'scrapped'. But on 2 September 1891 the *Morning Post* declared, 'London is once more in possession of a floating swimming bath.' In the intervening seven years the bath (apparently the same one) had been 'lying unused in the Surrey Commercial Docks, having been purchased by a syndicate' but it had now 'undergone a process of improvement, amounting almost to transformation'. The bath was moored 'within 50 yards' of Cleopatra's Needle and named the Cleopatra Swimming Pool and was 'entirely new in many of its features'. The main one was that the water no longer came from the Thames, but was 'drawn from the main of the New River Company, and as it is to be frequently changed the only serious objection to the old floating bath will no longer hold good'. This suggests the problem with the original bath wasn't just cost and weather, but concerns about the state of the water.

The bath's foundation weighed 750 tons, and piles had been driven 25 feet into the bed of the river. The water rose and fell with the tide, and the swimming area, said to be the largest in London, was 133 feet long by 25 feet wide, with the depth 'graduated by means of a false bottom'. Pumps heated the water, the bath was illuminated at night with electric light, there was 'a well-appointed café where bathers can obtain light refreshments', and it was open every day, including Sundays.

But again the bath didn't last long. In 1893 the Highways Committee turned down a licence renewal application, deciding that 'the retention of the bath in its present position, or the placing of it in any other position on the river near the Embankment, was not desirable, nor of any great advantage to the public; while, on the other hand, the structure itself was not, nor in their opinion could it be made, ornamental'. This was despite accusations that 'in this exceptional weather the Council was standing in the way of poor people obtaining at a cheap rate the opportunity to bathe in the natural stream', which was met with cries of 'No, no'.

In 1894 a proposal to 'moor or fix' the bath on 'the beach at Southend' was approved, but four years later it was sold to a ship breaker for £300. The original cost of the bath had been £23,000. But again the dream of a floating bath wasn't quite over and in 1899 the *Leeds Mercury* referred to 'a new club' for Londoners, anchored 'somewhere off the embankment', with a promenade deck 'whereon on sultry days in summer members can listen to sweet music and gaze romantically into the swift flowing, muddy Thames'. The river was 'dirty' but 'odourless', although there was an 'evil smell' coming from penny steamers whose smoke was said to be 'harmless'. For years, said the paper, London had had a floating bath but there had not been enough public support, because bathers didn't believe it could possibly be clean enough and instead took their 'morning dips elsewhere'. It's not clear what came of these new plans.

Today there is little on Thames swimming at the City of Westminster Archives Centre. Archivist Alison Kenney has searched numerous prints and photographs of river panoramas, 'but none of the index cards say anything about swimming apart from the one about the Charing Cross floating bath'. The one image they do have shows the bath neatly tucked to one side of the Thames, the surrounding water clear and calm. But if architect Chris Romer-Lee has his way, there could be floating baths on the Thames again. He's director and co-founder of Studio Octopi, which in 2013 was one of five practices selected for the Architecture Foundation's Open Call to develop ideas for the future of the river. 'Our idea was legal swimming in the Thames post completion of the Super Sewer,' he explains. Work is scheduled to begin on the Thames Tideway Tunnel – otherwise known as the Super Sewer – in 2015, if it gets planning permission. At twenty miles long, it will connect with thirty-four of the most polluting sewer overflows and by 2023 will 'catch 96 per cent of the current levels of sewage discharge'.

Studio Octopi's original plan was to design 'some slightly bonkers swimming enclosures that sit or float in the river at Blackfriars Bridge North Foreshore and King Edward Memorial Park Foreshore, two Super Sewer building sites. We've just got an idea that seems believable *if* a whole series of factors falls into place! If the Super Sewer doesn't get permission other clean-up options will be considered as they still need a solution to overflowing sewers.' However, until recently Chris wasn't aware of London's heritage of floating baths, although 'I've always loved swimming; it's a bit of a family obsession and there are stories that an elderly relative used to swim across the Thames at Hammersmith sometime in the 1980s.'

When he saw the Open Call, 'I was at Lake Zurich where they have swimming areas and lovely sophisticated changing rooms. I thought, why can't we swim in the Thames if the Super Sewer is going to make it cleaner?' It was only much later, after being selected for the Open Call, that he found out about the old floating baths at Charing Cross. At the Blackfriars Bridge North Foreshore the initial plan was for four pools, including one devoted to lane swimming and one for wild swimming, which Chris believed could be popular with City workers and tourists. At low tide there could be water cascading between the pools so 'it's not so murky'. The shallowest pool, at 500 millimetres deep, would be for children, while the deepest, at 1,500 millimetres, would be a semi-submerged floating pontoon, just as in Victorian times. Response to an article on the plans was mixed. One reader commented, 'Two words: Weil's disease', but another said they had spent their childhood swimming in London in the 1950s and even 'learned to snorkel in the Thames'.

By 2104 Studio Octopi's plans had changed; now there would be one site, at Blackfriars Bridge, and this time they wouldn't use Thames water. 'The response from the public and swimming community has been phenomenal,' says Chris, 'and although unfunded we're continuing to develop designs that address the biggest concern, water quality. What if the plans to resolve the sewage overflows into

Will swimmers return to the Thames in central London? Studio Octopi's new plans for floating baths at Blackfriars Bridge.

the Thames weren't tackled for another ten years? How could we get Londoners swimming in the Thames sooner, tomorrow even? The solution was simple. Build a steel pontoon with pools set within the structure, therefore physically separating them from the Thames water, yet maintaining a visual link with the river.' This would effectively give 'the illusion of swimming in the Thames when in fact the water was freshwater (rainwater or tap). We see these new proposals as a stepping stone to actually swimming in the Thames.'

The floating pontoon would offer a twenty-five-metre lap pool, a plunge pool and paddling pool all within a 60x10 metre structure moored off Temple Stairs along Victoria Embankment. Surrounding the pools would be a 'generous open-decked area for relaxing and enjoying the amazing views up and down the river', just as in Victorian times. Key to these proposals, says Chris, is seeing them as 'an extension to the civic spaces along the river, re-establishing a physical link between Londoners and the Thames'. The baths would be connected to the Embankment via a walkway, with changing and washroom facilities at street level. As with the original scheme, they would be 'enclosed by our now trademark native reeds and rushes. A visual sign that London's river is clean and healthy and given the chance plants will grow in this tidal stretch of the river.'

The floating baths, if they do happen, is yet another example of using the Thames in the same way as we did in the past, whether forming open-water swimming clubs or organising river races. Once again we are returning to the waterway with 'new' ideas, only to find out they're not new at all. Press coverage of Studio Octopi's plans has been substantial and, as with the Victorian floating baths, media reports expressed enthusiasm at a new place to swim, tinged with scepticism that the Thames is the place to do it. The context is similar, too; in 1875, when the Charing Cross bath opened, the new sewer scheme had just been completed, while Captain Webb's crossing of the Channel meant outdoor swimming was hugely popular. In the twenty-first century there are again new sewer plans, as well as a resurgence in outdoor swimming. Even the development of the plans is the same, initially using Thames water and then switching to tap water.

I cross over Charing Cross Bridge to the south side where there is a series of easily accessible small sandy beaches. One lies just by the National Theatre, on the Queen's Walk, where the air smells of cooking burgers and people stroll in the sunshine dodging low-flying pigeons. A locked gate blocks the steps to the beach, but the sand is pitted with recent boot marks. I can hear the waves at the shore, the tide has washed up seaweed and beer cans, the water is a uniform brown. 'See, here's a beach!' exclaims an American woman. 'Look at the sand!' 'I wanna go on it,' says her son. 'You can't go on it.' 'Why?' he whines but his mother has already walked away and so half-heartedly he starts to cry.

For a moment, in the sun, it's easy to imagine children cooling off here on a hot day, not caring about pollution or even if they could swim. An 1842 lithograph by William Parrott, one of the few images held by the Museum of London with evidence of Thames swimming, shows a group of boys undressing on the foreshore below Waterloo Bridge getting ready for a dip. But in modern times people were more likely to try and kill themselves here.

Actress Damaris Hayman remembers people jumping off London bridges 'to finish themselves' in the 1950s: 'a lot of people thought of it as a way to end it all, and people mostly picked Waterloo Bridge. If they were fished out alive, and they were quite often fished out alive, then they had shots, typhoid and so on. They had tetanus shots and everything you can think of. The fear of what they might have picked up was seen as a greater hazard than the actual drowning.'

This didn't seem to be a worry for the characters of Iris Murdoch's 1954 novel *Under the Net*, when one drunken night Jack Donaghue and friends decide to swim in the Thames. They check the time for high tide, set off down Upper Thames Street and find the river 'thick with scum and floating spars of wood, full to over-flowing in the bosom of London'. Despite this and a smell like rotten vegetables, they undress, keeping an eye out for river police. Jack shoots out into the open river, the sky above cascading with stars, behind him the black hulls of barges, 'the whole expanse of water was running with light. It was like swimming in quicksilver.' Eventually he feels the tide turn and it's time to leave, 'a tension had been released, a ritual performed', and like river swimmers before and after him, he is ready for the new day.

18

London Bridge

'The agile Agnes all proclaim
The lady champion aquatic,
And warm admirers hold her fame
To equal that of heroes Attic'
            'An ode to Agnes Beckwith', in *Fun*, 1879

I am standing on the north side of London Bridge, looking downstream towards the Tower of London, where Tower Bridge looks like a gateway to a medieval castle moored in the middle of the river. Everywhere are boats, from City cruisers to HMS *Belfast*, while a row of buoys bob in the water like swollen orange lozenges. There have been several bridges spanning this section of the river reaching back to Roman times, and when the Victorian stone-arched bridge opened in 1831 it became the busiest and one of the most congested points in London. By the mid-nineteenth century 100,000 people walked across it every day – an ideal spot then if you intended to swim from it and wanted a crowd. In September 1875 it was here that Agnes Beckwith plunged into the Thames from a rowing boat and sped all the way to Greenwich. She was just fourteen years old.

It was Agnes Beckwith who first sparked my interest in Thames swimming. I initially came across her in a British Library poster, an advertisement for a performance at the Royal Aquarium in 1885. She stands dead centre, wearing a satin costume, stockings

MISS AGNES BECKWITH. MISS EMILY PARKER.

Agnes Beckwith and Emily Parker, both aged fourteen, were set to race each other in the Thames from London Bridge to Greenwich in September 1875.

and boots, one arm resting casually on a beach rock. Just behind her in the water a man has both arms raised in the air, his mouth open in alarm; presumably in the process of drowning. Then I read a passing reference to a swim she had done in the Thames, with no idea what a trailblazer she had been. Here she was diving off a rowing boat in 1875 when most sailors couldn't swim and when 3,199 people had drowned by accident that year in England and Wales, 500 of whom were women.

Thanks to Captain Webb's crossing of the Channel the month before, long-distance events were the height of popularity and it was now that Thames swimming really came into its own. Swimming of any kind was in fashion: 'while the present weather lasts all England by sea and stream will take a periodical if not a daily plunge into the limpid element,' reported the *Penny Illustrated Paper*. It was 'the mania of the hour, and a very good mania too,' commented *The Graphic*. But few could match the skill and strength of Agnes Beckwith.

Born in 1861, she'd been swimming and performing since she was a few years old. Her father was swimming professor Frederick Beckwith of the Lambeth Baths, who'd spent several months

T. Wildgoose and children, a swimming family similar to that of Frederick Beckwith's 'family of frogs'.

training Webb for his Channel swim. In 1854 he'd been declared 'English professional champion', a title he held for six years, and had been connected with the Baths for nearly a quarter of a century. Frederick's 'family of frogs' started giving public displays in the early 1860s and in 1865 he included Agnes, introducing her as a two-year-old, although she was probably older. By the time she was nine she was performing with her brother Willie, himself a champion swimmer, as 'Les Enfants Poissons' in a plate-glass aquarium at the Porcherons Music Hall in Paris.

Frederick, like most swimming professors, was a lover of spectacle and a savvy promoter, issuing swimming wagers at indoor pools as early as the 1850s, and organising fêtes of natation. His daughter's swim in the Thames was both a publicity stunt and a money-making scheme. Just weeks earlier another professor by the name of Parker had advertised that his sister Emily would swim five miles from London Bridge to Greenwich. He'd placed a wager of £50 to £30; Emily had started training, her brother had even fixed a date. But Professor Beckwith got there first. On 1 September, just before 5 p.m., Agnes, 'of slim make, and diminutive stature', took to the Thames and 'at once commenced a rapid side-stroke, which she maintained to the finish', blowing 'kisses to spectators on the way'. The *Morning Post* reported, 'Swimming Feat by a Female', and noted that her time was 'remarkably fast'. The object was to 'decide a wager of £80 to £40 laid against her by Mr Baylis, the money being deposited with *Bell's Life*' a weekly sporting paper: 'the event created a great deal of excitement . . . a perfect swarm of boats accompanied, and indeed impeded, the swimmer the entire distance.'

Like Annette Kellerman some thirty years later, it was Beckwith's attire that was of just as much interest, 'a swimming costume of light rose pink llama trimmed with white braid and lace of same colour', and no future press report would be complete without reference to her clothing. At Horseferry Dock a salute was fired, and she was 'encouraged with lusty cheers'. Passing Millwall, she 'crossed to the north side and took advantage of the strong tide. At this point she was met by the saloon steamer *Victoria*, whose passengers were vociferous in their applause.' She arrived at Greenwich Pier to 'the spirited strains of "See, the Conquering Hero Comes!"'. She then swam 'some distance beyond the pier' before being taken on board a boat, having accomplished the distance in one hour seven minutes and ending 'almost as fresh as when she started, and to all appearance was capable of going considerably further'. She had also 'declined' the offer of brandy and port wine and therefore accomplished her swim with 'no stimulant whatsoever'.

Was it her idea or her father's to swim the Thames? What did she think about as she made her way down the river, and what were her mother's views on the matter? We'll probably never know, because there remain many gaps in the story of Agnes Beckwith. While university sports lecturers Dave Day and Keith Myerscough have recently uncovered a great deal, she remains largely unheard of, even in the world of swimming.

Her achievement would have been astonishing. No woman had ever done what she did in the Thames, and only one man. Byron might have boasted of his swim in 1807, but that was only three miles. In 1826 the party of printers had covered four and a half miles, the Eton Psychrolutes were swimming the Thames a couple of decades later, but they were ex-public school boys, and of course the aristocratic jockeys were getting away with naked races. In terms of truly organised events the one-mile amateur championship for men had only begun in 1869, while the Lords and Commons five-mile race wouldn't start until a couple of years later, and it would be another decade before the Amateur Swimming Association was formed. No one had succeeded in a Thames swim of this distance, except Webb the year before when he completed 'nearly six miles', watched by just three people.

The following year Agnes Beckwith swam three-quarters of a mile in the River Tyne, and then ten miles from Battersea Bridge to Greenwich. Once again hundreds assembled to watch when, on 5 July 1876, she reached Greenwich after two hours and forty-three minutes. 'Ladies who would learn to swim, take lessons of Miss Beckwith!' reported one paper. But it then added disparagingly, 'Miss Agnes, now you have given such ample proofs that you are a duck of a girl, stick to your proper vocation – that of teaching your sex to swim.' Beckwith did just that, forming her own 'talented troupe of lady swimmers', and in the coming years she taught many women to swim, with her pupils giving benefit shows.

She also returned to the Thames. In July 1878 her twenty-mile swim from Westminster to Richmond and back to Mortlake received huge press coverage. One journalist applauded 'little Missie Beckwith's marvellous swim . . . What girl will now remain

'The Lambeth Naiad'. Agnes Beckwith was a trailblazer in terms of Thames swimming, but is yet to be inducted into any hall of fame.

ignorant of swimming?' Press reports frequently mentioned her 'ease and grace' and she was nicknamed 'the Lambeth Naiad'. *The Era* reported that 'an immense number of spectators thronged' Westminster Bridge and the Thames Embankment, and 'accompanied' by the steamer *Matrimony*, gaily 'decorated with flags, and attended on by her father and redoubtable brother William in a skiff, the youthful water sprite, dressed in a closely-fitting amber suit, adorned with white lace, a jaunty little straw-hat, and fluttering blue ribbons, parted the waters and commenced her tedious journey at twenty-six minutes past twelve o'clock'.

At Coates's boathouse she was 'fired at by way of encouragement, which, no doubt, was very comforting, and was certainly greatly appreciated by those on board the steamer, who cheered lustily, and probably took the compliment to themselves'. She 'received an ovation as she glided prettily under Barnes-bridge that must have been highly gratifying', the 'merry young siren' then 'shot under Old Kew-bridge, laughing and keeping up an animated conversation with her friends'. An enormous crowd welcomed her at Richmond as she 'floated under the picturesque bridge' where she 'went through numerous elegant evolutions in the water that were greatly applauded'. It was then back to Mortlake where she was greeted with the sort of enthusiasm 'this young water-queen so unquestionably deserved'. She completed the swim in six hours twenty minutes, and it was only at Kew Bridge, after eleven miles, that she had paused to take a cup of beef tea.

The swim was preparation for an attempt on the Channel, an ambition she had stated in the press, which would again have been unheard of for a woman and wasn't attempted until nearly a quarter of a century later by Madame von Isacescu. But it appears this was too expensive for her father to finance, although he was now advertising her as 'Heroine of the Thames and Tyne'.

Like other professional swimming performers, Agnes Beckwith travelled the country giving exhibitions at seaside regattas and indoor pools. In July 1880 she spent thirty hours treading water at the Royal Aquarium, equalling a record set by Webb, in what was known as the whale tank – it had recently been home to a beluga whale which had died apparently because of mistreatment. She ate all her meals in the water and read the day's news reports on her swim. A few months later Beckwith stayed 100 hours in the tank and once this was done she remained at the Aquarium teaching 'ladies how they may save themselves and others from drowning . . . every afternoon and evening [she] shows the fair sex how to master the water, and swim and dive and float as dexterously as a Mermaid'. The Princess of Wales came to watch, bringing her children along, which meant Frederick could now promote his daughter as being 'patronized by the Royal Family'.

Agnes Beckwith (in the middle) travelled the country giving exhibition shows with her 'troupe of lady swimmers'.

In 1882 Beckwith was being billed as 'the premier lady swimmer of the world' at a farewell benefit at the Aquarium, before she set off for a tour of the United States where the *New York Times* commented, 'unlike most female performers, Miss Beckwith is pretty'. She swam in France and Belgium, and in 1887 took part in P.T. Barnum's Greatest Show on Earth at Madison Square Garden. The same year the Princess of Wales took her daughters to the swimming annexe of the Westminster Aquarium to let Beckwith 'inspire them with a love for the delightful art'.

Her impact on the world of swimming, as with her successors Annette Kellerman and Mercedes Gleitze, was enormous, but there has been no induction into any hall of fame for Agnes Beckwith. Yet her 1875 Thames swim was still well known nearly forty years later. In his 1914 book *Swimming*, Montague Holbein cites her in his chapter entitled 'Long-distance Swimmers and their Feats'. First comes Lord Byron, then Dr Beadale of Manchester, J.B. Johnson, Boyton, Webb, and Cavill, then finally Agnes Beckwith whose five-mile swim, according to Holbein, was for a wager of £100.

In 1916, when Eileen Lee swam thirty-six miles from Teddington, the British press still remembered Beckwith. She was the 'pioneer of long distance swimming for ladies' and her twenty-mile swim in 1878 had stood as a record until Lee beat it. The Australian press remembered her, too; an article in 1911 on 'LADY SWIMMERS SOME AMAZING FEATS' by the Adelaide *Advertiser* opens with: 'There must be people still living who looked on with amazement, one day in 1875, as Miss Agnes Beckwith stepped out of the water at Greenwich "fresh as paint" after swimming from London bridge.' It then quotes 'sporting baronet' the late Sir John Astley: 'If I hadn't seen it with my own eyes I shouldn't have believed it was possible ... After this I quite believe that the day will come when women will beat men in the water, whatever they do on land. I shall not live to see the day, but it will come.' The *Advertiser* then names Beckwith's rivals, Emily Parker, Lizzie Gillespie and Annie Johnson, and comments, 'the woman of today, where she has not improved on these performances, has proved a worthy successor of these pioneer mermaids'. The paper goes on to cite Ethel Littlewood, Lily Smith, Claire Parlett, Vera Neave (who, in 1914, was the 'best distance swimmer the world has seen'), Olive Carson and Mme Isacesen, before turning its attention to their own Annette Kellerman. So, while the British and Australian press once placed Agnes Beckwith firmly where she belonged, as the first woman to swim a notable distance in the Thames, who has heard of her today and how many of these other women are household names?

Just like Kellerman, Agnes Beckwith also had firm views on women and swimming, telling the press it was the 'best exercise', developed the figure 'to a marvellous degree', and improved 'the chest and arms wonderfully'. It promoted circulation and gave a healthy appetite, and for those who wanted 'to cultivate pure muscle' the overhand method was best. 'One of its little known advantages,' she said, 'lies in its being a preventive of rheumatism, and I don't know any swimmer who is troubled with that malady.

SWIMMING CARDS.
COMPLETE SELF-INSTRUCTOR
FOR BOTH SEXES,
With correct Illustrations and Practical Instructions.
" *Dulce et Utile.* "

PROF. H. BOCOCK.
GAINSBOROUGH.

By PROFESSOR HOBSON BOCOCK,
(Member of the Professional Swimming Association, Gt. Britain),
GAINSBOROUGH, ENGLAND.
Entered at Stationers' Hall.   (Rights of Translation and
Reproduction are Reserved.)
HANNAM, GAINSBOROUGH.]   1888.   [VOL. I.

Swimming professor Hobson Bocock whose 1888 'self instruction' swimming cards were aimed at 'both sexes' thanks to pioneers such as Agnes Beckwith.

It is also quite invaluable as a cold cure.' Again like Kellerman, she also linked swimming with weight: 'strangely enough, swimming has a fattening effect, and many of us find a difficulty in keeping down flesh.'

By now the press was urging that all girls and women should know how to swim; 'no girl's education should be considered complete before she is able to swim well,' declared the *Penny Illustrated Paper*. In 1899, for 'one night only!', Beckwith performed at the new Lambeth Baths as 'Champion Lady Swimmer of the World'. She was still holding exhibitions as well as teaching in the early 1900s. By now she had married theatrical agent William Taylor, their son was born in 1903 and five years later he was performing alongside his mother as 'the youngest swimmer in the world'. She performed for visitors to the Industrial Exhibition in Manchester in 1910, but a year later was calling herself an ex-professional swimmer.

What happened to Agnes Beckwith after this remained a mystery for a long time, and it took sports lecturer Dave Day and his partner Margaret ten years to establish when and where she died. Dave's original interest came through researching Frederick Beckwith, whose biography he wrote for the *Oxford Dictionary of National Biography*. It was only very recently that he was able to update Agnes' entry. After her first husband died she married again and then, widowed for a second time, she moved in with her son, William. In 1948 the family sailed for South Africa and settled in Port Elizabeth. Agnes Beckwith died at the age of ninety at Nazareth House, a care home run by Nazarene nuns, in 1951. She was buried in the South End cemetery, where her name appears on a memorial plaque listing patients cared for by the nuns. To Dave, it was her career that helped to 'pave the way for the British women who represented their country' in the 1912 Olympics.

Sports lecturer Keith Myerscough, meanwhile, first came across Agnes while researching the Blackpool Tower's Aquatic and Variety Circus. 'A programme for 1895 revealed an astonishing scene of swimmers conducting acrobatics in the water!' he says. 'I was hooked. Agnes Beckwith was a true pioneer of swimming for females. She alone was responsible for making swimming in public a respectable activity. Her amazing feats were the equal of most male swimmers, which gave her a mythical aura that legitimised swimming as a profession. Countless working-class females escaped the factories to earn a living in an activity – synchronised swimming – that would eventually become a sport.'

Emily Parker, meanwhile, whom Beckwith had beaten to her intended swim from London Bridge to Greenwich, also completed some major Thames swims. She was said to be just a few months older than Beckwith when in September 1875 she also set off from London Bridge, this time to Blackwall. Like Beckwith, she was a professional swimmer who had performed in many English towns, and again like Beckwith she had a brother, Harry, who was 'the champion of London'. The press reported that her appearances were made under his tuition.

At five o'clock on Saturday afternoon a river steamer 'conveyed the heroine of the evening' to London Bridge. Parker, 'dressed in appropriate costume, descended into a wherry with her brother and her pilot. At once the boat shot out into the stream, and having passed under the bridge . . . amid much cheering, which Miss Parker gracefully acknowledged, the young swimmer plunged quietly into the Thames.' The river police kept the Thames free from the obstruction of seventy or eighty wherries 'as well as they were able', while Harry stood in the accompanying boat 'with all his natatory honours thick upon him'.

Parker used a 'vigorous breast stroke' and never showed 'the slightest sign of fatigue'. River pistols, guns and small cannon were fired from various points as she made her progress down the Thames, and 'sailors in the ships cheered as the swimmer and the river mob which followed went past'. Just before seven she arrived opposite Greenwich Pier, where several thousands were waiting along the Embankment hoping to catch sight of her, but had to 'content themselves with cheering while the black patch on the water rapidly drifted in the gathering twilight towards Blackwall'.

In the 'half obscured light of the moon' Parker reached Blackwall Pier and was taken on board the steamer in a 'most vivacious mood'. Her time was one hour thirty-seven minutes. She had successfully eclipsed Beckwith's swim from London Bridge to Greenwich 'by going a stage further'. But, once again, the press were not entirely supportive. 'While we admire the endurance and skill of these young ladies,' commented *The Graphic*, 'we hardly like young ladies indulging in this public exhibition of their natatory abilities.'

Both young women were making a name for themselves, outdoors in the River Thames where everyone could see them, easily swimming five – even twenty – miles, and in conventional terms not wearing much in the way of clothing. No wonder the press were a little unnerved. But if male journalists didn't like to see young ladies indulging in public exhibition, others did, and how exciting it must have been to watch teenagers Agnes Beckwith and Emily Parker in the middle of the 'greatest metropolis in the world' swimming their hearts out.

The same month that Parker reached Blackwall Pier, she also swam from London Bridge to North Woolwich Gardens, using her 'favourite chest stroke' and covering around ten and a quarter miles. The *Morning Post* reported the tide was 'moderately good, but the wind, which was rather high, was dead against the swimmer, and the water very rough and lumpy'. At Greenwich 'a man named Buike, who had accompanied little Emily from London Bridge, gave up'. From Blackwall Pier to Woolwich 'the water was extremely rough, and the constant breaking of the waves in the face of the swimmer distressed her considerably'. At this point her brother Harry entered the water 'with a view to encourage his sister, who was working hard'.

When Parker arrived at her destination she got on to a boat and her brother then carried her up to the gardens. 'After she had partaken of some refreshment' – having not had 'any stimulant whatever while she was in the water' – she was presented with a gold medal valued at ten guineas.

Other noted Victorian swimmers also set off from London Bridge, among them Frederick Cavill, who attempted to swim to Gravesend in July 1876. The ex-Champion of the South Coast would 'start a little swim' said the press, intended as a 'gentle preparation' for a projected Channel crossing. Cavill, born in 1839 in London, had joined the navy, and seen action, before taking up professional swimming. In 1862 he'd won the English 500 yards swimming championship. This time he swam 'over twenty miles from London Bridge to Greenhithe, the longest distance to that time on the Thames', according to the *Australian Dictionary of Biography*. But Cavill failed to reach Gravesend because 'the ebb tide had run out' and he could 'make no head way'. There was no mention in any press reports of what he was wearing. The following month he swam from Southampton to Southsea Pier and from Dover to Ramsgate, before trying the Channel, but he was forced to give up three miles from the end.

Described as having a 'robust constitution, broad chest, and great muscular power', he tried the Channel again – and failed again – in 1877. He then migrated to Australia, settling in Sydney and establishing himself as a swimming professor, publishing a pamphlet, *How to Learn to Swim*, and successfully completing a number of long-distance swims. He must have also returned to England for in 1897 it was Cavill who won the Kew to Putney race, beating twenty-one other competitors. The British press described him as Australian, 'a wonderfully good man' who had now won 'his first success in England'. Cavill died in 1927. One of his sons, Arthur, was a professional champion of Australia and is credited with originating the crawl stroke, while another, Sydney, is said by some to be the originator of the butterfly stroke.

Meanwhile, other famous sporting men decided that, rather than swimming from London Bridge, they would dive from it. In 1871, J.B. Johnson made 'a sensational leap' in order to rescue a drowning man, a 'Mr Peters of the West-end'. But rumours abounded: was 'Mr Peters' none other than Johnson's brother, Peter, himself a professional swimmer? It appeared that 'his fall from a steamer' and his successful rescue were pre-arranged and the press concluded the whole thing was 'a got-up affair'. It might have been daring, but it hadn't been heroic. The brothers declined to comment. In 1872 Johnson became the first person ever recorded to try and swim the Channel, and although he failed it was his attempt that inspired

Webb. He went on to compete in many Thames races, such as the Putney to Hammersmith championships, and was immortalised in a ballad:

> Oh ! J.B. Johnson, I wish that I were him,
> Oh ! J.B. Johnson, he is the man to swim,
> And hasn't he the pluck? he floats just like a duck,
> I wish that I could swim, like J.B. Johnson.

Johnson's title the 'Hero of London Bridge' was short-lived, but others were quick to copy him. One Monday afternoon a man named Rawlins, whiling away his time in a local tavern, bet his friends a pot of beer that he would jump from London Bridge. He got on to the parapet and 'dived head foremost into the Thames'. The bridge was crowded with pedestrians and 'the excitement was intense' as Rawlins came to the surface and began swimming towards Old Swan steamboat pier. Several 'watermen, who thought it was an attempt at suicide', rowed after him. A captain from the London Steam-Boat Company threw out a rope and Rawlins, who was 'a first class swimmer', got on to the steamer. The police went after him, but he'd already made his escape.

A few years later, on 27 September 1889, it was seventeen-year-old Marie Finney's turn to dive when *The Graphic* reported, 'A LADY'S LEAP FROM LONDON BRIDGE'. 'Of course the act was an illegal one, and on that account the arrangements for the performance were kept secret. Beyond the customary gangs of loafers, no one was about at the time. It was decided that Miss Finney should leap from the first arch on the Middlesex side at 2.45 . . . A number of steamboats and tugs were passing at the time, and it was not until three o'clock that the signal was given to the fair diver. The course, so to speak, being clear, one male friend took her broad-brimmed hat, and another her long ulster, the lady

When Marie Finney dived from London Bridge in 1889, diving was still a new sport in England. By 1903 the Highgate Men's Pond on Hampstead Heath (above) was hosting high diving displays and Graceful Diving Championships.

immediately leaping on to the coping-stone. She was attired in a tight-fitting, dark blue navy jersey.

'After pausing for a few seconds to take her bearings, she dropped upon the projecting stone, a couple of feet below the parapet, and then dived down, striking the water beautifully. The whole business occupied only a few moments, and before the loafers could realise what had happened she was striking out for the boat. On reaching it she waved her hand to her friends, and was rowed to the shore none the worse for her immersion.'

Other reports added that just before she jumped a nearby policeman, busy regulating the traffic, was oblivious to what was going to happen, and that it was her brother who gave the all-clear signal from below, after which she was 'hoisted' on to the bridge. Presumably the press had been tipped off about the stunt beforehand. And what a stunt it was: diving was still a relatively new art form in England, and the country's first professional purpose-built diving stage wouldn't appear for another four years, at the Highgate Men's

Pond on Hampstead Heath which hosted the national Graceful Diving Championships. In the early nineteenth century diving had been more of a plunge and the aim was to dive in and go as far as possible underwater. Then in the 1890s Swedish and German gymnasts developed it into an art form until a dive meant the actual process of entering the water. The Swedes also brought in the swan or swallow dive, far more graceful than the 'English header', and fancy diving, adding more complex somersaults and twists. It would be another five years before Annie Luker dived from London Bridge and went on to perform at the Royal Aquarium, where her husband was too nervous to watch her; the Amateur Diving Association wasn't formed until 1901; diving for men didn't become an Olympic sport until 1904, and for women not until 1912. So Finney's 'leap' from London Bridge would have been the first time many people had seen a dive at all.

Born in Southport in 1872, Finney's brother James was a champion swimming professor and together they had been giving aquatic entertainments 'in a glass bath'. She was, said the *Penny Illustrated Paper*, a 'captivating young lady, as lissome as a mermaid under water' and, unlike Johnson's dive, there was 'no pretence of a rescue on the part of Miss Finney, who proved herself an exceedingly courageous damsel . . . this daring little Lancashire witch walked from a neighbouring hostelry on to London bridge . . . to all appearances out for a stroll'.

The following spring Finney wasn't so lucky. This time she was in Dublin and attempting to dive from O'Connell's Bridge into the River Liffey. 'Thousands of people assembled, but just as Miss Finney was clambering along the battlements, previous to taking the dive, she was seized by a policeman and arrested.' She was charged with obstructing the thoroughfare and fined £1.

But she went on to complete other dives, often off seaside piers, and together with her brother toured the United States giving exhibitions at theatres.

A few weeks after Finney's 1889 leap from London Bridge, another famous diver followed suit. Tom Burns' plan was to walk from his home city of Liverpool to London and back, diving from a bridge at each end of the journey.

'The Champion Diver of the World', as he would be known, first dived from Runcorn Bridge, and then swam eighteen miles along the Mersey to Liverpool, before setting off to London. When he reached London Bridge 'the police had to be evaded, while no little difficulty was found in procuring a recess from which to jump off. At length however, Burns saw an opportunity. The boatman below gave the signal, and in a few seconds Burns doffed his clothes, mounted the bridge and dropped on to the parapet. After a careful survey, with a loud shout he plunged.' Burns then swam the overarm stroke, and pulled himself into the boat, while 'hundreds of people watched him from the bridge and remained in earnest conversation all the time [he] was dressing in mid stream'. Then he started off on his journey home.

Born around 1867, Burns was a popular entertainer who amazed audiences at the Royal Aquarium where he dived 100 feet into a shallow tank of water. He'd learned to swim when he was nine, became a club captain and a swimming teacher, and won hundreds of awards for diving, swimming, running, walking and boxing, as well as numerous medals and awards for saving forty-two people from drowning. Seven years after his London Bridge dive, he is said to have dived from at least seven other London bridges. He also dived off bridges in Glasgow and Dublin, and was known for disguising himself as a 'farmer, miner, newsboy, old woman, and a female market worker' in order to evade police. However, he didn't always succeed and was sometimes arrested after a dive. He died at the age of thirty, after a dive went wrong in North Wales where 3,000 people had gathered to watch. The *Liverpool Echo* applauded his 'dare-devil exploits' and described him as an erratic genius: 'He had all the rough material in his composition out of which heroes are made.'

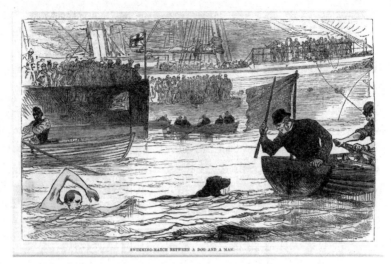

SWIMMING-MATCH BETWEEN A DOG AND A MAN.

A six-year-old retriever named Now Then outpaces R. Smith from Sheerness in a ten-mile swim from London Bridge in August 1880. The dog lasted two hours, the man forty-seven minutes.

London Bridge wasn't just the site for daring swims and dives, but, like Westminster Bridge, it was a place for novelty feats as well. In August 1880, for a wager of £50, R. Smith from Sheerness, a 'known aquatic performer', and a six-year-old black retriever named Now Then, said to have rescued seven people, set off to swim ten miles from London Bridge to North Woolwich Gardens. A newspaper illustration from the time shows the river full of boats, the dog calmly leading the way being spurred on by a slightly threatening looking bowler-hatted man in a rowing boat waving a stick. Smith started the race in front but was quickly overtaken and by the time he got to the Tower he was 50 yards behind. He gave up, 'much distressed', just off Limehouse after forty-seven minutes, while the dog continued to Deptford Creek 'none the worse for wear' after nearly two hours in the water. Of all the ground-breaking swims and dives from London Bridge, and particularly the women's, few are celebrated today. Instead it is this novelty race between a man and a dog that is more likely to be referenced in books about the Thames.

19

Tower Bridge and Tower Beach

'Children may now use the beach lawfully as well as safely, for the King has given permission for them to have this tidal playground for ever'

The Times, 24 July 1934

I leave London Bridge and head along the Thames Path towards Tower Bridge but the route is temporarily closed and so I stop, not wanting to take a detour right into the Tower of London. I walk down some steps to the shore where waves lap around ancient timber structures; two heavily tattooed men are roaming the beach while a woman concentrates on writing her name on the sand with a sharp stone. A Dutchman asks if I can take his photograph. It's not the beach or the bridge he's interested in: he wants to pose with the Shard behind him, the silver needle looming over London Bridge Hospital on the other side of the river. But it is Tower Bridge that attracts most people. Opened in 1894 it's still one of the most familiar bridges in the world, regularly featured in films and tourist literature. It's the only Thames bridge which can be raised, the middle section being lifted four or five times a week to allow large vessels to pass underneath. 'I want to go on the beach!' a man at the top of the steps shouts to his children and I think, why? There's nothing much to see down here.

But back in the 1930s, a little way downstream in front of the Tower of London, this was the city's very own 'sea side'. Here children of the East End traditionally played on the rocky foreshore at low tide, although this could be a fatal pastime. Officially they were also trespassing on land that belonged to the Crown. When Henry III received 'a white bear' from King Haakon of Norway in 1252 it was reportedly given 'a long leash' so that it could swim in the Thames and catch fish, but in the fourteenth century Edward III issued a proclamation against bathing in the Thames near the Tower 'on pain of death', presumably because it bordered royal land.

When the Tower of London Children's Beach opened in 1934 King George V promised the children of the East End would 'have this tidal playground for ever.' Here families enjoy 'London's Riviera' in 1952.

The 1930s children's beach was the brainchild of the Revd Phillip Thomas Byard Clayton, explains Rose Baillie, chair of the City of London Archaeological Society (COLAS), who has written a booklet on its history. Popularly known as 'Tubby', the Revd Clayton was a man of 'radiant spirituality, energy, good heartedness and charm'. In the summer of 1931 he came up with a plan for the foreshore which 'in summer is alive with families' and when 'venturesome children have from time to time to be rescued from the incoming tide by boats from Tower Pier, but warning will not keep them from their natural wishes'. 'Tubby' believed the area could be 'a genuine delight to the poor families who frequented Tower Hill'. He received the backing of Lord Wakefield of Hythe, a former Lord Mayor of London who made his fortune founding the Wakefield Oil Company, later Castrol, and who became president of the Tower Hill Improvement Fund. He bankrolled 'all the beach expenses pre-World War Two,' explains Rose, 'and a heap of other good causes as well'.

On 23 July 1934 the beach was officially opened with a grand ceremony attended by the Lord Mayor, the Bishop of London and Lord Wakefield. 'Now,' declared the Fund in a report entitled 'The Great Goal', 'on this very spot where, in the Middle Ages the penalty for trespass was also death for man, woman or child' there would be 'a safe playground for little ones'. King George V had been petitioned for permission to create the beach and, in a letter read out by Lord Wakefield, he assured local children that they would 'have this tidal playground as their own for ever'. Wakefield cut a white tape to open the beach and then, reported *The Times*, 'the ladder was lowered, to the music of cheerful siren-blasts from ships in the Thames'. Children rushed down to the beach, where free 'buns and chocolate and unlimited lemonade' were set out on long tables laden with casks and cardboard boxes of food.

The beach was used for paddling, swimming, building sandcastles and sunbathing. In the coming years there were toffee-apple sellers, entertainers and gala days, and thousands used the spot for their summer holidays. An estimated 70,000 children visited in the first year; in 1935 there were 100,000 children and adults. Most came from Stepney, others from Barking, Bermondsey, Borough, Shoreditch, Tottenham, Bethnal Green and Walthamstow. Teachers brought their classes to the beach as well, just as state school pupils would be taken to Thames baths at Oxford and Reading and public school boys would be taught to swim in the river at Eton and Westminster.

The ladder was lowered for up to six hours a day, between April and September, depending on the tides. There was a beach guard and during very busy days the St John Ambulance was on hand to help.

Safety, says Rose, was always a major concern. Leaflets were widely distributed, and a duty waterman was posted 30 yards downstream with a lifebuoy and pole grapnel to rescue those in trouble. His services were called upon three times in the first year. He was then joined by a commercial boatman who offered boat trips and rowing lessons. Yet while eighty-two accidents were reported in two seasons, most were minor cuts and scrapes.

The quality of the water itself, however, didn't seem to cause concern: 'we today are very conscious of the health risks of swimming in possibly polluted water,' writes Rose. 'Strangely enough, I have yet to find any indication that this was a concern for those involved with the Beach in the 1930s.' Instead, within a few years it was increasingly being used by hospital convalescents.

In 1936 deckchairs were introduced, as well as 200 cubic yards of 'clean Essex sand', which meant the beach was a little higher and so could be used for longer periods. The next year another 300 cubic yards of sand was added and on sunny bank holidays the beach was thronged with deckchairs as people sampled the delights of London's 'Riviera'. There were still accidents, however. Children were rescued when they got into difficulties swimming in water that was 12 feet deep, and at least two drowned near Irongate Stairs when they were swept away by the current.

In September 1939, with the outbreak of war, the beach was closed, as were other Thames bathing spots. By then it had been used by an estimated 400,000 people, such was Londoners' love of holidaying by the Thames, even within the City. In July 1946 it reopened with new ladders, taken from the SS *Rawalpindi*, and that year Pathé News filmed 'Tower Bridge Pleasure Beach', with '800 feet of beach right in the heart of London'. There was 'plenty of good, soft sand', to 'build fairy castles' or to laze on, with deckchairs 'for mum to snooze in and dad to read the paper in'. But it had been a close call; the PLA had wanted to remove the sand, saying it interfered with shipping.

There was also a sandcastle-building competition judged by Tessie O'Shea, the actress and singer whose 'theme tune' was 'Two Ton Tessie from Tennessee'. A picture from 1949 shows children eagerly queuing up to enter the beach on 26 September, the last day of the summer season. 'It was pure joy,' remembers one visitor, 'it was freedom, it was a day out, it was our Southend. It was something you looked forward to.'

'As a kid I was taken to Tower Beach a lot,' says Ron Osborne, 'as it was near to Mile End where we lived, having moved from a rundown tenement flat in Shadwell to a proper house in Mile End to avoid the bombing of the Docks in the war. In the 1950s Tower Beach was very popular and was packed at weekends if the sun was out, or even if it wasn't.' The Thames might have been declared biologically dead, but the shore was still a social place to meet for lunch and have a singsong, and parents were still taking their children there in the late 1960s with 'bucket and spade and sandwiches and bottles of pop'.

Yet the beach never quite regained its former glory; the boatmen had gone although there was still an attendant. No more sand was added and, explains Rose, there was growing awareness of 'the dangers of bathing in a sometimes polluted and strongly flowing river'. In 1971 the beach was closed because of cost, pollution and safety fears, and it stayed shut as 'an anti-terrorist measure'. Then in 1990 a committee was formed to campaign for the beach to reopen. There was to be a two-month trial and the idea was to truck in more sand and open it for twelve days a month, taking up to 500 people at a time. The committee's medical adviser, a professor from Guy's Hospital, told the press that 'the water quality of the Thames was probably at least as good as most British beaches, and better than some'. However, the plans were dropped after the death in 1991 of one of its chief instigators, Labour politician Donald Chesworth, and the beach remained closed.

In the end London children didn't get the tidal playground for ever as promised by the King in 1934, but such is the pull of the Thames that we've found new ways to use the foreshore. 'Londoners appear to have forgotten that they have a river,' says Rose, and few would 'contemplate crowds bathing in the lower Thames'. But with increasing interest in the shore as an environmental and archaeological resource, the Tower Beach is now open for two days a year with free activities organised by Historic Royal Palaces, COLAS and Thames 21. The event began in July 1998, with access by Irongate Stairs, which the tide reached sooner than the rest of the beach. It was then repeated in 2000 and this time people were allowed to use the Queen's Stairs. The weekend is intended mainly for children, but anyone can search for treasures washed up or buried on the shore during two hours or so of low tide, the only time of the year the public is allowed access.

On the last weekend in July, I come back to the Tower of London where at ten o'clock on a Saturday morning there is already a queue of about thirty people. Some are mudlarks, I'm told, wearing sturdy boots, camouflage trousers and kneepads, carrying rucksacks and trowels. The original mudlarks were nineteenth-century children and adults who scavenged the banks of the Thames at low tide, looking for coal, iron, brick, copper, canvas, and bones to sell to dealers. In the early twentieth century the word was used to describe schoolchildren who begged passers-by to throw coins into the Thames mud for them to retrieve. Today's mudlarks search the riverbank for objects of historical and archaeological interest and are more likely to use metal detectors – but they are strictly forbidden at this event. There are around seventy licensed mudlarks, of whom just seven are women.

Everywhere I look are large Health & Safety signs, a warning about Weil's disease and a long list of rules – 'Children must be accompanied by an adult. WALK – do not run. The beach is very rocky in parts – be careful how you move. There may be sharp objects on the beach – be vigilant. Do not touch your mouth or eyes after being on the beach.' Anyone with an open cut or graze is to ask for a plaster, and 'if you find yourself in deep mud stop and walk back out the way you went in'. The warnings seem excessive to me – how dangerous can it really be to go down to a beach? – but presumably an event like this can't be run without them. Even sadder is the idea that 'venturesome' children's freedom to play has to be curtailed, as if we can't trust kids to run around on the sand any more (and perhaps dodge a few rocks and survive some cuts and scrapes) when, after all, that's what beaches are for. Today's rules would seem very strange to those who used the beach before us. Now banning swimming and closing down old bathing spots is seen as an easier option than the effort required to create safer places to swim.

COLAS have set up tables on the grass on the other side of the Thames Path, where I meet Rose Baillie. 'This foreshore,' she says with a sweep of her hands, 'was always a place where children played.' She points behind to the green spire of All Hallows church, one of the oldest in the City of London, where Revd 'Tubby' used to preach. 'He saw kiddies nearly drown,' she says, 'but instead of saying "let's ban it", he said "let's make it safer".' And he did.

I rejoin the queue and chat with a woman from Yorkshire. 'My dad worked here in the sixties for a construction company and he found this.' She pulls a small cannonball out of her pocket. Her father died recently and she seems to have brought the cannonball with her as a memento of his life and the very reason she's here at the Thames. Suddenly there's activity on the Queen's Steps: they're being cleaned with a hosepipe. I lean forward and see the water is right at the bottom of the steps, and I wonder how long it will be before the tide recedes and we're allowed down. More mudlarks arrive, skilfully managing to join the front of the queue, with 'hey, mate' and hearty handshakes.

Now we have to sign a Health & Safety form and put on blue surgical gloves. At last, an hour later, a Yeoman Warder in full regalia says we can enter the Queen's Steps. A woman shouts, 'don't run' and then asks me quite sharply if I have gloves and if so why I haven't put them on. The stairs are steep and wet but I manage not

Today the old children's beach at the Tower of London is open for two days a year. Children no longer swim, but it's an opportunity to find riverbank artefacts.

to slip, and then I start walking along the beach, with no idea what I'm looking for. There is something dreamy about looking down on stones, strolling on a hot day by the Thames in central London, right at river level for once. I try to conjure up what it would have been like here in the 1930s at the city's Riviera, with deckchairs and sandcastle competitions, toffee apples and unlimited lemonade.

Then I see a man wearing a bright yellow jacket and, assuming he's a volunteer, I go up to ask for tips. He turns out to be Graham Keevill, a consultant archaeologist and one of the initiators of the foreshore event who has worked at the Tower for twenty years. He is Historic Royal Palaces' professional supervisor for the beach open day and is known as Mr Archaeologist. 'It's a thrill,' says Graham, 'even after thirteen years.' I ask him what people normally find: 'clay tiles, pottery going back to Roman times. It's a piece of history, our history, and we don't mind people taking it away with them.' A volunteer approaches; he says the tide will be in in an hour and the water will get to the stairs, 'then we have to get people out. But there will still be a bit of beach and they don't realise they are getting cut off at the steps, because they don't want to leave.'

Graham says people particularly like picking up bones; 'you see them with armfuls, it's some sort of dinosaur fixation'. Others find cannonballs and broken cannons – the Tower supplied the royal army with weapons from medieval times to the mid-nineteenth century – as well as coins. The Tower was home to the Royal Mint for 500 years until 1812. 'There is a sense of the people who were up there,' Graham points to the Tower, 'and down here,' he points to the beach, 'this was the Tower's own private dock.' To archaeologists like those involved in today's event the Thames is a keeper of our history, preserving relics from bygone days on its shore, fragments from the past, signs of industry and battle, even of England's old place in the world. And now at last, after nearly thirty years, the public is allowed to come here again.

Someone once found a Roman oil lamp, Graham tells me, and there are plenty of clay pipes. 'That red stuff,' he gestures down at my feet, 'is brick or kiln material.' 'What, like this?' I ask, picking up a big chunk. 'That,' he says, 'is a Roman tile, you can tell by the ridge that it was an end-of-roof tile.' So far all I've found is a chocolate wrapper, a plastic water bottle and lots and lots of stones. But then, as he's talking, I suddenly see a coin-sized piece of pottery with a pretty blue and white design, and then fragments of clay pipes, which I'd thought were bits of discarded tubing.

The beach is busy now; everywhere is the sound of people scraping in the sand, kids filling up buckets with stones and bones. Volunteers have set up a table with pictures of animal skeletons; I hand over a bone and am told it's a sheep's metatarsal. Next I present a piece of pipe; it has quite a big central hole so that makes it nineteenth-century, then a green bit of pottery which I'm told is a piece of border ware from Surrey or Hampshire made in the sixteenth or seventeenth century, and would have been used for cooking or storing food. By now my arms are aching with all my treasures, the heat is overwhelming and it's time to make way for the children behind me queuing at the information table, some with bones as big as their hands.

It's clear that the reopening of the children's beach at Tower Bridge, even for just one weekend a year, has been a great success, giving us free access to an area we want to explore. Other places could follow, with recent calls for a year-round beach on the Thames. The campaign group Reclaim the Beach argues that 'with the water cleaner every year, it will soon be fit for swimmers again' and suggests one could be below Victoria Tower Gardens and another on the South Bank.

Artist Amy Sharrocks also has a dream for Tower Beach. She has been 'making work about people and water' for around ten years and her projects include SWIM in 2007, an 'all-access swim across London', and Museum of Water at Somerset House in 2014.

For the past few years her plan has been to organise a swim across the Thames. 'I'm doing it to try and get a different sense of London; it's a conceptual art piece, a dream. I'm not doing it for charity. It's an artwork. It's crucial to think about this river and how we use it.'

Swim the Thames is scheduled for 2015 and would start from the south side of the river, ending underneath the Tower of London, where the children's beach used to be, probably in September, as 'we need a dry month, before the rain and the sewers overflow'. It would begin about thirty minutes before low tide; swimmers will be pulled by the current, catch the slack water and then be taken around in an arc. At the moment Amy is 'marshalling people. I have around a thousand names of people who want to do it. Everyone's like, "Oh I want to swim the Thames, where do I sign?"' But when she asked the PLA 'if I could swim from Vauxhall, or anywhere really, they said "no way, no one touches the Thames". I'm not doing a guerrilla swim: I want them to recognise our right to it. In Roman times London was a water city. Now we're leading dry lives alongside an oasis of water.'

She had aimed to do the swim in 2012, but this was suspended because of the Olympics, and now the new by-law is in place. 'They close London off if it's a race or if it's to raise money,' she says, 'but this is just for the joy of doing it. If just once a year they could stop industry for a swim . . .'

Others are attracted to Tower Bridge, too, not for art but for stunts. In July 2009, twenty-seven-year-old Australian freestyle motocross star Robbie Maddison performed a spectacular back-flip over an open Tower Bridge. 'People say I'm crazy,' he told the press, 'but I just love taking on these huge challenges.' Tower Bridge also remains a good spot for a demonstration. In July 2012 a man said to be a taxi driver dived head first off the bridge during a protest by London taxi drivers who wanted to be allowed to use the Olympic Games Lanes. A group of drivers travelled slowly across Tower Bridge tooting their horns when, at around 4 p.m., a man apparently wearing a white Stetson hat, jumped. He was pulled from the river by the marine policing unit, having, according to the BBC, almost been hit by a tourist ferry and arrested for a public order offence – just like Victorian divers Tom Burns and Marie Finney who once dived upstream at London Bridge.

20

London Docklands

'We loved everything about the river . . . it was our playground, our life'

John Daniel, Thames lighterman, 1950s

Downriver from Tower Bridge the River Thames now begins to enter London Docklands, once part of the Port of London and the world's largest port, and an area where people have been swimming and bathing for at least a century, including in the docks themselves. In Roman and medieval times ships docked at small quays in the Pool of London, between London Bridge and Tower Bridge. Then, in 1696, the Howland Great Dock in Rotherhithe was built, providing a more secure place for large vessels. The Georgian era saw the opening of the West India Dock in 1802, followed by several others, while more docks were built in Victorian times, mainly further east, such as Royal Victoria and Millwall. Some were for ships to anchor and be loaded or unloaded; others were for ships to be repaired. 'Lightermen' on small barges carried the cargo between ships and quays, while quayside workers dealt with the goods onshore. In 1909 the PLA took over management of the docks, replacing a number of private companies, and built the last of the docks, the King George V, in 1921.

The docks suffered heavy bomb damage during the Second World War and while trade recovered in the 1950s they weren't big enough to cope with larger vessels transporting cargo in containers, so they began to close. In 1981 the London Docklands

Development Corporation was formed to redevelop the area, today a centre for business and luxury apartments. It's also home to the Museum of London Docklands, on the side of West India Docks on the Isle of Dogs.

I arrive to find a grand old Georgian sugar warehouse, with spiked bars at the windows giving it a Bastille-like air, flanked by restaurants and bars, while down at the waterside an old boat is dwarfed by a huge glass building housing a bank. The Museum opened in 2003 and tells the history of the Thames and Docklands with twelve galleries spread over four floors. I walk around looking at artefacts, models and pictures, an atmospheric recreation of nineteenth-century riverside Wapping and a gallery explaining the city's involvement in transatlantic slavery. But I can find little reference to swimming, except for a poster from 1870 announcing a fête at West India Dock.

'The Thames, from London Bridge onwards, is a difficult and dangerous place to swim,' says Tom Wareham, currently Curator of Community and Maritime History, 'but people did. You weren't supposed to bathe in the docks or the entrances to docks, but there is evidence that people drowned while bathing. Most drowned in winter when conditions were icy or smoggy, but there was also a peak in the summer. There was usually a beach, a stretch of silt, at the entrance to most docks, and kids were drawn to it.'

I follow him to a small meeting room where he's arranged a number of documents on the table, including photocopies of Victorian ledgers written in beautiful cursive script and modern colour-coded bar charts. Such was the concern at the number of fatalities in the late nineteenth century that the docks committee ordered an investigation. An unnamed clerk looked at fatality reports from four sample periods between November 1873 and December 1891. The results were alarming: nearly three people drowned every month – 176 deaths over a seventy-one-month period. This was despite the fact that the various private dock companies encouraged their employees to learn to swim, and even offered lessons in an outdoor tank at the West India Docks.

Of the known causes of death, five boys drowned while bathing. But far more fell from barges and ships; one boy was knocked into the water by a rope, a stevedore missed his footing coming ashore, a ship keeper slipped off a gangway ladder. Records from the winters of 1873–4 and 1879–80 show that most drownings happened at West India Dock, which was one of the biggest areas of water with a large number of people living close by.

In the early 1900s police paid young boys half a crown for every body they retrieved from the Pool of London, with many deaths the result of swimming under a boat and getting trapped. But soon amateur swimmers were racing in the docks and newspaper photographs from 1895 illustrating 'A Swimming Fete at the Docks' show nine bathers, all apparently men, about to leap off a floating wooden board on which stand two suited officials. One swimmer is already in the water; behind the raft is a rowing boat full of people, while the sides of the dock are dense with spectators. Another image catches two divers in midair, having just thrown themselves off a temporary diving stage.

In 1906 the London and India Docks Swimming Club held their gala at Millwall Cutting, and again pictures show a row of men about to dive off a raft, although this time it seems to be covered in clothing as part of the '50 yards wet shirt handicap', with corner poles holding up bunting. By the early 1930s the docks had become the setting for swimming events run under ASA rules. The Port of London Authority Swimming Club had an annual open-air gala at the Millwall Cutting, starting at 3.15 in the afternoon, complete with printed programmes costing threepence. The *Daily Mirror* featured a front-page photo of 'Dock as Swimming Bath' showing the fifty yards championships at the PLA's swimming gala at the Millwall Cutting. The dock looks vast, like a lido, with concrete sides and a group of officials at one end, all set against a grey background of warehouses, bridges and ships' funnels.

'A Swimming Fete at the Docks'. It's not clear which dock this is, but the date is July 1895.

I'm surprised the Docklands Museum hasn't anything much to commemorate these old events, until Tom tells me they have three silver cups (not on display), won by Kathleen Ralphs (née Elgar) in the PLA Swimming Club Ladies Championships between 1932 and 1934. They also have a transcript of an oral recording of her memories.

Ralphs was born in 1913; her father was in the navy and his father worked as a granary foreman in the old Surrey Docks. When she was seventeen she joined the PLA as a typist. 'The social life was wonderful,' she recalled, 'the main thing I can remember is the swimming club they used to have [and] swimming galas there in the West India Dock.' She belonged to the Lewisham Ladies Swimming Club, separate from the PLA but which was invited to take part in the galas. The day before an event a section of the dock was 'skimmed off' and a boom put across the entrance so 'nothing else could float in'. The dock was decorated with bunting, there were tugs to undress in and 40 feet of water to swim in. 'I used to love swimming in the dock,' she remembered, 'because although it had been skimmed it was still very oily and it made you feel tremendous. You just shot through the water at twice your normal speed.' The river had a distinct odour: 'it wasn't a dirty smell but it was a certain smell when the wind blew in our direction' and her mother was 'always waiting with a dose of sennapods' (the seed of the senna plant used as a purgative) when she got home from a swim, because 'she said, "you don't know what you might have swallowed"'.

As a child Ralphs' father also used to swim in the docks, where one swimmer was 'a very good swallow diver' and later ran a club for local boys. Ralphs' father had a silver medallion for life saving and she had bronze. 'I always used to think now I've got this medallion and I must make use of it. So I was just dying for someone to fall in the dock so that I could rescue them.' Everyone working for the PLA had to swim. 'In those days swimming was a pastime that everyone indulged in . . . everybody swam as a matter of course.'

People continued to swim in this area of the Thames after the war, and Tom has someone he wants me to meet. Downstairs at the entrance to the Mudlarks Children's Gallery is Museum guide Brian Gover, wearing the distinctive bright pink shirt required of employees, which he's not overly fond of. He opens the gallery door and children rush in to the interactive play area, some heading for the sand bowl, others for the water area or the model ship.

Brian makes sure they're settled, before telling me of his swimming experiences. He was born on the Isle of Dogs in 1941 and remembers two areas where you could swim officially, Tower Bridge and Greenwich. 'It was strange really, we were allowed to swim but if a worker on the river fell in he spent three days in hospital under observation. But we grew up in post-war London and our playground was the Thames. You could find so many things on the river. If you needed a new rabbit hutch then you could pick up timber, and we used to raid the barges for peanuts.'

Dives in progress during a dock swimming fête in 1895.

Some children dived from barges or from the steps off the causeway; others just waded into the water. 'No one had swimming costumes,' says Brian, 'or if you did then you were lucky. Mums knitted them and once they were wet they hung by your knees, so people didn't bother wearing them.' He remembers only boys playing in the Thames and 'we would wave at American tourists on the pleasure boats and they would throw us money'. But everyone knew it was potentially dangerous. 'We were warned not to swim, the police would come around the schools and tell us not to. But the river was the only place to play. The barges moved up and down, bobbing in the water, and a lot of children died from jumping off them or getting stuck underneath.'

As for the water, 'it was absolutely filthy and full of oil, we all had boils. It was polluted, no doubt about it. There was a lot of glass and you cut your feet. The older lads went to the Thames with air guns to shoot the rats. You'd see a cow going up and then the tide changed and you saw it come back again . . . twice the size! You also saw dogs, cats, trees, horses . . . and boats chucked everything, all the waste, overboard.' As he got older, 'we just grew out of it, and they shut up the stairs and built up behind them. The stairs were for ships mooring, there were jetties for the seamen to walk up and we used them, there were no barriers then.'

John Daniel, who worked as a Thames lighterman in the 1950s, also experienced the dangers of the river, as recorded by his son, Peter, who is educational officer at the City of Westminster Archives. Daniel's family worked on the Thames in one form or another for many generations. 'We loved everything about the river . . . it was our playground, our life.' In 1953, at the age of fifteen, Daniel left school and got a job on a Thames sludge boat; he was then apprenticed as a Thames lighterman with Humphrey and Grey Ltd, based at Hays Wharf and at one point employing more than 200 men, with seven tugs and 400 barges. As the weeks progressed Daniel learned the skills of a waterman, using the natural currents of the Thames. The river then was 'completely different. There were so many craft afloat, so many barges that you could almost walk across some of the docks by stepping from one to another.'

The river shaped Daniel's life and he met his future wife thanks to the Thames. One day he was with a friend who'd invited 'a lovely redhead named Pat . . . to join us for a day's sailing at Greenwich'. But as Pat was about to 'step into the dinghy to take her ashore she slipped and found herself waist-deep in the water. I gallantly fished her out . . . Forty-six years, four children and five grandchildren later I think that was the best day's work I ever did on the grand old river.'

This stretch of the Thames still draws swimmers, like journalist and former Conservative politician Matthew Parris who in 2010 decided to cross the river a little way upstream from the Museum

In July 1906 the London and India Docks Swimming Club held their gala at Millwall Cutting, including the 50 yards wet-shirt handicap.

of London Docklands – and got into quite a bit of trouble. Matthew had never swum in the Thames before, although he did once rescue a dog, 'but that doesn't count as a swim'. The rescue took place on a late February night in 1978 when he was walking home after work from Westminster. 'I saw a little boy and girl near the river and they were crying. They said they'd taken their dog out for a walk and it had climbed over the parapet and fallen in. It was dark, the tide was high and it was windy. I was brought up in Africa; I didn't know how cold it really was.' But he plunged in and saved the dog, and a few months later was awarded an RSPCA certificate for bravery, presented by then leader of the opposition, Margaret Thatcher, on Westminster Bridge.

Some thirty years later Matthew took his first planned swim in the Thames, although it was something he'd been mulling over for fifteen years. His decision was inspired by the part of London in which he lives, on Narrow Street in the East End. 'I look across to the Globe Stairs,' he explains, 'and I wanted to swim across the river. People didn't believe me, I was always boasting about doing it. They said, "take a life jacket, have someone in a boat, tow a life belt", but to take the means to save you, well, that's cheating. I didn't think it was risky, and I don't think so now. There was no traffic, only the occasional barge. You can see up both arms of the river for around half a mile, and I wasn't doing it alone.'

Matthew, who describes himself as no great swimmer, decided to make his crossing in high summer when the water was warmest, and at high tide as it turned. He would start from the stairs at Globe Wharf and swim straight across to the Ratcliffe Cross Stairs at Narrow Street. His lodger, Tom Mitchelson, would flash a light from the balcony to show the coast was clear, and when Jonathan Weir, a twenty-year-old student, heard Matthew wouldn't be taking a life jacket he said he would come, too. One night they finally put their plan into action. Matthew had checked online tide tables; he would go at slack tide (the period before the tide changes direction), at 03.35 on Thursday morning. So he had a few hours' sleep, put on trunks and an old singlet and some discardable flip-flops and then just after 3 a.m. called a minicab to get to the other side of the Thames under the Rotherhithe Tunnel. Along with Jonathan he crept down the Globe Stairs and undressed. A barge slid past, a light from the balcony light flashed and in they jumped. The water was choppy but Matthew, swimming breaststroke, couldn't feel any current. 'It wasn't cold, it was very different from 1978, but the waves seem higher when you're in it, you feel them slap against your face.' Then, when he turned to look for the Globe Stairs behind him, he saw they were far over to his right; the two men were being carried speedily upstream.

They decided to stay close together and keep swimming towards the opposite bank but without fighting the current. Soon they were almost past the King Edward VII Park, and approaching some moored sailing boats at Wapping, when Jonathan managed to grab a rope and Matthew a rudder. They then reached the stilts of a riverside boardwalk, pulled round to a little creek, and climbed a ladder on to a road. 'I would have carried on if I hadn't managed to get out at Wapping,' says Matthew, 'there are big warehouses so the next place I would have been able to get out would have been another mile or so.'

They'd been in the Thames for around half an hour, and they were about three-quarters of a mile upriver from Limehouse. Barefoot, wet and freezing, the two men 'ran down the highway' for home, with Matthew's underpants full of mud. Tom, still waiting at the flat, told them, 'I reckoned you'd either drowned or you hadn't, there was no point calling the police. Anyway, I had the strongest of hunches you'd be OK.' It was then that Matthew realised navigational tables are in GMT. He'd got the time wrong; high tide was an hour later than he'd thought. Yet he was overjoyed that he'd done what he'd set out to do and, as for any effect on his health, 'I did swallow a lot of water and it tasted slightly salty which was a surprise, but both of us were fine.'

Matthew got plenty of press coverage, mainly because he wrote about his swim in *The Times*, and also because of people's response. He began his article with, 'First, don't try this at home. It could have ended in disaster. It was ignorant and it was dangerous. But it was not impetuous.' Today he says, 'I knew people would condemn me, I was not surprised by people saying it was dangerous, but I didn't think it would get so much reaction, I just thought it would raise a few eyebrows.'

And what does he think of the new by-law that would now make his swim illegal? 'Stupid. There are millions of places in Britain where it would be dangerous and they can't prohibit swimming in them all, it's your own decision.' As for the PLA's argument that a swimmer poses a danger to boats, he says, 'mostly it is dangerous in the Thames, but any object could pose a potential hazard to boats, there are all sorts of things in the river like huge logs. It could be a hazard if a boat swerves to avoid you, but that's far-fetched.'

The reaction to his article was mixed. Explorer Bear Grylls said he'd once swum in the Thames towing a canoe on a long line; he'd ended up one mile downstream and wouldn't do it again. Photographer Brian Griffin said it was 'an absolutely crazy thing to do . . . I've seen the stuff that is dumped in it, and what is washed up on the beach. I've seen bodies, I've seen the whole lot.' But as with Victorian swimmers, Matthew was also applauded for his daring. Playwright Steven Berkoff, who swam at the Tower Bridge beach as a child, called it an 'audacious, dazzling, daring piece of derring-do'. Kate Rew, founder of the Outdoor Swimming Club, praised Parris' sense of adventure, while politician Vince Cable admired Parris' 'pluck'. However, he added that considering the Thames 'takes sewage from overflowing storage tanks and acts as home to various microbiological nasties, I shall stick to boats'. At the time Matthew said he would never do it again, but would he? 'I think I may,' he says, 'especially as it's illegal now. But I won't write about it. And I'll get the tide right this time.'

21

Dock Swim

'The charity element of swimming the Thames is huge'
Alex Jackson, Great Swim operations manager

The PLA galas in the London Docks presumably ended around the outbreak of the Second World War, and were never resumed. Today, however, there's a new opportunity to swim here with the launch in 2009 of the Great London Swim, an annual one-mile event in the Royal Victoria Dock. The Great Swim series started in 2008 with one mile in Lake Windermere. That was a good year for British open-water swimmers at the Beijing Olympics, with Keri-Anne Payne's silver and Cassandra Patten's bronze in the women's marathon ten-kilometre open-water event, and David Davies' silver in the men's. The Windermere swim was such a success that the series was expanded and now there are five events. The Royal Victoria Dock was chosen because of its location, with its backdrop of the O2, plenty of transport links, space for medics, changing areas and a charity village, and the opportunity for swimmers to cover a mile.

I've signed up to do the swim for several reasons; it will be my first experience of a mass-participation event and I'll be in the water with hundreds of others, many of them determined racers, when I don't like the idea of crowds and hate the notion of competing. It will also be a very different experience from my lush upper Thames swim through the Oxfordshire countryside from Buscot Lock to

Radcot Bridge. This will be a city swim, and I want to get a sense of what it might have been like swimming in London's dockland seventy years ago, and to understand who does it now and why.

But then on the evening of Thursday 29 August I get an unexpected email. Forty hours from now I'll be arriving at the Royal Victoria Dock for 'the UK's biggest mass-participation open-water swimming series', only something's gone wrong. The email informs me that 'Following recent tests . . . the water has been found to be unsafe for immersion sports, such as swimming.' So the venue has been changed to Millwall Dock. This puts me in a bit of a panic; I've visited the Royal Victoria Dock, interviewed people who've swum there, and watched numerous YouTube videos. I felt I was well prepared for my first mass-participation swim, and now I'm not. The email explains: 'despite multiple clear test results in recent months . . . activity related to construction work in the immediate area has resulted in the reduction in water quality'. The organisers assure me that my 'safety and comfort' is their number one priority. None of the Great London Swim literature has mentioned Millwall, but now we're told it 'has always been on standby as a suitable alternative'.

Then I realise what a gift this is, because it was Millwall Cutting where a gala was held in 1906 and where the PLA hosted their swimming events in the 1930s. So, rather than swimming at the Royal Victoria Dock, I'm actually going to be further upstream on the Isle of Dogs, right next to the West India Docks where Kathleen Ralphs won her silver cups.

First opened in 1868, Millwall Dock was mainly used for timber and grain. It's an L-shaped construction with an outer dock, where the swim is held, and an inner dock at the end of which is Millwall Cutting. Today the area is a commercial business district, its office towers home to technological, publishing, legal and financial companies. The three West India Docks, meanwhile, were closed to commercial traffic in 1980 and are now the site of Canary Wharf.

The Royal Victoria Dock was chosen as the original venue for the first Great London Swim, a one-mile course that attracts thousands of swimmers every year.

The new venue for the swim is Docklands Sailing & Watersports Centre, at the west end of the outer Millwall Dock where it used to be connected to the Thames by a channel that was filled in during the 1920s. But although I'm keen to swim near where Kathleen Ralphs once raced, I'm still a little anxious that I haven't seen the venue and that I'm going to be in the water with thousands of others. That night I dream I've lost my designated swimmer's hat, then I have my hat but there is no number on it and I'm walking down an urban road in the dark in my wetsuit insisting it's too cold to swim.

The next morning I get to Millwall Dock to find a mass of people crossing back and forth on Westferry Road, with volunteers holding up ropes to stop traffic. It all feels a bit haphazard; I'm not sure where to go and all I really want is to see the course. The dock looks big to me, although it's smaller than the Royal Victoria. The water is calm and sprinkled with sunshine; there is barely a ripple. There's no bunting as there was in the 1930s, but there is a carnival atmosphere. I can hear music in the distance and smell frying onions from a nearby food tent. People stand in front of brightly coloured flags and banners advertising the event sponsors, holding up cameras and jostling for the best view.

I've been told by one swimmer that in the early days of the London Triathlon, which held swims in the Royal Victoria Dock in the mid-1980s, it was a grim place, a barren wasteland with dead dogs and cats in the water. The docks have certainly improved since then, the landscape no longer a scene of Depression-era warehouses with a section of the West India Dock skimmed off with a boom to stop anything floating in.

The first of today's swimmers started at 9 a.m.; we're split into 'waves' and I'm in the 11 a.m. 'white wave', which means I wear a white hat with my number on it. I watch a group of people in wetsuits walking down a jetty; they look like upright beetles as one by one they go in. I can see the course runs down the right-hand side of the dock, past a series of yellow buoys resembling bouncy castles, then the swimmers seem to disappear before returning along the left-hand side. Unlike in Ralphs' time, there's no floating platform in the middle of the dock for people to dive off.

I've been warned about dehydration, so I drink a bottle of water before going to change; there are no tugs to undress in as there were in the 1930s, instead there are large canvas tents across Westferry Road. But I'm stopped at the entrance to the women's tent and asked to produce my hat. I've left it in another bag with my daughter, and now they won't let me in. This is my bad dream coming true. I sit on a small stone wall by the toilets and put on my wetsuit, then return to the starting area. 'Look, Mum,' says my daughter as she hands me my hat, 'look at the faces of everyone getting out, they're smiling!'

I chat to a woman behind me who has just done the Great Swim in Windermere. She seems seasoned and sympathetic and I must look worried because she asks, 'Have you ever swum outdoors before?' It's now 10.30 a.m. and time to check in for the white wave. I fix the timing chip provided around my ankle, secure the Velcro strap, give my name to someone with a clipboard and am told to rest my ankle against a block. This is nothing like my upper river swim; the challenge here seems not so much to swim in the Thames but to do it as speedily as possible. We all mill around near the start, helping ourselves to water. I drink two bottles, so now that's three I've drunk and I really need the toilet. We've been advised not to drink any alcohol the night before, but I overhear a woman saying she had three beers and a curry.

We're let into the acclimatisation area, a roped-off section of the dock next to the starting pontoon. This is a chance to get used to the water, and we're told to swim clockwise. I walk down what appears to be an underwater ramp. 'When you get to me,' says a man in a red t-shirt, 'you can swim.' I get to him and throw myself in, hoping I've cleared the ramp. The water isn't too bad, it's 19.5 degrees, just half a degree colder than Gospel Oak lido has been this week, but I hear a man behind me say, 'Shit, it's cold.' I start to swim leisurely, not wanting to use up any energy. Then I feel a sharp pain in my side as someone overtakes and when I look round someone else kicks me in the foot.

We're herded out of the water and a man takes a microphone to welcome us. The fastest time so far has been just under twenty minutes but for some it could take two hours. 'In twenty minutes,' he says, 'you'll wonder what all those sleepless nights were about. An hour from now, you'll be in the pub.' He asks the newbies to put up their hands; nearly everyone in this wave of around 200 people is doing it for the first time. But one or two have done all the Great Swims this year; this is their last and the warmest. The man expertly mixes jokes with information and reassurance. He tells us about the people in kayaks, the lifeguards and volunteers. If we have any problem at all, we just stop and put our hand up. Then he passes the mike to a woman who launches into a manic group exercise routine.

I wonder how the dock events would have started in the 1930s, whether a gun was fired before the swimmers in their one-piece knitted costumes leapt in. There would have been no safety canoes back then, and probably no written warnings about the state of the water either. My 'on the day guide' advises that all cuts or abrasions should be covered, to try not to swallow any water, to take 'a full

Lining up to enter the Millwall Dock. I'm fourth from right and about to start my first mass-participation swim.

shower at the earliest opportunity' and 'if you feel unwell for a period of up to three weeks after your swim, visit your GP and advise them you have been swimming in open water'. Unlike my SwimTrek trip, however, there is no specific mention of Weil's disease.

Thankfully, there isn't a scrum to get into the dock. In previous years, I've been told, people ran in and smashed into each other and so I've been advised to stay right at the back. As the hooter sounds we're let in, one small group at a time, with everyone walking politely. But why is the PA system playing an Olly Murs song, 'Troublemaker', with the refrain 'I swear you're giving me a *heart attack*'?

I'm in the last six as we head towards the waters of Millwall Dock. Then off we go, and I think, it's easy after all, it's just swimming. It feels a little like being in a pond, the water is dark and smells of bracken and when I open my eyes underneath I can't see a thing. I wonder how deep it is; there's no chance I could put my feet down here and feel mud between my toes as I did near Buscot Lock. I swallow some water by accident and it tastes like metal, but it's clear enough for me to see my hands in the water, with a faintly yellow tinge.

All around me the dock is being churned up by swimmers, arms and legs thrashing, and I can't quite get the right rhythm, unable to decide which stroke to use. In the upper Thames I tried to follow the curves of the river; here there's a set course I have to follow. The warm-up man has told us that after the first buoy at 200 metres we will be fine but it's not until I reach the second one that I calm down. I seem to be veering near the wall where people are standing cheering and waving. It's strange being watched while I'm swimming, it makes me feel self-conscious and so I tread water and take in the views: a tree-lined walkway on my right, ahead a single chimney rising up over a small park with bushes like giant bunches of broccoli, on my left the sun bounces off the reflective windows of shiny office blocks. I want to take in this city swim experience, to lie and float and think about things, but I have to keep an eye out for everyone else. A woman is doing a strong backstroke seriously off course; she's heading my way and she can't see me and I stop as a man on a kayak puts her back on track.

I get to the end of the dock and swim alongside boats, some like old-fashioned tugs; on one a couple are sitting having their breakfast as hundreds of people swim past. I turn on to my back; there are no overhanging trees here, no bright blue dragonflies, instead I see a man high up at an office window, leaning out, smoking a cigarette. I feel like I'm part of some bizarre entertainment as still the people on the walkways cheer and shout. Then I reach a bridge, behind which is the inner dock and after that Millwall Cutting. Now I'm on the final stretch, swimming towards the finishing line through two large buoys. I'm enjoying it more now, because I can see the end and nothing has gone wrong except my bladder is ready to burst. I tread water as discreetly as possible and at once a man in a kayak zooms over and asks if I'm OK. 'I'm fine!' I tell him. But my daughter later says, 'You didn't look like it, Mum, you looked like you were drowning.'

I see a digital clock face ahead of me. It's 11.50 a.m. So I've been a bit slower than I thought, although I have had quite a few stops and floats. But I can speed up now, I don't have to worry about getting tired and suddenly it feels like the most brilliant day to be swimming round a dock.

A man helps me out of the water and on to the exit ramp. I'm a bit dazed; although I don't feel the euphoria I had with my upper Thames swim.

I'm given a finisher's bag and follow a sign to a shower. Then I start to cough, and soon I'm coughing so much I'm nearly retching. I think of Kathleen Ralphs' mother, waiting at home with a dose of sennapods because of what her daughter may have swallowed while swimming in the dock. But I also think how proud she must have been to have won three silver cups, just as my daughter asks, 'Have you got a medal?'

I walk back to the tent to get changed and it's now I appreciate how well it's all been organised, the venue was transformed in less than two days, thousands of people are being carefully supervised swimming round a dock in half-hour waves. An hour later I'm home and the first thing I want to do is have a bath; I have an urge to wash off the Thames. Then I look at my Just Giving page. Entrants to the Great Swims are encouraged to raise money, helped to create a Just Giving page and nominate a charity, so I've put down Solace Women's Aid. I see that in five days I've raised £520. If the majority of people swimming today were doing it for charity, and if the average pledged is a few hundred pounds, then today's event could have raised £100,000.

In Victorian times people made wagers on swimming races across and along the river, in the 1930s they competed for silver cups in the docks; now we actually pay to swim here (the London Great Swim fee is £39) and make money for charity in the process.

'The charity element is huge,' says Alex Jackson, Great Swim operations manager. Thirty per cent of swimmers today were raising money, although it's not the main motivation. Twenty-six per cent want a challenge, a quarter are looking for a good time and/or to beat a personal best, while 12 per cent do it to raise money. Men make up 51 per cent of the swimmers, overall 32 per cent are aged 26–35; there are 20 per cent in my age group of 46–55, four per cent over 61 and 12 per cent under 25.

'Initially some people did think, "hmm, a dock: do I want to swim where people throw their rubbish?",' says Alex, 'but we're very vigilant about testing the water.' While the organisers were aware of a tradition of people swimming in the London Docks, 'to be honest, it was more about having a good product and wanting to put it on and find a location; we've missed the history element a bit. But we've come full circle, from leisure use to industrial use and back to leisure.'

The morning of my swim, after I've had a bath, I check the comments on the Facebook page. People say the venue was excellent and want Millwall again next year; many boast they beat their personal best; others want to know when the results will be up. A few hours later I search for the timings; the category 'Elite Men and Masses' is topped by a man who did it in nineteen minutes and one second. But there are women listed here as well, and when I ask Alex if they are 'the masses' he assures me he'll look into it.

I put in my name; I did the mile in forty-seven minutes fifty-two seconds. The quickest in my wave did it in twenty minutes thirty-eight seconds, the slowest in one hour ten minutes. My overall position is 1806. Now I'm tempted to come back next year and be a bit faster. How many minutes did I waste before actually starting to swim and what about all the times I stopped to take in the views? It's only the next day that I open my finisher's bag. Inside there is a snack bar, shampoo, a small tube of toothpaste, nuts, a t-shirt – and there it is, right at the bottom, my medal. Here is the proof that I swam in the London Docks, just as people have been doing since the 1930s when the oil was so thick that Kathleen Ralphs shot through the water during the PLA Swimming Club Ladies Championships at twice her normal speed.

22

Greenwich–Woolwich–Grays–Gravesend

'How pleasant from that dome-crowned hill
To view the varied scene below,
Woods, ships, and spires, and, lovelier still,
The encircling Thames' majestic flow!'
William Gifford (1756–1826), 'Greenwich Hill'

It's a muggy summer's morning when I come out of Woolwich Arsenal station on my way to the Royal Arsenal, once one of the world's leading centres for manufacturing munitions. There are only around forty miles left of my journey down the Thames and today I'm heading for the Greenwich Heritage Centre, on the hunt for swimming stories and in particular the history of Greenwich Beach. Few people are out today on this recently redeveloped site; a woman is walking a dog; another pushes a crying child in a buggy. I walk down a wide paved boulevard past expensive looking apartment buildings and then Firepower: The Royal Artillery Museum. In the distance, by the Royal Arsenal Pier, there seems to be a group of soldiers and it takes me a while to realise they're rather menacing cast-iron statues. At the pier itself there's the usual warning sign, 'Danger of injury, strong currents and deep water', but when I look over the wall the Thames is motionless and the water silky.

In Victorian times this was the site, just east from here, of the *Princess Alice* disaster, then described as 'one of the most fearful disasters of modern times' and today as the largest loss of life in peacetime Britain. On the evening of 3 September 1878, several hundred passengers were returning from a 'Moonlight Trip' from Swan Pier, near London Bridge, to the Rosherville Pleasure Gardens in Gravesend. The *Princess Alice* was one of the London Steamboat Company's largest saloon steamers and at around 8 p.m., in sight of North Woolwich Pier, it collided with a Newcastle-bound collier, the iron-built SS *Bywell Castle*.

The *Princess*, said to be as 'thin as eggshell', split in two and sank in less than five minutes. Many passengers were trapped in

THE TERRIBLE DISASTER ON THE THAMES

On the evening of 3 September 1878 the paddle steamer *Princess Alice* sank in less than five minutes after colliding with the coal ship *SS Bywell Castle*. Around 700 people died, many because they were unable to swim.

the wreckage and drowned; others died in the river in which an hour earlier raw sewage had been released from sewer outfalls at Crossness. Hardly any of the passengers would have been able to swim, only 'a few' were reported as having made it to shore, and the paddle steamer was barely equipped with life belts – the press reported 'a dozen or more lifebuoys onboard'. Around 700 people died, just 100 were rescued. Newspaper reports painted a horrific scene, with 'the river for a hundred yards full of drowning people screaming in anguish and praying for help'. The captain of a nearby ship launched a rowing boat and although he managed to save eleven people the vessel was so swamped by crowds 'shrieking and drowning' that 'it was necessary to quench their hopes by knocking them off the sides with the oars'.

As a result of the tragedy, new safety rules were put in place, as they would be again after the *Marchioness* disaster in 1989. All ships would pass each other on the port side, and there would be enough life belts for everyone on board. The Thames River Police's rowing boats based at Wapping were replaced with steam launches, there was a new plan for dumping sewage at sea, rather than releasing it downriver, and treatment works on shore.

A few years later, on the northern side of the Thames from here, the Royal Pavilion Pleasure Gardens (now the site of the Royal Victoria Gardens) was the starting point for a race which 'severely tested the strength of amateur swimmers,' reported *The Times*, 'as they had to go nearly across the river and back again'. But by the early twentieth century newspaper reports on Thames swimming in this area tend to focus on tragedies. In the summer of 1920 two men jumped into the river at midnight 'for a wager' and attempted to swim across, with fatal consequences. The same year a man was seen swimming fully dressed before he sank opposite the North Woolwich Pier. As ever with the story of the Thames, the river has been the scene of pleasure, sport and, because of lack of swimming ability and pollution, tragedy.

Upstream from here, to the west, is the Thames Barrier, one of the world's largest movable flood barriers, run and maintained by the Environment Agency, and where the PLA swimming 'ban' from Putney ends. The barrier opened in 1982, spanning 520 metres across the Thames, and is said to protect 125 square kilometres of central London from flooding caused by tidal surges.

This was a memorable spot for Kevin Murphy during his 1980 swim, when he ran out of tide. 'They were building the Thames Barrier at the time,' he explains, 'and I had to fight to get through the pillars, the workmen were cheering and shouting me on but I couldn't get through. I spent six and a half hours going nowhere. I might have gone backwards a bit. The water was really, really black and sludgy. What I didn't know then, what no one told me, was I was stuck at the sewage works, which was probably why I got ill.'

Lewis Pugh's Thames swim around a quarter of a century later, to raise environmental awareness, was rather different. When he reached the barrier he had no problem getting through, but was shocked at what he saw: 'the Thames Barrier is supposed to save us from climate change and a storm surge, but when I got there I realised how small it is, it's nothing.'

I leave the Royal Arsenal Pier and walk back up the boulevard to the Greenwich Heritage Centre, which houses the local history library and the Royal Borough of Greenwich's museum. There's nothing on display about swimming, but archivist Jonathan Partington has some documents in the search room where the local studies collection is kept. It's quiet inside; there are the usual filing cabinets, wooden tables and the obligatory blue carpet. I sit by an open door, hoping for a breeze; outside I can see a courtyard where a group of primary school children in full camouflage gear are being told to stand in line.

Jonathan hands me a thin manila folder labelled 'Swimming'. Inside there is just one newspaper article, dated September 1895, which explains, 'we announced that Sam Martin, of Woolwich

Baths, would attempt the great swim from Blackwall to Gravesend. He has done it – that is the attempt. But he did not quite succeed in the task.' Only two others had managed this nineteen-and-a-half-mile course, Captain Webb and Fred Bownes. Martin almost made it; he only had half a mile to go when the tide turned and his friends persuaded him to stop. 'Unless a man can swim 3¼ miles an hour with the tide for six successive hours,' noted the paper, 'he has no chance.'

Jonathan wheels in a trolley with three old books of council minutes, as well as a huge cardboard box of photographs labelled 'Greenwich beach, pier and power station'. Then he brings a box of Thames riverside pictures, and yet another until I have five boxes on the table in front of me. This is the best photograph collection I've yet to see in any Thames-side archives.

I've already read that in the 1930s an official beach was created at Greenwich, and, like the beach near Tower Bridge, it became a popular place for those who couldn't afford to get to seaside resorts. Children went beachcombing, collecting pieces of chalk and selling them, while families spread out on the sand to have tea. I've also been told by Dr Pieter van der Merwe, General Editor and Greenwich Curator at the National Maritime Museum, that in the hot summer of 1933, in the depths of the Depression, 'when to provide some holiday opportunity for people who had no means of taking one, Greenwich Council imported thousands of tons of sand and – presumably with Admiralty agreement – spread it on the Royal Naval College foreshore'.

I open the box of Greenwich beach photos and pick up an undated picture showing a tiny narrow strip of sand with a short flight of stone steps leading down from the Royal Naval College. Another photo, dated 1930, shows groups of children and women – most fully clothed in coats and hats – picnicking on the foreshore. Some of the children are paddling, their trousers and dresses hitched up. Then I bring out a copy of the same photo, only this time it's labelled 'the children of Greenwich enjoy a day on their beach in the late 1920s'. So perhaps the beach was only officially opened – or extended – a few years later, as the foreshore was clearly being used well before the 1930s.

An illustrated newspaper clipping from June 1933 describes 'the beach at Greenwich where little Londoners love to play at being at the seaside'; women sit on the stone steps; children and dogs play on the sand. The background is heavily industrial, full of building and boats, for the southern side of the Thames from Rotherhithe to Woolwich had long been a place of shipbuilding, although the naval dockyards at Deptford and Woolwich had closed in 1869. Postcards were produced of the beach; one also appears to be from the 1920s, in the foreground a young man in shorts seems to be towelling himself dry and it suddenly strikes me that so far no one is actually swimming in any of these pictures.

Another postcard of Greenwich Beach shows the same landscape – the beach, the steps, the boats – only this time it's Edwardian, judging by people's clothes. There's a similar Edwardian bathing scene at low tide in the pages of a guide to Greenwich, issued by the council in the mid-1920s, and now there are two naked boys in the foreground who appear to be getting dressed after a swim. The beach 'is at the eastern end of the Pier', a long stretch of 'shingle which at low tide and, of course at the proper season, affords facilities for bathing, paddling, etc., of which the juvenile population eagerly avail themselves'. Greenwich had 'long been noted for the hospitality it extends to strangers,' notes the guide, with hotels and private apartments, tea gardens and 'temperance restaurants galore'. In all 'there is an enjoyable and inexpensive holiday awaiting the visitor at Greenwich, and a variety of interests such as can hardly be found in any other place in the kingdom'.

Outside in the courtyard I hear a man shouting, 'foul language? Do we tolerate it?' 'NO!' shout the children in their camouflage

The beach at Greenwich where 'little Londoners love to play at being at the seaside' pictured in 1935. The beach was in use from Edwardian times, by the 1930s guards were on duty to ensure better safety, and children still used it in the 1960s.

outfits. A few moments later the sun comes out and they start doing star jumps.

I pick up the books Jonathan has put on the trolley, three volumes of the *Greenwich Minutes of Proceedings of the Council* between 1929 and 1933. There are references to an open-air swimming bath in Blackheath and a public bath and washhouses on Trafalgar Road, where mixed bathing had proved very popular, with 1,196 people on a single day in July. But there is no mention of any beach. However, there is one last reference in a newspaper clipping. In August 1938 the *Kentish Mercury* explained that the Greenwich Life Guard Corps, a group of volunteers linked to the Royal Life Saving Society, had started work on Greenwich Beach on August bank holiday to 'prevent loss of life'. As with Tower Beach, children may have always played here but by the 1930s there was more emphasis on safety. A bell tent had been erected for guards to use in an emergency and the 'latest apparatus in resuscitators' was kept at Greenwich Pier. The guards were drawn from 'all ranks of competent swimmers', most with life-saving awards, including members of the police, Sea Scouts and swimming clubs attached to Greenwich baths. First aid had already been given to 'numbers of children who have cut their feet while paddling on the foreshore', as well as to a boy who 'had his head cut with a swimming bucket'. A few years earlier a boy had been saved from drowning here and his rescuer given a shaving set in recognition of his valour. The guards were on duty from 10 a.m. to 8 p.m. and 'their presence has given a feeling of security to many parents this week for during the hot weather hundreds of children have been using the beach'.

Like other Thames bathing spots, the Greenwich beach would have been closed during the Second World War, although again children continued to use it in the 1960s. One visitor remembers playing on the beach and coming home 'with at least one item of clothing (and some skin) coated in sticky tar. I think it came from ships flushing out their fuel tanks.' Fast forward some fifty years and in 2012 the Greenwich peninsula, upstream from Woolwich and now home to the O2, was to be the site of the longest artificial city beach in Europe, catering for up to 5,000 people with tonnes of sand ferried by barge from Norfolk as part of a Peninsular Festival. But this never materialised and the company concerned went into administration. I leave the heritage centre still puzzling about the history of Greenwich Beach: when was all the sand shipped in and where did it come from? In the case of the Greenwich peninsula, our attempt to reclaim the Thames ended in failure.

I get the Docklands Light Railway to Greenwich, turning left out of the station to where the *Cutty Sark* is marooned on dry land. Greenwich, a World Heritage Site with several famous maritime landmarks, has long been a popular ending place for endurance swimmers. The National Maritime Museum, however, has no specific objects or documents relating to Thames swimming, although it was at Greenwich that Agnes Beckwith arrived in 1875 from London Bridge and Annie Luker from Kew in 1892.

There are also records of people bathing here since the early 1800s, and as with other places along the Thames it could be dangerous. On one summer's Sunday afternoon a young boy was 'suddenly taken with the cramp, when he sunk to rise no more', while another ended up in hospital after diving into the river and 'his face was severely cut and his head injured by a stone at the bottom'.

But, as usual, it was naked bathing that the local authorities viewed as a bigger concern. In 1835 a 'gang of fellows' were seen bathing on the banks of the river at Greenwich 'in defiance of the order very properly issued by the Lord Mayor'. The nuisance had 'recently become intolerable', considering the number of passing passengers 'hourly conveyed by the steam-boats', and the press hoped the police would step forward and 'do their duty'. The river would hardly have been clean. In 1859 Greenwich's Medical Officer noted several epidemic diseases, scarlatina, measles and cholera – the latter in part attributed to 'the emanations from the waters of the Thames' which had the summer before reached 'a putrid condition' with hundreds if not thousands of houses draining their sewage into the water.

In 1871 one case of indecent bathing did go to court when the police arrested sixteen-year-old Edward Vinten who, along with two other boys, had been seen 'in the river near the Ship Tavern, preventing several guests from being seated on the lawn'. The Ship was one of several celebrated waterside hotels by the Thames (and now the site of the *Cutty Sark*) known for its 'public dinners' and particularly its whitebait. These were caught in the river until pollution drove fish – and the local fishing industry – out of the area in the 1860s. Another hotel, the Trafalgar, was famous for its 'Ministerial fish dinners' when cabinet ministers travelled to Greenwich to mark the close of the parliamentary session. This was the traditional Liberal venue, while the Conservatives favoured the Ship.

As for the issue of naked bathers, at the time of Vinten's arrest there had already been 'numerous complaints made to the police', and the Chief Commissioner of Police had issued placards 'cautioning persons against bathing within sight of public highways or resident houses'. Naked bathing was also common among those visiting 'convalescent small-pox patients' on board the *Dreadnought* hospital ship. The young men – aged between fifteen and twenty – were in the habit of 'standing on barges and exposing themselves', driving the Revd F. Clarke to write to the police authorities.

During the trial Vinten's mother explained her son was 'not a disobedient lad', and was about to enter 'upon a seafaring life'. The judge said he could well understand the desire to bathe during hot weather, but there were baths at Greenwich 'where bathing could be carried out without any offence being committed'. Greenwich baths and washhouses had opened in 1851, while the Greenwich Hospital School had its own 'spacious swimming-bath', an open pool built in 1833 and later covered, where pupils were taught to swim. In the end Vinten was fined ten shillings on condition of good behaviour for three months.

I walk around the *Cutty Sark* and turn right along the Thames Path and there it is, right in front of me, a scene straight out of the archive photographs I've been looking at all morning. Here is the exact same strip of beach, the same unchanged set of stone steps. But there are no children playing on the sand or families having picnics, no guards or bell tent. The scene in the distance is still industrial, building cranes and boats, black smoke in the air, but far less grim than it would have been in the 1930s. A clipper boat passes by; it's not a paddle steamer but those on board are still travelling down the Thames for pleasure, although they don't need to avert their eyes from naked bathers.

I walk past the Old Royal Naval College where people sit on benches enjoying the sun, and stop at the steps; there is an open gate at the top, but also a large sign warning these are 'Dangerous steps! Descend at your own risk'. The stone surface towards the bottom is green and slimy, and so is the chain handrail, but they don't seem particularly dangerous. The beach is covered in grainy beige sand, on which someone has drawn a love heart, dotted with rocks, stones, shells and a piece of broken glass, while in the water bobs a deflated football. I decide to paddle as children used to do, take off my sandals and roll up my jeans, even though the water is swirling shades of brown and I can't see the bottom. It doesn't feel too cold; I'd like to get in and swim. The only thing that puts me off, aside from not having a costume, is what might be underfoot after all the stories I've read of children getting injured.

Apart from this beach and the one at the Tower, there was another beach on the Thames, some twenty miles downstream in the town of Grays. It officially opened far earlier, in July 1906, with barge loads of sand from Great Yarmouth. The plans had started in 1902 when the suitably named Councillor A.W. Boatman suggested a permanent memorial to mark Edward VII's coronation, complete with public baths. A few years later the pool was dug, providing work for the unemployed in a town where 'the distress of the poor was severe' and a councillor presented a pair of swans 'to be placed in an enclosure whilst bathing was taking place'.

The formal opening took place on the evening of 30 July, with 'tremendous crowds and unbounded enthusiasm'. Traders and households decorated roads with flags and fairy lamps; there were fireworks, music provided by the town band and a swimming display of 'ornamental and scientific swimming' by Mrs W.B. Knight, gold and silver medallist of the Royal Life Saving Society. The 'pond', as it was known, was 91 yards long by 50 yards wide and contained 616,500 gallons of water. In the two weeks before the formal opening, 3,535 had paid for admission. Yet incredibly, considering it was 1906 and women already had a swimming club at Kingston and their own Thames pool at Reading, only nineteen of these were 'ladies'.

By 1912 the pond was open daily during the summer, with private dressing boxes for hire, and, as with other Thames pools, local schools used it for swimming lessons. But the tide washed the sand away, the beach had to be renewed several times and by 1930 vandalism had become a problem. Within a couple of decades the sand had gone and there was rubbish everywhere. In 1999 the beach was redeveloped as a children's playground and the pond filled in with sand. Today it's part of the New Grays Beach Riverside Park, which includes a beach, only this time behind the sea wall. This seems to be in keeping with the way the Thames was once used at Grays; the city beach on the Greenwich peninsula might never have materialised and the Tower Beach is now only open two days a year, but here the foreshore is still for children, even if it's no longer officially for swimming.

There is an even longer tradition of organised bathing a few miles downstream, on the southern side of the Thames at Gravesend. The Gravesend Bathing Establishment had warm and cold salt-water baths on shore, as well as bathing machines in the river. An advert from around 1800 explains 'the Warm Baths may be had at a moment's notice in Summer or Winter', while the machines were used 'at all times of the tide, and may be subscribed for by the Month, Quart or Season'.

Aside from river bathing machines, Gravesend was another ending point for endurance swimmers in Victorian times; Frederick Cavill, for example, arrived here in 1876 after his twenty-mile swim from London Bridge. But the only recorded long-distance swims *upstream* from Gravesend were by two British Channel champions – Captain Matthew Webb and, in modern times, Alison Streeter.

'Swimming is not unnaturally in vogue this month,' commented the *Penny Illustrated Paper* as it reported on Webb's ten-hour swim between Gravesend and Woolwich on 12 July 1878. Webb, accompanied by two 'Gravesend boatmen', dived in at 7 a.m., reached Woolwich just after midday, turned with the tide and swam back to Gravesend. He covered around forty miles, 'probably the longest distance ever accomplished in fresh water', and 'took no alcoholic stimulants during his swim, his only refreshment being a little beef and some coffee'. The press devoted just a paragraph to this swim, and there was no mention of any crowds. Perhaps, considering he'd done the Channel three years earlier, it wasn't seen as a major feat. In comparison, at the time of his Channel crossing, the Mayor of Gravesend had presented Webb with a purse containing £75, the Assembly Rooms were full to capacity, and the Mayor hoped Webb's achievement would mean soon 'every waterman in the town' would be a swimmer, whereas at the present only 'one in 50' knew how to swim. Swimming, as elsewhere along the Thames, was beginning to be seen as a key life skill.

On 2 August 1878 when Webb set off for a 100-mile swim, this did receive more coverage. The plan was to start at North Woolwich Gardens, swim down the river, 'probably reaching Gravesend about low-water', turn with the tide and swim back to Woolwich. As the tide turned again, so would Webb, reaching Gravesend at about midnight and then North Woolwich that evening. The press noted that this was 'an expedition which, should it prove successful, will, as a feat of endurance, be far greater than his former feat of swimming across the English Channel', during which he'd been in the water for nearly twenty-two hours. But Webb's plan to swim 'continuously, without any rest whatever', for an intended thirty-six hours, wasn't to be.

He set off with a powerful breaststroke and, hugging the Essex shore, headed towards Gravesend. Two hours later he 'partook of slight refreshment' and was 'swimming in capital condition' when he reached North Woolwich. But 'the wind then had increased so much that there was quite a sea on, and Webb consequently left the water by the desire of his friends'. He landed at North Woolwich Pier after nine hours, a fraction of his intended time.

It would be more than a hundred years before anyone attempted anything similar. This time it was Alison Streeter. In 1985 she had swum from Richmond to Gravesend; the following year she decided to do it the other way round. She went back to the PLA, intending to swim from Gravesend to Richmond but 'they didn't want to give permission, they said no one has ever gone *up* the Thames,' laughs her mother, Freda: 'don't issue Alison a challenge!'

This swim, which raised money for breast cancer research, 'was fraught with difficulties. She would stop so I could feed her and the river was so fast that she went back half a mile, by the time she caught up it was time to feed her again. Around the Woolwich Ferry the tide was due to change and it didn't. We phoned the PLA and said, "when is it going to change?" They said, "it has". I said, "don't tell us that, we're in the middle of it and it hasn't!" An hour later we phoned them again and they said "it's changed" and we said "it hasn't".' Eventually it did. During the downstream swim there had been strong tides and Alison had to move to the sides, while on the upstream swim 'everything was coming towards her, the water was foul. I don't even want to talk about what was in it. She was ill for six weeks afterwards. Before the end she was beginning to go a funny bluish colour. But there was a friend and her family on a bridge and they yelled and she saw them and that seemed to do it, because she rolled on her back and then she flew into Richmond.'

In 1991 Alison Streeter was awarded an MBE for swimming and charity fundraising and, like Mercedes Gleitze, she is one of very few women inducted into both the International Swimming Hall of Fame and the International Marathon Swimming Hall of Fame. The former currently has thirty-six British honourees, of which nine are women, and the latter has fifty-one individual British swimmers, of which thirteen are women. 'After she stopped swimming Alison was a Channel pilot,' explains Freda, 'but it was too close for her so she sold her boat, changed her name and moved to a farmhouse in Wales.' But Freda continues to train Channel swimmers at Dover harbour and in 2005 she herself was inducted in the IMSHOF as an Honour Observer in recognition of the hundreds of Channel swimmers who owe their success to her training, support and advice. 'Open-water swimming is so big now,' she says. 'Thirty-three years ago I started training Channel swimmers, there were six people. Last weekend I had a hundred and twenty.'

23

Southend

'The estuaries of rivers appeal strongly to an adventurous imagination'

Joseph Conrad, *The Mirror of the Sea*, 1907

It's 9 a.m. in mid-July, the first week of the school holidays, and I seem to be the only person on the train from Barking to Southend Central. The longest heatwave for seven years has just come to an end with dramatic thunderstorms, but the air is still hot and humid. As the train stops at Benfleet and then Leigh-on-Sea I catch glimpses of foreshore and boats moored on land like metal crabs, while at Chalkwell the tide is so far out there are miles of mud. I get off at Southend where the paved pedestrian street is deserted and a lone seagull screams in the air. Southend is a seaside town not yet open for the day. Only it's not really a seaside town, it's an estuary town, where the River Thames meets the waters of the North Sea in one of the largest coastal inlets in Britain. A major shipping route for oil tankers, ships and ferries, it's tricky pin-pointing where exactly the estuary ends or begins. The western boundary is said to be Sea Reach, near Canvey Island, while the eastern boundary is a 'line' drawn from North Foreland in Kent to Harwich in Essex. It's that imaginary line (or variations thereof) that has posed a serious swimming challenge both in the 1920s and today.

For novelist Joseph Conrad the Thames Estuary was a perfect place for adventurers, a route both to and from the empire. He lived upstream in Stanford-le-Hope in the 1890s and *Heart of Darkness* opens on board the *Nellie*, a cruising yawl: 'The sea-reach of the Thames stretched before us like the beginning of an interminable waterway . . . leading to the uttermost ends of the earth.' Conrad's later novel *The Mirror of the Sea*, published in 1907, has much the same theme, with the estuary promising 'every possible fruition to adventurous hopes . . . Amongst the great commercial streams of these islands, the Thames is the only one, I think, open to romantic feeling.' Unsurprisingly, considering its location, there is a long tradition of swimming in Southend, for both competition and pleasure, and it was the training ground for two noted Channel champions.

Its reputation as a resort began in Georgian times, and its beaches and good rail links with London led to an influx of summer visitors. In Victorian times Southend was mocked by comic writers for its 'cockneyism and vulgarity', but it was a clean, quiet town according to *Dickens's Dictionary of the Thames*, the air fresh and invigorating, 'a well-built, well-arranged, and old fashioned watering–place'. ''Arry occasionally descends upon the place in his thousands', and was to be found on the pier where 'arrayed in rainbow tweeds, he delights in fishing for dabs'. The bathing machines on the beach were well used 'although the strict rules of decency are not observed as well as could be wished'.

The bathing machines are long gone, of course, but the famous pier and its railway line still stands. I get the first train of the day, ducking my head to get into a carriage with shiny brown bucket seats. It rattles off like a ghost train ride, and there must be plenty of ghosts around this pier, first built out of wood in 1830 and then replaced with iron in the 1870s. It has survived fires, collisions from barges and boats and two world wars. Yet here it still is, the longest pleasure pier in the world at 1.33 miles, and it's had a tram (and then railway) running along it since 1890.

From the window I see patches of water, clean and clear, then mudflats, and then finally the estuary proper. It looks broody today; a low purple cloud hangs over the landscape like a bruise. I get off the train and walk to the edge of the pier and put 50p in a talking telescope. A recorded voice tells me I'm opposite the Kent coast and the River Medway. There doesn't seem much to swim towards except for what look like factory chimneys. At the far end of the pier is the RNLI station, and before that a restaurant with a large decked terrace. No one seems to be around and there isn't much traffic on the water either; a sailing boat passes by and I can see a dredger in the distance near Canvey Island. To my left is the North Sea, a shimmering horizon lit up in a sudden burst of sunshine interrupted only by a single silhouette of what looks like a huge building. To my right the river heads towards London, to distant chimneys and the crest of a low hill. There are, as Conrad wrote over a hundred years ago, 'no features to the land . . . no conspicuous, far-famed landmarks for the eye'.

As I walk back along the pier the air is silent but for the water gently sloshing underneath, the flap of tape warning about wet paint, and the rattling clatter of the returning train. The mudflats near the shore look like a sheet of ice. Unlike other piers, such as in Brighton, there isn't actually anything to do on the long walk back except enjoy the views. There are places to sit, and two drinks machines with a big sign saying 'Thirsty?' and then a smaller sign saying 'Out of order'. There is little evidence of modern life, but for regular no smoking signs, until I come to the end and there is the carnival of Adventure Island, an amusement park opened in the 1970s. I turn back and look along the pier; the 'building' I thought I saw near the North Sea is now clearly a massive boat.

A council booklet on the history of the pier makes no mention of swimming, yet it has been associated with races since Victorian times when the town hosted summer regattas with rowing and other events. In 1873 the press reported that 'the annual aquatic festival was conducted . . . with even more than the usual spirit, and passed off with the accustomed eclat . . . the swimming, considering the state of the water, was most excellent' and 'there was the usual laughter splitting walking the greasy bowspit for a pig in a box'.

In May 1894 the Southend Swimming Club was formed and it ran an annual long-distance swim from the pier head. In the summer of 1909, the course, presumably along the length of the pier, was completed in fifty-five minutes.

The most famous club member was Norman Leslie Derham and in 1926 he was chosen as their candidate for an attempt to swim the Channel. Lord Riddell, owner of the *News of the World*, then the largest circulation paper in the world, was offering £1,000 to any English person who could beat the time set by an American swimmer. In other words, Gertrude Ederle, who that year had swum from France to England in fourteen hours thirteen minutes. In 1923 another American, Henry Sullivan, had swum from England to France in twenty-six hours fifty minutes.

Southend Swimming Club's most famous member was Norman Derham. The future Channel champion trained in the Thames.

Derham's archives are housed in the Southend Museum where Ken Crowe, Curator of Human History, has left them out for me. I'm expecting a few press reports; instead I find a large cardboard box on a table in a top-floor office. The first item is a neatly folded letter, several typed pages written by Derham's daughter, Penny, who describes her father as 'perhaps the last of the great adventurers'. I can't believe my luck, I'm actually going to read about him in the words of a family member. Born on the Isle of Wight in 1897, his family originated from Germany, and were 'lower landed gentry' with a long naval tradition. In his early teens he was a midshipman cadet and before he was twenty he had 'travelled three times around the world'. Conrad unsurprisingly was one of his favourite writers. During the First World War Derham joined the Royal Flying Corps, while in the Depression he worked as a pig farmer, an iron and brass bed manufacturer and a distributor of Fyffe's bananas.

He later travelled to Canada and spent a season exhibition swimming with Johnny Weissmuller, the swimmer and actor who became known for playing Tarzan, before he went to Germany to become a glider pilot.

I'm entranced by Derham's story, until I turn the page and Penny suddenly declares that her father was an admirer of Adolf Hitler, because of what he 'was doing for the material welfare and advancement of his then bankrupt country', although he also warned that the German leader was a 'mad dog bent on conquering Europe if not the world'. Then Penny feels the need to confess something; sounding hesitant and asking for her father's spirit to forgive her, she writes that he had 'a tendency to Anti Semitisms'. I stop reading, feeling shocked; what does she mean by a 'tendency'? But then she adds that this 'did not prevent him from volunteering to swim around the "St Louis" [in 1939] when it was off Plymouth to assist in picking up the Jewish Refugees who had planned to join hands and jump into the water rather than return to Nazi Germany when no port due to International Red Tape would allow them to land'. The way around this was if they were picked up out of the water. Her father's view was that when you saw someone drowning 'you don't stop to ask his religion and look at the colour of his skin' but get in the water and try to rescue them.

I refold Penny's letter, still wondering about Derham's character and prejudices, and put it back in the box, to find the next document is his very own thirty-one-page 'my life story'. He could swim by the age of six and at seven had made up his mind 'that I should swim the Channel and do the same as Captain Webb had done ... I could stay in the water and swim for hours if they would only let me.' As a twelve-year-old he swam a 'few miles' to East Cowes from Newport, and in 1911, when Thomas Burgess swam from England to France, this 'again fired my imagination to conquer the Channel'. Taking advantage of his parents being away he swam for six hours from Osborne Bay to Calshot Point.

In 1921 Derham moved to Southend, still aiming to do the Channel, and a few years later he set 'myself the task of swimming the Thames Estuary'. On 4 June 1925, he made his first attempt, giving up after four hours because of cramp, but earning the name Sinbad the Sailor as 'several miles from the shore a large porpoise rose to the surface beneath me, lifting me completely out of the water'. A porpoise? I stop reading again, picturing Derham midway across the estuary riding for a moment on the back of a harbour porpoise.

Then, on 10 June, he managed the crossing of thirteen miles in five hours and modestly explains, 'I may mention that this was the first and only time that the Thames Estuary had been conquered.' He doesn't describe his route; one press report says his five-hour swim was from Southend to Sheerness, another that on his third attempt he 'successfully swam across the estuary from Sheerness to Westcliff ... starting on the Kent side he had 500 yards' expanse of mud to walk' and ended at the Southend swimming bath. So perhaps Derham tried it in both directions.

Either way, his stated aim now was to beat Montague Holbein's fifty-mile Thames swim of 1908. Derham was clearly aware of the swimmers who had come before him; first he wanted to emulate Webb, then he was inspired by Burgess, and so, unlike many women Thames swimmers, he saw himself as part of a glorious tradition. He knew what other men had done and he wanted to beat them; his motivation was to set a new record, to achieve fame like them, and, considering that he later took up the challenge from the *News of the World*, to make money as well.

On 2 August, in pouring rain, Derham started from Putney Bridge and swam to Woolwich, but was forced to give up after twenty miles, again because of cramp. 'They fed me with tomatoes and anything they had,' he explains, 'and it is a wonder that I did not sink long before I reached Woolwich.' He then swam twenty-one miles from Blackwall Pier to Gravesend but 'the condition of the water [was] terrible'. The press explained that with just three miles to go he was 'made to swallow more of the odoriferous and heavily chemical laden water of the lower Thames than was good for him' when tugs and steamers went past just after the Woolwich Ferry. At Barking Creek an outward-bound Belgian steamer 'saw fit to open her bilges just as she was level with the swimmer . . . it made [him] terribly sick and although bodily he was strong, he looked as though he had been poisoned'. Derham was ill for three weeks and decided he'd had enough long-distance swims for that year.

In July 1926 he began his first Channel attempt, but a heavy storm meant he stopped five miles from the end. His next attempt came on 2 September. 'A London paper had offered a prize,' he explains, 'and I was advised by my wife to start from France . . . she said "why not go the easiest way and win the money?"' He started from Cap Blanc Nez but only two miles from the end fog 'robbed me of a certain victory'. On 16 September he tried again, covered in 10 pounds of grease, and this time he made it despite being so dazed and exhausted that just 15 yards from land he rolled on his back and lost direction. Then finally his feet touched bottom: 'I shot up my arms and proclaimed to the World that I had conquered.'

Pathé News was there to see Derham arrive, filming him yards away from shore, where he was making no progress at all until a group of women swimmers enter the water, clapping and urging him on. Out he trudges, his limbs almost flopping as he emerges on to land. A few shots later he is fully dressed and combing his hair, beaming uncontrollably. And no wonder: he was the first Briton to swim from France to England, from Cap Gris Nez to St Margaret's Bay, in '13 hours, 55 minutes', and the third British man to cross the Channel after his heroes Webb and Burgess. And, of course, he had beaten the American Gertrude Ederle, knocking around forty minutes off her time. Naturally the British press was ecstatic and he was photographed leaving the *News of the World* offices both 'chaired' and cheered.

I leaf through the rest of the items in the box; someone has certainly put together a treasure trove of memorabilia, perhaps it was Derham himself. Postcards show him with slicked-back hair and a black swimming suit with the Southend Swimming Club badge; others depict his final moments as he reached shore. There is also an envelope of congratulatory telegrams sent to 5 Holly Gardens, Southchurch Road, Southend, just a few minutes' walk from the museum. One is from the founder of the Webb memorial, Alfred Jonas, who congratulated him 'on your regaining the glory for England'; another is from the president of the Otter Swimming Club. There is also a telegram sent from Derham himself, 'DONE IT WHAT DO YOU THINK OF THE OLD MAN NOW HOME TONIGHT LESLIE +'. Presumably these brief but triumphant words were sent to his family. The 'old man' had finally proved himself.

Derham received an enthusiastic welcome in Southend: flags were hung out, there was a civic welcome by the Mayor, dinners in his honour and a parade around the local football pitch. But, like

Webb before him, now he had to come up with something new. His daughter, Penny, recalls him setting off from Tower Bridge to try and break a world record for canoe paddling, having designed and built 'a sort of canoe with broom handles for paddles'. He began on the tide 'one very murky peasouper evening' and was nearly run down three times in the estuary before giving up. The press headlined the attempt: 'Reckless Adventurer or Bizarre Suicide Attempt?' The date isn't clear, but in April 1928 he set off from the sunken garden at Southend in a collapsible boat with a passport in his pocket intent on reaching France. But a mile from the pier head a large wave overturned him and two hours later he was rescued. The following month the *Southend Pictorial Telegraph* shows him in a small Gaskin Ships' lifeboat leaving Westminster Bridge to 'conquer the channel again'. Presumably this ended in disaster, too.

In 1929, after having 'a complete rest from long distance events', Derham again decided to return to the Channel. He was also training a 'Mrs. Coleman' of Kentish Town in London, who was preparing for her Channel swim 'under his supervision' at Southend. Coleman had already shown 'that she possesses the requisite stamina in a number of long-distance trials from Tilbury down the Thames'. Another paper reported 'BIG SWIMS BY MOTHER AND DAUGHTER' with 'Mrs. Coleman, the well-known swimmer and her wonderful eight-year-old daughter, Edna, who recently swam five miles in the Thames in remarkable time, are now in Southend training for two big swims'. Edna Coleman would tackle Southend to Sheerness; her mother would attempt Tilbury to Southend. By now another swimmer called 'Mrs Inge' had created 'a record for a Thames Estuary Swim' in 1928 between Gravesend and Southend. She swam ten miles in two hours forty-three minutes, in the face of a strong easterly wind.

By 1938, however, Derham was working as a swimming pool superintendent. 'I thought I was made,' he told the press, 'but the world forgets quickly. For a year or two I have lived like a lord, but in the long run I lost money over it. And then I had to find a new career.' Now he had another idea: he would be the first to glide across the Channel 'from a straight take-off . . . And then I think that will be enough records for me.' It doesn't look like this was successful and, when Derham died at the age of forty-seven, the local paper described him as 'Southend's greatest ever swimmer'. His club, Southend-On-Sea Swimming Club, still exists today; members train in indoor pools not in the Thames, and it has fielded a number of Olympic swimmers, including Mark Foster and Sarah Hardcastle.

Norman Derham attempts to boat down the Thames and 'conquer the channel again' in 1928.

I leave the archives and head back to the pier, thinking of another champion Channel swimmer, East End insurance clerk Edward Temme, known as Tammy, who also chose the Thames Estuary as his training pool. He became the first person to cross the Channel in both directions; in 1927 he swam from France to England and in 1934 from England to France. Tammy, who trained at Leigh Creek, was 6 feet 2 inches and weighed 200 pounds and was said to 'romp across the surface of the sea like a porpoise'. He was also a member of the British water polo team at two Olympic Games.

Other would-be Channel swimmers similarly came to Southend to train, such as Eva Coleman – it's not clear if she was related to the 'Mrs. Coleman' whom Derham trained. In 1933 the press reported 'Girl to Attempt Channel Swim Training Diet of Steak and Peaches', describing Coleman as having 'big brown eyes, black hair, an infectious laugh, and a swinging, supple-limbed stride'. Coleman worked as a cashier at a hotel in the Strand in London. Her mascot song was 'This is My Lucky Day – l'm Going to Win Through', and she was determined to have it playing on a gramophone on the accompanying boat, saying she could swim much better to music. Her motto was 'No slimming for swimming'; just like Agnes Beckwith and Annette Kellerman before her the effect of swimming on women's weight seemed to be of some interest, although perhaps she was just answering a question from the press. She was said to 'hold a few records', including a twenty-one-mile swim in the Thames, and a 'seven hour test' at Southend.

Some swimmers, meanwhile, attempted to swim upstream from Southend. Pathé News filmed a race to Gravesend, 'up the mouth of the River Thames' sometime between 1920 and 1929. Competitors, both women and men, can be seen swimming against the current, although the water looks eerily calm. In modern times there is only one person who has officially swum across the estuary and that is Peter Rae who, in 2003, swam from Southend to All Hallows in Kent and then back to Leigh. The idea started as a bet, just as many other Thames swims have done, whether Victorian races or the modern Chiswick swim. Peter was having a pint with friends one day on the *Bembridge*, the headquarters ship of the Essex Yacht Club, when someone proposed a challenge. Could he swim across the Thames Estuary and then return to the Essex shoreline within one tide? This meant he had about five hours before the water retreated and there would be a mile and a half of mudflats again.

Peter thought he could. An experienced open-water swimmer 'with a fair few miles under my belt', eighteen years earlier he'd crossed the Channel. While this swim would be much shorter, he could similarly expect cold water, jellyfish, strong currents and tide. The main hazard, however, would be crossing busy Sea Reach shipping lanes. While Peter swims competitively, and started Masters swimming in 1994, he says he prefers just doing it for enjoyment. 'Open water I like the best, I just enjoy the freedom, it's almost a form of meditation.' However, he hadn't swum much before in the estuary.

It took him five months to plan the trip, liaising with the PLA and raising around £3,000 in charitable pledges. 'I assumed I would have to go to the PLA, and because of my sailing experience I knew the shipping channel. I produced a plan and explained how I would be accompanied, and what my abilities were. I had no problem at all with the PLA. I'd done a lot of homework.'

His correspondence bears this out. In July that year he wrote to the Harbour Master to seek 'advice and support' for a sponsored swim to raise funds to convert HMS *Wilton*, due to replace *Bembridge* as the headquarters of the Essex Yacht Club. Sponsorship would be based on the number of completed miles, with a further bonus for completing the swim within one tide. He was originally to start from Jocelyn's Beach in Leigh 'as soon as there is sufficient water', and the swim would be abandoned 'if wind strength exceeds Force 3 or visibility is below 4 miles'. Unlike Derham and Tammy before

Peter Rae's swim across the estuary in 2003 started as a bet; could he swim from Essex to Kent and back within one tide? Here he's about to strike out from the beach in All Hallows for the return leg to Leigh on Sea.

him, Peter would have a whole series of safety measures in place. He would be accompanied by a yacht, *Uncle Ronnie*, carrying a ladder, life belts, life jackets, flares, fixed and portable radios, and equipment for hauling a body both horizontally and vertically from the water. The skipper would be Stuart Silcock, a qualified Offshore Yachtmaster, and Peter would be supported on board by at least three crew, one of whom would be 'dedicated to monitoring and supporting the swimmer'. Both the local Coast Guard (Shoebury) and RNLI (Southend Pier) would be fully informed before and during the swim and 'while the traffic in the Sea Reach should be minimal on the planned date the Yacht/Swimmer will ensure that they do not present any hazard to shipping in the channel. If necessary the swimmer will exit the water well before a potentially hazardous situation arises.'

Peter would wear a full-body neoprene Tri-suit and yellow swim cap for warmth and visibility, and be provided with isotonic drinks at regular intervals. Finally, he explained he was forty-nine years old, of excellent health and fitness, and had recently competed in the 2003 European Masters Swimming Championships where he took a bronze in the 400 metres freestyle and silver in the 5,200 metres open-water swim. Peter was then ranked first for his age group in Great Britain and, aside from his Channel swim in 1985 in just over eleven hours, he'd also made an eight-hour double crossing of Lake Geneva.

He got the go-ahead and at 12.20 p.m. on 14 September he started next to the Westcliff-on-Sea casino, the air temperature was 18 degrees, the sea a 'positively balmy' 16 degrees. He set off to cross the estuary 'in two feet of water, but it was just enough to swim in'. After one hour and fifty minutes he was standing on the beach at All Hallows, having avoided a large tanker in the main shipping channel. 'A dredger was coming down,' he remembers, 'ships had been warned there was a swim in progress, it was not a close shave but the dredger had to be contacted by phone. The PLA had given notice about my swim to shipping but maybe the dredger didn't heed it. It wasn't dangerous but there are a huge amount of ships and with the new container port there will be even more.'

Curious well-wishers came out to welcome him at All Hallows, where he had a chicken sandwich and a cup of tea, replaced his cap and goggles and struck out for the Essex coast. 'No one was expecting me, people at the yacht club came out to say "hi", but I was only there for five minutes.' Things then turned tough and he had to fight increasing wind, waves and another hour of incoming tide, as he was pushed towards the Shell Haven oil refinery behind Canvey Island. But he recovered his energy and, using the strengthening outgoing tide, the *Bembridge* was now in sight. After four hours and twenty-five minutes, covering eleven miles and with 3 feet of tide still available, he landed on the east slipway of the Essex Yacht Club to a 'rapturous champagne welcome' from members supporting and sponsoring the swim.

His advice to others is that the Thames Estuary is 'for someone who enjoys a challenge. It's not a particularly tough swim, it was not too cold, and it's not big seas, though it can get choppy, and I was going with the tide.' But he says Derham's crossing in the 1920s 'would be a no-no now, you couldn't take the course he took because of shipping'. Just as with Matthew Parris, who swam across the Thames in central London, Peter says, 'Yes I would do the estuary again; living here and looking at it every day . . . I just need to pick a nice day.'

Another famed swimmer to arrive in Southend was Lewis Pugh, at the end of his swim along the length of the Thames in 2006. A crowd of 'more than 250 people turned up to watch him finish,' explained the press, and 'as the polar explorer and endurance swimmer emerged from the water onto the slipway cheers and shouts of "well done" rang out'. Lewis' main memory of his final leg of the Thames from the barrier to Southend, however, was 'plenty of jellyfish'.

Charlie Wittmack, the American adventurer who swam the Thames in 2010 as part of his world triathlon, had a rather different experience near Southend where he discovered first hand just how dramatic tides in the Thames can be. First, like Lewis, he swam through lots of jellyfish: 'it felt like I swam through them for an entire day, and got quite a few stings', but then 'across from Southend' he got stuck in the mud. 'It was unexpected; we calculated the tides wrong so the swim took a lot longer than we thought. The sun was setting, we were nowhere near where we needed to be, so we pulled up to the shore to make a phone call and take a look at the GPS. As we were standing there, over the course of just a few minutes, the tide really truly went out, and we realised we were essentially stuck in the mud. It was getting dark, we couldn't see where we were, and the scariest thing was we really couldn't work out where the water was going to end up being, it was just cutting back so dramatically from where we thought the shore was. So we got in touch with the rescue boat service and within an hour or so they had picked us up. They even gave us a place to stay, they were very encouraging, it was kind of a lot of fun.'

Meanwhile, although Peter Rae gained official permission for his estuary swim, at least one person has done it without. 'I have always wanted to swim the Thames,' says Wouter Van Staden. 'I always had the idea that if you can see something then you can swim to it. I live in Basildon and, being in Essex, when you get to the coast you can see Kent, so I wanted to swim there.' Wouter comes from Pretoria, South Africa, and knew 'a bit about the Thames' growing up, but it 'wasn't big on my radar' until he came to England. In 2007 he settled in Reading, and 'for around six months I tried to find information if I could swim in the Thames, but I only heard stories about sickness. Then I read about a pensioner swimming near Maidenhead and I was convinced the Thames was swimmable.'

On 23 May 2010 he swam from Canvey Island to All Hallows-on-Sea, covering just over two miles. 'I read about rights and permissions and figured I needed to speak to the PLA but in the end I thought there was a chance they would say no, so I thought I would just risk it. I moved my kayak to Canvey Island the day before. I just knocked on someone's door and said, "can I please leave my kayak in your garden?"' The next morning he went back to get it with his wife, Anecke; 'she was to be in the kayak and she was not entirely willing but everyone else I had asked couldn't do it. We did it in the early morning to avoid the pleasure craft, so there would just be big ferries and tankers. There is a short dredged section of around 400 metres wide with big craft and so it was sort of safe and sort of not, because if they come across you they have nowhere else to go. After the central channel a ferry did pass and I believe it notified the coastguard that there was a swimmer in the estuary, although I had already passed the channel by then. They sent out a boat and I saw it roughly as I got to Kent; it was too shallow for the boat to come any closer but I noticed them and as I headed back I went straight for them. They asked what was going on and "are you fine?" They said they were obliged to stay with us until we reached land. They offered to quicken the process and so we put the kayak on their boat and they gave us a lift back. I wasn't going to swim both ways anyway. I had missed my train and started late so it took longer than I thought.'

It took him around two hours. 'The tide had moved too much to swim back to Canvey so I was kayaking anyway. They interviewed us and asked what safety precautions we had and took our names and numbers and address, which my wife was not happy about, but I didn't break any rules or regulations.' But he says since then he has always been in contact with the PLA, and he still does long swims, but along the shore and sometimes to the Mulberry Harbour. Here there is a 'Phoenix' caisson, lying on a sandbank off Thorpe Bay, part of a temporary harbour intended to be used in the Normandy landings following D-Day. But it sprang a leak and was brought into the Thames Estuary and allowed to sink. 'It's visible from the shore and so I wanted to swim to it,' says Wouter, who has now done the route twice, along with others. 'We notify the coastguard, saying when we are going and where and how many of us there are and we tell them once we've arrived back. I'd definitely like to swim the estuary again and I probably would, but I don't have a lot of time.' He works for a car rental company and with the new Southend airport is very busy. But he has more plans to swim the Thames, this time through London. His aim is to travel the length in sections, and he's already done a three-day swim from Cricklade to Radcot Lock. 'I'd like to swim to Southend. If you time it with the tide you can do large distances in one go.' He would swim through central London doing 'a twenty-kilometre stint at night and I could do it in three or four nights', and this time he says he will approach the PLA first.

While the Southend area is clearly home to some experienced

and ambitious swimmers, others can be reckless, as Richard Sanders, pier and foreshore supervisor, knows only too well. He meets me where the pier train begins and I follow him down to offices below. We walk along a corridor and stop at a conference room where Richard opens the door a little cautiously, saying he's looking for the two 'ship's cats' as they have a habit of opening doors. That's when I realise it feels as if we're on a boat; even his white uniform gives him the air of a sea captain. A long, thin table runs the length of the narrow room, like a ship's mess, while in the corner is a big display board 'Visit Southend – town, shore and so much more'.

Richard is from Southend but doesn't swim in the Thames; his swimming memories are of his dad taking him to the indoor baths on Sundays. 'There were bad news stories when I grew up,' he says, 'about sewage and tall tales about people contracting things.' But he stresses that maritime law has changed a lot, and now passing passenger ships and tugs can pull up at the end of the pier and their sewage is pumped to the shore, not dumped into the sea. The method is described as 'ship to shore' but is otherwise known as 'shit to shore'.

As evidence of its cleanliness the estuary is well populated with flat fish like sole, there is a nearby colony of seals, and in 2008 the Zoological Society of London found a breeding population of endangered seahorses. 'Our waters have improved massively,' says Richard, 'the Thames is not the dirty urban waterway it used to be.' He compares the estuary to places like the Maldives, 'which is seen as paradise, but while one side is, on the other they dump their sewage'. As for the tradition of swimming, he points out of a row of small, partly frosted windows in the direction of the Westcliff-on-Sea casino: 'there used to be swimming baths there, there was an inlet that was tidal-fed, and people have told me about swimming in the 1950s.' There was also a sea-fed dolphin pool and boating lake east of the pier with two dolphins.

Southend has a long history of Thames bathing; in the 1920s people enjoyed open-air swimming baths complete with slides.

When it comes to swimming today, 'there are incidents,' he says carefully with what turns out to be great understatement; 'people swim to the shore against the tide and they swear they are Olympic-standard swimmers and end up going backwards. The tide is six knots and most people can't do that.' The Hadleigh Ray, a body of water near the pier in the direction of the casino, can be particularly dangerous. 'People walk to it, it has quite a gentle edge, but part of it falls into the estuary. At the shore there is soft mud, at the Ray it's hard-packed sand, and one of its edges is a sheer eight-foot drop.' In other words, someone could think they're having a paddle, and drop straight in. It's mainly 'day trippers and people who don't know about tidal estuaries,' says Richard, who once rescued two 'big lads in their twenties' who fell in and the current took them out. You should, he says, always try and swim across the current, but 'they tried to beat the tide' – and nearly died.

There are other hazards, too: 'a lot of time you're standing on oyster shells', then there's boat wreckage, trawler wire which is used to hold the nets and 'some just push it over the side, so we find coils of wire in the mud, as well as wartime debris, anti-aircraft shells, plane wrecks and once a pre-1900s cannonball. It's not unknown for an angler to walk into the casino and say, "look! I found a mine".' Richard recently saw one 'sitting on the mud the size of a smart car' although a leak meant it was harmless. Those that still pose a threat are sometimes blown up on Ministry of Defence land at Shoebury.

Some people also attempt to jump off the pier and can be dragged under it by the current, where there are mussels, barnacles and shellfish, in which case 'you wouldn't have much skin left,' says Richard calmly, 'and you will bleed because barnacles release an enzyme that stops blood from clotting'. Then there are sunbathers who 'cook themselves' all day in the sun, as well as having a few drinks, jump into cold water and suffer cardiac arrest. Traffic's another danger; near the shore there is a speed limit for jet skis, but once they reach a quarter-mile out from the sea wall then it's boat territory and 'they go extremely fast'. There are also container ships, such as the one I saw earlier emerging from the North Sea, and boats doing thirty to forty knots 'and no swimmer can outpace that'.

Richard is certainly putting me off having a swim around here, and recent reports from the Southend Lifeboat Station confirm the risks, with children found stranded on a sand dune with the flood tide coming in fast, and two people stuck in the mud underneath the pier head. Then there are the swimmers; a capsized catamaran had two people on board, 'one of which had swum from Canvey Island to assist his buddy who he had just witnessed capsizing!' There was 'a possible person seen drifting west' which turned out to be a white plastic container, a person suspected to be swimming from Canvey Island to Kent, although no one was found, and a swimmer thought to be in trouble offshore of Canvey Island who in fact was 'a very good swimmer who takes to the water every day'.

The best time for a sensible swim, says Richard, is slack water and he goes into some detail about low and high tide, measurements and depth, and the role of the moon. I ask him if he feels the water outside these windows is a river or the sea. 'I know it as a river, I can see the opposite banks, but a lot of people think it's the sea,' he laughs. 'People think it's Calais opposite. Actually it's Snodland on the Isle of Grain, you can see the chimney.' Then I ask him where the Thames ends. He points behind me, in the direction of the North Sea. 'The Thames ends where it ends, when it becomes the sea, it ends.' And when does it become the sea? He gets up a little wearily and traces a finger along a map on the wall. 'I've been all round the coast and I feel you're really at the end of the Thames there, once you're around Wallasea. It feels like Clacton and Margate are still on the Thames, although they are not. Clacton to me is the absolute limit of the Thames.'

Richard is, of course, happy to negotiate with sensible swimmers, such as the organisers of the Great Pier Swim which began in 2008. But when he heard they wanted to swim from the pier head, his horrified reaction was, 'ah no! You can't swim the shipping channel, it's one of the busiest in the world.' Then when a local swimmer, Iain Keenan, got in touch, interested in setting up a swimming club in nearby Chalkwell, with a designated area and starting point for events, Richard thought, 'right, OK, we've got a swim club, that's better than a walking on the mud club'.

Having filled me with horror stories, Richard takes me to another room, as big as a warehouse, where the equipment is stored, including an amphibious boat which is used to rescue people from both mud and water. Finally, he bids me goodbye at the entrance to the pier, where I'm getting increasingly worried about the swim I'm doing this afternoon with the Chalkwell Redcaps Open Water Swimming Club. I fancied a pleasant dip; now all the way back to the railway station I have visions of stinging barnacles, lacerating oyster shells, zooming jet skis, lethal currents and buried wrecks.

24

Crowstone Swim

'If you love something you don't want to keep it to yourself'
Iain Keenan, founder of the Chalkwell Redcaps

When I get off at Chalkwell Station the transformation since I first glimpsed the foreshore from the train window this morning is breathtaking. Gone is the mud, now there is an ocean of water. The beach, however, looks dull and overcast; family groups are having a day out, but no one is actually swimming, just a handful of children splash and paddle, some clutching big inflatable toys. Perhaps they're put off by reports of strong tides and dramatic rescues, as well as the recent advice from the ambulance service that deep water is cold enough, even on a hot summer's day, 'to take your breath away, possibly leading to panic and drowning'. On the other hand, unlike other spots on both the upper Thames and in central London I can't see any warning signs about swimming, and there's no information about lifeguards either.

I walk along the shore; the sand is as dark as Demerara sugar and I'm so intent on following directions to the Chalkwell Redcaps hut that when I spot, ahead of me, an obelisk in the water I almost don't pay it any attention. But this is the Crowstone that marks the end of the PLA's jurisdiction over the River Thames. The marker on the Kent side is the London Stone on the Isle of Grain, while the western marker is the London Stone just above Staines. There still remain questions as to where the Thames ends, though not nearly

THE CEREMONY AT THE BOUNDARY-STONE, AT LEIGH.

A ceremony held at the Crowstone in July 1849 when a pledge was given to preserve the City of London.

as many as where the river begins, but it's the Crowstone that I'm swimming to this afternoon.

In Victorian times the stone was the limit of the powers of the Thames Conservancy Board. In 1858, the year after it took control of the river, Board members paid a visit to the estuary and found the Crowstone 'having been comparatively recently placed there, is a prominent object, and is discernible at great distance'. Over a hundred years later, in the mid-1960s, *Essex Countryside Magazine* described it as, 'standing tall and solitary on the foreshore at Westcliff-on-Sea'. It was, according to J. Blundell, an 'obelisk with a difference' and 'uncommonly situated, its very presence demands explanation'. Erected in 1836 (although some reports say 1837), it joined a much earlier stone of 1755 (which itself replaced an earlier limit mark). Both stones stood together until 1950 when the PLA presented the older one to Southend Corporation for preservation in Priory Park, where it still stands today. The derivation of the Crowstone's name isn't clear. It may come from Crowes, a nearby settlement existing in 1536, or it could be because the stone was a favourite lookout post for beachcombing crows, which may explain how Crowes got its name in the first place. Starting in 1842, Blundell writes, there were ceremonial visits paid to the Crowstone and Sir John Pirie, then Lord Mayor, 'first held the City sword and colours' against the stone, which was then circled three times by boat or on foot. Wine was served, a pledge given to 'God preserve the City of London', and these festive occasions took place every seven years but ended when the Thames Conservancy Board took control of the river. An 1849 edition of the *Illustrated London News* includes an image showing 'the ceremony at the boundary-stone' where a man stands, a massive flag held high, next to the Crowstone. He's surrounded by people celebrating, some wading in the water, others pushing a boat, while he perches on top of the smaller, older stone that now stands in Priory Park. Other events were held here, too. In the summer of 1900 a local Baptist pastor baptised 'four candidates by immersion in the sea near Crowstone, in the presence of the regular congregation and of witnesses'. So it's a stone that has inspired a fair bit of ritual over the years.

I reach the Redcaps' hut, marked by a red and black flag, open a side gate and walk in. Iain Keenan is waiting for me, as are his wife, Rachel, Ben Jaques, Jane Riddle and Jane Bell. 'Do you want to swim now or later?' asks Iain. 'Now,' I say, because I'm hot and sticky and desperate to cool off. They all look well kitted out, with endurance-style costumes, hats and goggles, and I feel a bit underprepared, especially as I've forgotten to bring a towel. But Iain lends me one and I get ready in the club's wooden hut.

We walk a few steps to the beach and he explains the plan is to swim out to the Crowstone from in front of the hut, and then back. Suddenly I'm a little unsure; it looks a bit far away. But then again I can't wait to get in, because although the water looks grey, back in February this year I was standing in my wellington boots at the official source of the River Thames in the meadow of Trewsbury Mead and here I am over 200 miles later. I've followed the course of the river at Oxford, Henley, Windsor and Eton. I've been on a boat to Hampton Court, strolled through Richmond and Kew, crossed the bridges through London and paddled at Greenwich. I've visited Victorian bathing spots and the sites of twentieth-century seaside city beaches, and at last I've arrived where the massive waterway ends. And now that I am about to end my journey I'd rather it went on. I want to go back upstream and visit the places I've missed in this story of the river. I'm a Londoner born and bred, so the Thames has never been far away from me, yet I've not really thought about it as a place to swim, even though I'm standing here in my swimming costume about to jump into the estuary.

I step over a small stone wall, walk down the beach and launch myself into the water. It's refreshing, but at 22 degrees only just, and the taste of salt takes me by surprise because it's been a while since I was in the sea. There are a series of poles in the water with green hats on top that mark the end of the groynes and serve as a warning to swimmers that there's an underwater hazard between here and the foreshore. I'm told we will swim out to the last pole, go round it, and then turn left towards the Crowstone. The route on the way there will be easier than the return trip, as to begin with we will have the tide in our favour. As we set off the water is choppy and there is a strong swell and I realise I'm swimming across the incoming tide. It doesn't seem to be helping me much; instead I'm being buffeted from the right, waves constantly slapping against my face. It's not a difficult swim, but I am swallowing a lot of water and I think of Norman Derham in the 1920s and then more recently Peter Rae and Wouter Van Staden and how they set off to cross the entire estuary.

We're being accompanied by a man in a kayak now, Jason Curtis, the founder of the Great Pier Swim. I think he's just having fun, but it's only later that I realise he's my safety escort. It's strange swimming with other people in the sea; it's not something I usually do, except for when playing with family and friends. I have the urge to head off, but I'm already aware that the Redcaps know these waters and I don't. Iain tells me to watch out for two windsurfers who suddenly appear in the distance and seem to be heading our way. If I was alone and not wearing a brightly coloured cap I don't know if they would even notice me. Later he tells me we have right of way – but do the windsurfers know this and would it make any difference?

It takes some effort to swim, although the further out we go the water feels colder and that's a relief. Now I'm reassured by the presence of the others: Iain is on my right, in his bright cap and goggles, the two Janes are ahead. One of them races off and I follow, but still it's a bit of a battle. Then at last we get to the Crowstone and at once I'm thrust up against it: there is nowhere to cling, it's so wide I can't grasp it. So I touch its gritty edge, tread water and look up to its pyramid-shaped top. My first impression is that it's so old, this grey monument that rises majestically out of the water. Letters are carved deep into the west side of the stone: 'Right Honourable William Taylor Copeland Lord Mayor, John Lanson Esq, David Salomons Esq. Sheriffs, God preserve the City of London 1836'. On the east side is a list of names including Aldermen, Sheriffs elect, a solicitor, water bailiff and common cryer, presumably those who took part in the 1842 ceremony held by Lord Mayor Pirie whose names were then engraved on the stone. The writing on the south side, however, which faces the oncoming tide, is too worn to read.

Swimming back is meant to be harder but it isn't, maybe because I made it and it wasn't far at all, only a 500-metre round trip. When I get out of the estuary I feel something sticky against my leg; for a second I think it's a barnacle, but it's only a sweet wrapper.

Inside the Redcaps' hut a curtain divides women from men. 'You're really lucky having this on your doorstep,' I say to Iain's eldest daughter, Olivia, who joined us on a surfboard at the end of our swim. She's thirteen and is concentrating on brushing her hair before a small sink, 'I know,' she says in absolute appreciation. We sit outside to have tea and biscuits, while the children of the various

A view of the west side of the Crowstone, with the words 'God preserve the City of London' carved deep into the stone.

Redcaps play. To my far right two women are bowling; we're at the end of their green. This Chalkwell open-water swimming club is just four years old and already the largest of its kind in the country. Just how did it start?

'I began open-water swimming with friends and my daughters, Olivia and Maria,' explains Iain, who lives a short walk away from Chalkwell Beach, 'Olivia was nine then and she said put it on Facebook. I just thought it would be fun to start a club. I wanted a family activity; people don't often swim in the sea as a family. She came up with the club name, in the sea you need something visual, so we called it the Redcaps.'

Swimming to the Crowstone with members of the Chalkwell Redcaps Ben Jaques and Jane Riddle, the stone is so wide it's impossible to grasp. The club used the stone as a marker to swim round during their first estuary dip in 2010.

Ben Jaques, one of the first members, joined because 'I'd thought about doing a similar thing, it's nice to see people in the water. Triathlons have become more popular but people are still a bit scared to go in the sea, it's a cultural thing, we're told to swim in pools with lifeguards. The club gives you a way in.' The group first met up on a bank holiday in May 2010, with twelve people, all of whom were locals, and decided to use the Crowstone as a marker to swim around. Iain contacted Richard Sanders at Southend Pier; 'he said we could use a temporary buoy, so we would swim up to the Crowstone, across to the buoy and then back, making a loop. But we hadn't quite anchored the buoy that first year and it drifted out and someone had to swim after it, he swam towards it, and there it was, still floating out . . . because he hadn't realised it wasn't tethered.'

The club then approached the council about the disused hut at the end of the bowling green, and were given a five-year lease, with an annual rent of £1,000. Club membership is £10 a year, and as well as paying rent and meeting other expenses they make an annual donation to the local lifeguard team. At the end of the first season they had forty people and it was then, just as with the new swims in Henley, Maidenhead and Chiswick, that they decided to make it 'more legitimate', rather than just a social event, and approached the lifeguards for support.

The Chalkwell lifeguards are a volunteer beach search and rescue unit, formed to help prevent incidents on the mudbanks along Leigh Creek and Hadleigh Ray. They are affiliated to the Royal Life Saving Society and have a kayak and foot patrol, but the volunteers only work on Sundays and bank holidays between May and September. The lifeguards were in existence by at least 1938, but were disbanded during the Second World War, and in 1978 they re-formed.

Nick Luff, club captain, later tells me there is a sign on the beach that refers to the presence of lifeguards, and more information is put up when they provide cover for the Redcaps' events. 'We're trying to develop,' he explains; 'the other day someone asked, "are you new?" "No," I said, "we've been going thirty-five years."'

There are normally plenty of swimmers on the beach: 'a couple of old boys have a ten-minute swim every single day and we see regulars every Sunday. Most are locals. The people from London, the day visitors, are more of an issue, they don't know the area and they don't know how to swim sometimes.' But they have only had one serious incident in the last few years: 'two girls were walking on the wooden groyne and one stepped off, her sister went in to save her, they were both in trouble. The coastguard rang us and when we got there, there were helicopters, air ambulances, fire engines, the lot.' The girls had already been pulled out and saved, and just as in Victorian times neither knew how to swim. Nick is a police officer by day, but says there is no life-saving training for police any more: this stopped twelve years ago 'to save costs'.

Meanwhile, Iain knew that as the club got bigger he would

have to tackle the issue of public liability. He went to the Amateur Swimming Association, 'but they couldn't work out what we were doing, they gave me regulations for an indoor swimming pool club!' So then he approached the British Triathlon Federation, the club became a member and by the end of year they were officially affiliated. The Redcaps bought a kayak and more buoys, and set out a schedule from April to October. They now have ten Crowstone Crawls a year, a 200-metre loop that is a social swim, attracting up to seventy people. Other events include a Christmas Day and New Year's Day swim, a club relay, aquathlon and a championship race. The Christmas Day swim started in 2010, and raises money for charity. 'A woman in a bikini, elves, a snowman and Santa were just some of the colourful characters who plunged into the chilly Thames Estuary,' reported the local press on the swim's second anniversary. 'The Chalkwell Redcaps open-water swimming club proved they were made of tough stuff by braving the icy waters.' Sixteen members met opposite the Arches café on Westcliff-on-Sea seafront for the charity challenge, 'hardy members managed to stay in the water for several minutes while others, after being fully submerged in the water, didn't stay quite as long'. They now have 240 members aged between seven and eighty-two. Women make up the majority of the club; the overall average age is between thirty-five and forty-five, and there are twenty junior members.

'The club gives you a network,' says Iain; 'to do something like what we've done today, inviting members to come to the hut at 2 p.m. for a swim.' But it is hard work, especially as he's a full-time nursing lecturer at Essex University. 'My reasons are personal, there are very few things we can do as a family and the Thames is on our doorstep.' It was also personal reasons that led him to come up with forty open-water swims to mark his fortieth birthday, with at least two every month, all without a wetsuit. Again, he started it for pleasure and fun, then people learned of his swims and offered sponsorship, so he swam on behalf of the cleft palate charity Smile Train. His penultimate swim meant packing his work clothes in a dry bag and swimming 1.4 miles to Southend Pier. He then put on his work clothes and set off on a five-minute walk to the University of Essex's Southend campus.

The Redcaps now work with the organisers of the Great Pier Swim, launched by Jason Curtis at Havens Hospice. Initially this was three kilometres from Jubilee Beach near the pier to Thorpe Bay, then they linked up with the Redcaps and came up with a new route. The challenge now goes from Chalkwell Beach to Jubilee Beach, and means swimming under the longest pleasure pier in the world, just as in Victorian times the Southend Swimming Club held its annual long-distance swim from the pier head.

Jane Bell has done the Great Pier Swim four times in a row, and before she joined the Redcaps she 'had little knowledge of how the tides work in Southend, as I didn't grow up here. I was perhaps a little reckless, swimming alone straight out from the beach rather than in a group along the shore as we generally do now.' Jane Riddle, on the other hand, has lived in Leigh all her life: 'I remember the tide coming in around me when I was only about five years old and a man having to rescue me from the mudflats. That memory has stuck in my mind all these years and I'm now forty-six!'

I ask if they ever come across jellyfish. They all nod; everyone here this afternoon has been stung. Jane Bell's turn came at 1.30 a.m. when she was stung on her face by a jellyfish the size of a hand, but while she wouldn't want to experience that again, swimming in the estuary is a passion and it hasn't put her off.

The sun is going in again, I've dried off and it's time to go. I ask Iain if he feels the Redcaps are bringing back an old tradition of swimming at Southend. 'That tradition has been wiped out,' he says. 'The big issues today are Health & Safety and safeguarding kids. You didn't have that in Victorian times. What we're doing is writing a whole new chapter.'

If this is where my downstream trip ends then, like Iain, it's time to look to the future, and every time I think I might have gathered enough stories about swimming the Thames, I come across new ones just about to happen.

25

Andy, Ness and the OSS

'There is absolutely no reason why women can't swim the
length of the Thames'

Ness Knight, adventurer, 2013

The Thames has always been regarded as a challenge. That's why
Captain Webb and Mercedes Gleitze used it as their training
ground before crossing the Channel, and why Jules Gautier and
Agnes Beckwith dived into the river when they wanted to show
Londoners feats never seen before. For over a hundred years it's been
the site of human endeavour and this is a tradition that continues
today. In the summer of 2013, when two endurance swimmers
decided to set new world records, they launched themselves into
the Thames. Andy Nation, the first person to swim the length of
the non-tidal river, would this time swim from Teddington all the
way to Calais, while Ness Knight would attempt to become the first
woman ever recorded to swim from source to sea.

I meet Andy at his home in Knebworth a few months before his
trip starts where he explains he got the idea from a neighbour who
commented after his 2005 swim: 'why not carry on to France?' The
only problems the sixty-three-year-old foresees this time around
are boat discharge, tides and bigger waves. 'Endurance events are
about a state of mind rather than your body,' he says. 'You just
keep putting one arm in front of the other for six hours a day.'
However, once again he had a battle with the PLA. 'I wanted to

In 2005 Andy Nation was the first person to swim the length of the non-tidal Thames. Here he's pictured at Barkingside Pool during his first charity swim in 1970.

go through London but they said stop at Vauxhall and get in at Barrier Gardens, after the Thames Barrier. I suggested getting out at Westminster and then in again at the Tower but in the end I decided to comply, as the new by-law gave them the whip hand.'

This time his 147-mile swim is to raise £1,000,000 for Herts Air Ambulance and Hertford MS Therapy Centre, and he shows me his Autograph Book of 'People of Our Time', to be auctioned at the end of the swim. The plan is to gather hundreds of autographs from around the world, including those of royalty, presidents and prime ministers, stars from stage and screen, 'real-life heroes' and corporate leaders. Andy's wife, Lieva, appears with tea and I ask what she thought about his first Thames swim. 'I felt the distance was too much,' she says, 'it was the worry of it all. As a family it was a risk. When he got unwell I said, "that's it, get out". But he bucked up.' Lieva, who 'hates water', is similarly concerned about this swim. 'I'm worried about the dangers and I resent the amount of time it takes up in our lives. The first swim took two years to organise. This one has taken three years, and then because of Andy's accident it will be five years. So I said, "you get on with it, I'm not prepared to do as much admin and preparation". But of course at the actual swim I'll be there.'

The accident she refers to happened in June 2012, shortly before Andy originally planned to start his swim to Calais. He went down the garden one afternoon to talk to Lieva, who keeps bees, picked up a bit of honeycomb and was stung on the forehead. He then ran across the lawn to escape 'a particularly persistent bee', fell over and ended up paralysed from the neck down. Andy had surgery, with his vertebrae realigned and fixed with a graft of bone from his hip, as well as a titanium plate and screws. Incredibly, he recovered and, although very weak, started training again. His previous average time for a mile was thirty-two minutes, now it was fifty, but eventually, despite extreme pain, he got that down to 33.5 minutes, and then he set a new date for the Thames. He takes me on a quick tour of the pool house he's built (which as yet doesn't have a pool), pointing out the lane rope he will use so he won't zigzag too much, and a Jacuzzi he's installed that he bought off eBay and which 'used to belong to Hugh Grant'. Then, after wishing him good luck, it's time to say goodbye.

His swim begins well; on 19 July he started from Teddington Lock and swam to Vauxhall Bridge. Day two was a non-swimming day, as he and his six-member team walked fifteen kilometres to Thames Barrier Gardens, but then a 'dodgy pie' meant he spent the night throwing up, putting a stop to the day three swim. Back in the river once more, Andy set off swimming from the Thames Barrier and under the QEII Bridge, with a PLA boat accompanying him to Gravesend. He then reached the mouth of the Medway. 'Tomorrow,' said his Facebook page, in language reminiscent of Victorian newspaper reports, 'he'll be attacking a 23 mile stretch to reach Herne Bay. He's in very good spirits and looking forward to getting back in the water tomorrow!' At Herne Bay he 'mud-walked to shore' to meet Lieva; here he was hosted by the local 41 Club from the Round Table. On day six he swam to Ramsgate and then came day seven, 'the LAST day of this epic swim taking him to Dover. After that he'll be heading home for some well-deserved recuperation in preparation for the Channel crossing.' But then on 9 August I turn on my computer to see a newspaper headline: 'KNEBWORTH man Andy Nation has been forced to pull out of a 147-mile charity swim just 10 miles from the end.'

I can barely bring myself to ring him, imagining how crushed he must feel, but when I do he simply says, 'The swim was good, it went according to plan.' That is except for the meat pie he ate at the O2, which he is certain is what made him ill. As he'd expected, the main difference compared with his earlier swim was the size of the waves, which he found crashing over him, especially from Herne Bay to Ramsgate, but 'there was very little wash from boats in the tidal Thames, whereas there had been a lot in the non-tidal river. The Thames was bigger than in 2005, and I stopped for feeds more often. In the non-tidal river I would stop at the locks, whereas in the tidal I had to stop for prescribed pain medication.'

The water wasn't always nice, however. 'There were a couple of places where it was really nasty; there were huge bands of seaweed with an inch of brown froth on top and I had to swim through twenty to thirty feet of it a number of times. I thought, "my God, what is this?"' His highlight was going under the QEII Bridge: 'that was especially gratifying. I later drove over it and looked down at that vast expanse of water either side, and I thought "yeah, I've swum that, brilliant!"' While he wore a wetsuit for the Thames part of the swim, 'I decided to dump it to go across the Channel', so the swim would be recorded by the Channel Swimming & Piloting Federation, and wore just trunks, cap and goggles. 'I began at

Shakespeare Beach and for the first five hours it was looking to be a twelve-hour swim, but at seven hours my pace had slowed. I was told my position in the water had changed and I was now looking at a twenty-four-hour crossing. My legs were dropping and I had pain in my spine and my neck. I thought, "that's not good news, but I'll carry on". However, my spine got even more sore and with my pace not improving I decided at seven and a half hours my health was more important than raising money for charity. It was a painful decision and I was bitterly disappointed. But, yes,' he laughs, 'my wife was very pleased.' As for the future, he says he's set a new world record by being the first person to have swum the entire length of the River Thames, because his 2005 swim started higher upstream than anyone else, but 'now my wife has my feet nailed firmly to the ground, although I'm still swimming and training'. I think back to what I saw in his autograph book, where someone wrote, 'why stop at France? Why not New York?' and think perhaps this could be his next swim.

Nearly a month after Andy began his Thames journey, Ness Knight was getting ready for hers. I first speak to her around ten days before her swim is scheduled to start. Born in Johannesburg, she moved to the UK when she was fifteen and has never swum in the Thames before. She did, however, accompany adventurer Dave Cornthwaite on his 1,001-mile paddleboard trek down the lower Missouri the year before. 'As an adventurer and endurance athlete, people think you need to go to the ends of the earth,' she says, 'but that's not true, because we have epic terrain on our doorstep. When you think of Great Britain you think of the Thames. My mum always told me London was the centre of the world, as a child I read books with awesome tales about London and the Thames.' So she decided to come up with a unique round-Britain triathlon, first swimming the Thames, then running 400 miles from Big Ben to Land's End, and finally a 1,000-mile cycle to John O'Groats. 'I've had mixed reactions,' she says.

'When you think of Great Britain you think of the Thames.' Adventurer and endurance athlete Ness Knight.

'Open-water swimmers understand it's a beautiful river, others, and unfortunately the media, don't.'

As for where she will begin her swim, 'I have an enormous map of the Thames on my living-room wall; I will possibly start at Cricklade, it's hard to say because of things like rainfall. When I started to plan this, I started to hear stories about other swimmers and the history of swimming the Thames and it brings a richness to the journey. I don't know any woman who has done this. A lot of women email me and say "thank you, I'm inspired, I didn't think it was possible because it's all men out there." There is absolutely no reason why women can't do it. It's part of the whole issue of women in sport, such as the Tour de France. We're making progress but we need to get more women out there. The hardest part of something like this is making the decision to do it. Sometimes I tell people what I'm doing and they blank me and move on, they think it's a joke. I do get dopy questions. It's such a male-dominated scene, but the support from women has blown me away.' Her motivation, just as with Agnes Beckwith, Annette Kellerman and Lily Smith before her – champion swimmers she's never heard of – is to 'encourage more women to do it'. Beckwith in the 1870s and Kellerman in the early 1900s both felt swimming was an ideal sport for women and one of the few in which they were allowed to compete, while Smith – an outspoken believer in women's suffrage – believed her swims would 'put a stop forever to all this twaddle about the weaker sex'. Similarly, over a hundred years later, Ness sees herself as a possible role model; if she can swim the Thames then other women can too.

The main challenges she foresees are loneliness and river traffic. 'It will get quite busy; the paddle person will guide me through. I will be doing crawl pretty much the whole way, but I've been told when I get to London to do breaststroke, and keep my head out of water!' Her initial aim was to be the first woman to swim from source to sea, then she found out about the by-law. 'I was only aware of it after I'd decided on my triathlon journey. I knew years ago people could swim the Thames and it's incredibly frustrating.' In the end she decided to stop at Putney.

Ness started as scheduled on 10 August, running from the official source at Thames Head, and for the next few days all went well. But then on 20 August she was struck by a bout of 'Thames tummy'. A couple of weeks later I read that she successfully ended her 155-mile swim at Putney Bridge on 7 September. That makes her the first woman ever recorded to have swum this far, but, unlike the champion women who came before her, the press coverage has been virtually non-existent and I haven't found a single report except in the online triathlon world. While Andy was interviewed by the press and appeared on local TV, Ness was not.

I finally speak to her again after she's completed the running section of her triathlon. 'The first few days of the swim were OK,' she says, 'but in the long term it was a funny old journey. I had a struggle to find the source, my GPS wasn't working. We asked the locals and they gave us different directions and we got there late afternoon, it was heading to dusk. We ran from there, but you can lose the trail and it's hard to follow the river. I got chased by a bull, stung by nettles, and my partner stood in cowpats. It was an adventure.' On day one she ran seventeen miles to Castle Eaton, near Cricklade, and the next day she started her swim. 'We assumed it would quickly get deep enough to swim and so did the locals, but, boy, were we wrong.' She then waded to Lechlade; 'the weather had been bad, there were lots of fallen trees, my wetsuit really suffered', and so day two meant six miles of reeds, sludge and water 'like an ice bath'.

As with other Thames endurance swimmers, Ness had to battle with sensory deprivation. 'There was the issue of boredom. I can deal with time alone, I loved cycling across America alone in 2012, but in the Thames there was no stimulation. Fifty per cent of the time you're looking at brown muddy water, and the other 50 per cent you're looking to the side and seeing the edge of the paddleboard. My goggles were all fogged up, I had earplugs in so I couldn't hear anything, I couldn't talk to anyone . . . I don't mind going solo but this was tough. Sometimes I deliberately swam to the side of the river just to feel the reeds, anything to find stimulation! You get a different perspective of a river when you're swimming, you feel it, smell it, you are immersed in it and every sense is alive, but in terms of communication you are in lockdown.

'I set myself short-term goals, and at least the Thames is not the ocean so every few miles there is a lock and that was a chance to break it up. I'm very food-driven so I'd look forward to getting out, taking off my goggles, having something to eat, seeing the world and interacting and having a treat. If you think about the end goal and how long it is before you get there that's when your mind goes to a very dark place.'

What also struck her was the fact that 'all the way people thought I was a man; even with a pink hat on, no one was expecting a woman. You should have seen the shock on their faces! It was a really big deal for them to see a female swimming the Thames. People weren't shocked to see a person in the water, only that it was a woman – everyone said, "oh you're doing a Walliams?" We used to bet how many people would say that every day. So the shock factor of doing the Thames has gone, except that I was female.' I ask why, if people were so fascinated at seeing her, she had no media coverage. 'With my previous journeys there had been lots of coverage,' she explains, 'and it's easy to get bogged down with organising and contacting press and it can take over. I was doing this for me, a personal experience, I didn't want the distraction of the PR side of it.'

She found the river 'beautiful and winding and so clean', but by the time she got to Reading she was feeling ill and from Marlow she had to swim one day and take the next off. Things improved at Teddington, however, where she was 'literally swept out on the peak of the tide, I whizzed through London. There had been no flow up to then, when I'd stopped swimming I had basically stood still, then I felt the pace and the *sweep* of movement. But it was bittersweet, because then I didn't want my swim to be over.' She also came across quite a few unexpected sights on the way, such as a snake in the water just before Oxford, as well as eels and shopping trolleys, while one day she found her foot inside someone's shoe. Sadly, Ness had to postpone the cycle part of her triathlon, because of a long-running hip injury, 'but I have huge pride that I am the first female in history to swim the Thames. I just love telling people that. I've put it on my CV. It's a challenge but I did it.' For Ness the draw of the Thames was its epic terrain; it was a place she had read about in books as a child, and as she began to discover the history of other Thames swims it brought a richness to her journey, just as it has to mine.

Shortly after these two Thames adventurers finished their trips, a group of other swimmers completed what for them had been nearly a three-year journey along the non-tidal river. This was not to set any record but simply to enjoy the waterway and the sense of community that comes from swimming. The Outdoor Swimming Society's Thames group, a loose-knit group of swimmers, started at the source at Kemble in Easter 2011. 'We have walked, waded, crawled and, once deep water was reached at Lechlade, swum our way towards Teddington,' explains Jeremy Wellingham. 'We swim at least once each month, winter and summer, rain, hail, snow and, if lucky, sun, and twice a month in the summer.' They have a core of around ten people and publish the swims on Facebook so others can join in. 'We've had more than a hundred people come along at one time or another, sometimes just as we swim past their locality. It's very much a social event, although some of us – not me – are quite fast. We meet up, swim a bit, stop for tea and cake – some of our partners walk along the bank with us and carry drinks – and finish off with a pub lunch. In the summer we also have swim weekends when we camp overnight on the riverbank.'

The idea started with a winter swim in December 2010 when a group met for a swim at Godstow when there was ice on the Thames. They vowed to swim at least each month of the year. 'The idea of swimming the length of the Thames put some structure around deciding where to go each time – where we got out last time,' explains Jeremy. 'Sefryn, my co-organiser, and I were rather surprised at how many people it has attracted and although we keep it informal and pleasantly chaotic, there is a degree of coordination, if only to ensure the pub is expecting us for lunch. We don't really have a finish date for everyone. Some people join us as we're in their locality for a few swims, others have joined us later on and once in London we had another surge of interest. It feels like a travelling circus! We'll just keep swimming the Thames once or twice a month. Our group is quite evenly balanced gender-wise and a lot of our "better" swimmers are female, which makes a nice change from the normal male-dominated sporting activities. We didn't have any comments from passers-by about women swimming – we were all thought of as equally slightly mad.' By October 2013 the group had completed fifty-six swims from Lechlade to Teddington, 'so we have finished the route as a group but only seven of us have done all fifty-six sections. But there are plenty of others that have a few sections missing that they want to catch up on to complete their own Thames journey. We're still swimming sections to keep company with the people doing the catch-ups and more importantly because we enjoy it and to try and keep together all the friends we've made along the way.' The OSS group will continue their Thames journey and no doubt others will join them as they swim every month in sun or snow, fast or slow, savouring the social aspect, the camaraderie and the sensual pleasure of being immersed in one of England's greatest rivers; a favourite bathing spot for centuries for everyone from royalty to East End children.

Swimming the Thames: Then and Now

'The Thames has never really been considered a friend of the swimmer. But it is more than the danger of pollution that acts as a deterrent. It is some deep fear of its nature that seems to prevent its use'

Peter Ackroyd, *Thames: Sacred River*, 2008

The story of Thames swimming is an ongoing one; there is no particular date at which it started and as long as the Thames still exists there is no reason for it to end. Instead, barring a major catastrophe such as the floods of early 2014, it will become even more popular. Because wild swimming is back; in rivers and in the sea, in lakes and ponds, we have rediscovered the joys of swimming outdoors. Today there are open-water clubs, books, blogs and magazines all devoted to swimming outside, and if Peter Ackroyd was right when he wrote in 2008 that 'some deep fear of its nature' prevents us from using the Thames, then this has certainly changed.

Back in 1867 Charles Steedman felt driven to write a manual on outdoor swimming in order to provide tips and advice; now we have bestselling guides to wild swimming spots across the country. When Archibald Sinclair commented in 1885 that 'open-water bathing has not been encouraged so much . . . as it ought to be', he attributed this to the Baths and Washhouses Act that gave people indoor places to bathe, just as in the 1960s and 1970s when another

A picture postcard of Maggie Scott, one of many champion swimmers from the early 1900s.

surge in the construction of public indoor baths helped to drive us away from the river. But to Sinclair, as to all 'wild' swimmers, a plunge in the open is something to be remembered, 'the body glows all over . . . the spirits become light and elastic'.

Some people started swimming in the Thames when they were children – and their parents and grandparents before them – and continue to do so, others have only turned to the river in the past few years and now they can't keep away from it. They describe the thrill of seeing life from water level, of being part of nature; they're surprised at how clean it is, they enjoy the wildlife, the current and the tide. In the past ten years or so, after decades of avoiding the place, we have come back to the Thames in numbers not seen for a long time.

We might have lost the old pontoons, pools, lidos and bathing islands that once lined the river, due to finances, Health & Safety, fears of pollution, and a preference for warm indoor pools. But although we don't compete in the Thames like we used to, there are now mass-participation events at the very river spots that fell into decline during the Second World War and were largely abandoned in the 1960s, at Windsor, Eton, Henley, Maidenhead, Chiswick and the London Docks. Access to the river has become harder in many places, but people still swim alone and with families, and are just as likely to form small informal groups, while every year at least 10,000 people sign up for organised swims in the Thames.

In some cases the tradition remains virtually unbroken: the Otter Swimming Club, formed in 1869, still races in the Thames. In other cases we've come full circle, resurrecting traditions we didn't know we once had, like open-water swimming clubs in Henley, Maidenhead and Chalkwell, and plans for a new floating bath in central London.

While the history of once famous swimmers has been buried over time, modern swimmers are replicating what their forebears did, even if they've never heard of them, and going much further. In July 1878 Agnes Beckwith swam twenty miles from Westminster to Richmond and back to Mortlake, dressed in an amber suit and a jaunty little straw hat. In 1916, Eileen Lee swam thirty-six miles, in modern times Alison Streeter has set two Thames records downstream and up, while in 2013 Ness Knight became the first woman to swim the non-tidal Thames, completing 155 miles.

It's a similar story when it comes to male swimmers; in 1876 Frederick Cavill swam twenty miles, Captain Webb topped that with forty and in 1908 Montague Holbein managed fifty. Now new records have been set by Kevin Murphy, Lewis Pugh and Charlie Wittmack, while Andy Nation has swum further along the Thames than anyone else. In 1925 Norman Derham swam across the estuary, while nearly eighty years later it was the turn of Peter Rae and Wouter Van Staden. In the summer of 2014 Lewis Pugh was back in the Thames again, this time as the final leg of his Seven Seas swim to highlight the need for protected areas in the world's oceans. He swam forty miles upstream from Southend to the Thames Barrier, having already completed swims in the Adriatic, Aegean, Black, Red and Arabian seas. He then delivered a petition to Prime Minister David Cameron.

There have been regulations about Thames swimming since Victorian times, along with warnings about strong currents and tides, the depth and the cold, pollution and boats. 'No swimming' signs remain, while the latest form of legislation is the by-law introduced in 2012 which prevents swimming through central London. But London Mayor Boris Johnson, who once jumped in at Chiswick – 'it was lovely and cool . . . and didn't do me any harm' – argues that if people want to swim in the Thames 'then they should be allowed to indulge their preferences in peace'. In February 2014 he approved a £40,000 feasibility study 'scoping for a major new initiative on the River Thames – a London Lido'.

There have, however, been major differences in the way we swim the waterway. The first is clothing and equipment, particularly the wetsuit, which has changed significantly since the modern version was invented in 1952. Once river bathers went naked, then people were made to cover up with drawers, tunics and pantaloons, followed by hand-knitted one-piece costumes which women had to keep covered until they entered the water. Now we have 'fastskin' racing suits, high-tech goggles, fins, neoprene gloves and boots. Wetsuits keep us warmer, able to swim throughout the year and more buoyant in case something goes wrong. They have made us faster and capable, perhaps, of doing longer distances, and their popularity is mainly due to the rise in the triathlon, now recognised as an Olympic sport, while open-water swimming was added to the Olympics in 2008.

For some the swim is initially the most challenging part of a triathlon, and then they find it's their favourite and just keep going. Arguments remain over whether open-water swimmers should have to wear wetsuits in organised events, but with equipment comes sponsorship, and now mass swims have a host of sponsors, from wetsuit brands to drinks and food manufacturers. Detailed entry forms asks participants what sort of wetsuit and goggles they wear, what drinks product they use for training, racing or recovery, and what they eat beforehand. Athletes no longer swim in the Thames, like Captain Webb, sustained by alcohol, or like Agnes Beckwith on beef tea; instead there is a whole array of sports supplements, energy gels and bars, and numerous books and articles on diet.

Swimming may no longer be seen as the new art form it was in Victorian times, but it is regarded as an ever-improving science. There are classes for those who want to swim outdoors for the first time, swim studios, coaching sessions for triathletes who want to better their stroke and speed. Perhaps those like Shaw Method instructor Phil Tibenham, who loves to swim near Grafton Lock, are our new professors of swimming, using the principles of the Alexander Technique to teach 'greater body awareness', just as Victorian manuals once gave us hand-drawn illustrations on strokes and techniques.

The growth in mass-participation events means swimming in the Thames has become a business, but balance this with the fact many people swim to raise money. And this is the second biggest difference when it comes to swimming the Thames, that a lot of us do it for charity. A decade ago few charities offered swims as a way to fundraise; now most do, in lakes, the sea, indoor pool swimathons and, of course, the Thames. People use Facebook to link up with others, post intended swims, join in events and share experiences and, unlike most social media users, people then meet up in real life – with one joint purpose, to swim.

We are far less likely to drown in the Thames now, because in general compared to 150 years ago more of us can swim. When Agnes Beckwith started her Thames swimming career, around 3,000 people drowned every year in England and Wales. In 2012, twenty-six people died while swimming in the UK, according to the National Water Safety Forum, including four in a river. The number of people who drowned while angling, however, is similar (twenty-four), while ten people died in a bath, Jacuzzi or hot tub. When Victorian teenager Emily Parker raced the Thames and

By the 1920s women bathers no longer had to cover up at the seaside but could wear the sort of one-piece costume advocated by Annette Kellerman in 1907 when she was arrested on an American beach for indecency.

Annie Luker dived from bridges, most of those working on the river didn't know how to swim, whether lightermen or sailors, and for years swimming professors and the press urged for better and cheaper ways for people to learn. Yet today many of the nation's lidos have closed and the teaching of swimming, as a way to save your own life and somebody else's, has fallen by the wayside. In the 1870s it was seen as a key life skill for men and boys, and then eventually for everyone. Now increasing numbers of children don't know how to swim because they receive little or no instruction at school, and few are taught how to dive because most diving boards have been removed. So while fatalities are down, drowning is still the third most common cause of accidental death (along with fire and smoke) among children under the age of fifteen in England, after transport and asphyxia. Swimming might be included in the national curriculum, but a third of children can't even cover

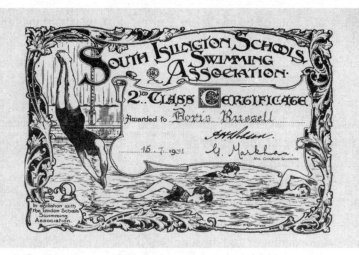

A school swimming certificate from 1931. Today a third of children can't swim 25 metres by the time they leave primary school.

25 metres by the time they leave primary school, according to the ASA. This means their lives are at risk and they're not able to really enjoy the water, whether indoors or outside.

As for the future of organised Thames swimming, many look forward to the day when open-water swimming has its own governing body, just like British Triathlon. At the end of 2013, at a meeting convened by *H2Open* magazine, safety at open-water events was a major concern. 'Open-water swimming is growing fast,' says editor Simon Griffiths. 'The biggest events now attract several thousand swimmers, but that growth has led some to question the direction the sport is taking and whether an organisation needs to oversee the development of open-water swimming clubs and to provide guidelines for event organisers.' Unlike triathlon, where organisers can ask the British Triathlon Federation to sanction their events, nothing similar exists for swimming.

Simon believes the development of clubs is essential to the sustainability of the sport. He launched *H2Open* after 'I'd been doing triathlons for a few years and really liked the open water component. Then, around 2009, I saw the Great Swim Series was taking off. Lots of people swim and not just in triathlons, and there was no magazine for them. I could see a gap in the market. If you're not experienced then you want a controlled, managed environment and some recognition at the end like a medal. There is a fear about open water and what's underneath you. Swimming for anyone under fifty is what you do in heated pools, but there's been a reawakening of interest in open-water swims. We are warned against the Thames and open water, more so than we need to be.'

There are times, however, such as the heavy flooding in late 2013 and early 2014 when England and Wales suffered the wettest winter since records began, when we're right to be cautious. Thousands of homes were damaged and the sewage network was overwhelmed by floodwater. 'It's sink or swim in the flooded Thames Riviera,' read a headline in the *Telegraph*, swans were seen swimming over a football pitch in Windsor, two people used a gondola to travel through a flooded village square in Berkshire. The advice from the National Health Service began with 'never swim in fast-flowing water'.

But as the floods receded, the swimmers returned. Because nothing has ever quite stopped us from swimming the Thames, not bad weather or war, not pollution or legislation.

Of the three swims I've done, the upper Thames, the Millwall Dock and the Thames Estuary, it would be hard to choose which was best because each offered a different way of experiencing the river, its water, landscape and history. Now I've decided an annual Thames swim will be my treat to myself and next year I'll go to Marlow where villagers once bathed before breakfast and where Jerome K. Jerome wrote parts of *Three Men in a Boat*.

As long as the Thames still flows through England there will always be new challenges to meet – who can swim downstream, upstream, across and along, who can swim the furthest, who will be the youngest, the oldest? The glorious story of swimming the Thames has only just begun; it has always been, and always will be, a swimmer's friend.

Bibliography

Sources/further reading
Books:

The Art of Swimming, Captain Webb, 1876, Pryor Publications, 1999

Badminton Library of Sports and Pastimes, Vol 19. *Swimming*, by Archibald Sinclair and William Henry, Longmans, Green and Co.,1893

The British Olympics, Britain's Olympic heritage 1612-2012, Martin Polley, English Heritage, 2011

Can we have our balls back please? How the British Invented Sport, Julian Norridge, Penguin, 2008

The Crossing: The Curious Story of the First Man to Swim the English Channel, Kathy Watson, Headline, 2000

Dickens's Dictionary of the Thames 1887, Old House Books, 1994

Down by the River: The Thames & Kennet in Reading, Gillian Clark, Two Rivers Press, 2009

English Hours: A Portrait of a Country, Henry James, 1905, Tauris Parke Paperbacks, 2011

The Eton Book of the River, L.S.R. Byrne and E.L.Churchill, Alden & Blackwell, 1952

Fighting the Current: The Rise of American Women's Swimming, 1870-1926, Lisa Bier, McFarland & Company, 2011

Great Lengths: The historic indoor swimming pools of Britain, Dr Ian Gordon and Simon Inglis, English Heritage, 2009

The Great Swim, Gavin Mortimer, Short Books, 2008

Haunts of the Black Masseur: The swimmer as hero, Charles Sprawson, Vintage, 1992

How to Swim, Annette Kellerman, William Heinemann, 1919

Hung Out to Dry: Swimming & British Culture, Chris Ayriss, Lulu.com, 2009

I Love the Thames: Notes for a Summer of Swimming, the Outdoor Swimming Society, Michael Worthington, 2009

I Never Knew That About the River Thames, Christopher Winn, Ebury Press, 2010

The Kingston Book, June Sampson, Historical Publications, 2006

Life on the Upper Thames, H.R. Robertson, Virtue, Spalding and Co., 1875

Lifesaving. The Story of the Royal Life Saving Society, Ronald Pearsall, David & Charles, 1991

London's Bridges, Peter Matthews, Shire Publications, 2008

London on Thames in Bygone Days, George Henry Birch, 1903, openlibrary.org

Lost Olympics: The Hilda James Story, Ian Hugh McAllister, emp3books Ltd, 2013

Manual of Swimming, Charles Steedman, H.T. Dwight, 1867

Margaret Rutherford: Dreadnought with Good Manners, Andy Merriman, Aurum, 2010

Memoirs of the Colman Family, R. B. Peake, London, 1841

Memoirs of Robert Patrick Watson: A journalist's experience of mixed society, Smith, Ainslie, 1899

The Million Dollar Mermaid, Esther Williams with Digby Diehl, Simon & Schuster, 1999

The Oarsman's and Angler's Map of the River Thames from Its Source to London Bridge, 1893, Old House Books

Old and New London, Walter Thornbury, 1873–74, http://www.british-history.ac.uk/catalogue.aspx?gid=79

The Original Million Dollar Mermaid, the Annette Kellerman story, Emily Gibson with Barbara Firth, Allen & Unwin, 2005

Our Old Home: A Series of English Sketches, Nathaniel Hawthorne, Houghton, Mifflin and Co., 1883

Our River, George D. Leslie, Bradbury, Agnew & Co., 1881

Pleasure Boating on the Thames: A History of Salter Bros, 1858-Present Day, Simon Wenham, The History Press, 2014

The Port of London Authority: A Century of Service 1909-2009, Nigel Watson, St Matthew's Press, 2009

Prezza: My Story: Pulling No Punches, John Prescott, Headline, 2008

Professionals, Amateurs and Performance: Sports Coaching in England, 1789-1914, Dave Day, Peter Lang, 2012

Putney and Roehampton Past, Dorian Gerhold, Historical Publications, 1994

Swimming Against the Stream, Jean Perraton, Jon Carpenter Publishing, 2005

The Swimming Instructor: A Treatise on the Arts of Swimming and Diving, William Wilson, 1883, BiblioLife Reproduction Series

The Thames from source to tideway, Peter H. Chaplin, Whittet Books, 1982

Thames: Sacred River, Peter Ackroyd, Vintage Books, 2008

Thames Valley Villages, Charles G. Harper, Chapman and Hall, 1910

This Time Next Week, Leslie Thomas, Constable & Co., 1964

Three Men in a Boat, Jerome K. Jerome, 1889, Penguin Books, 2004

The Tower of London Children's Beach, Rose Baillie, COLAS, 2009

Under the Net, Iris Murdoch, Vintage Classics, 2002

University Life in Eighteenth-Century Oxford, Graham Midgley, Yale University Press, 1996

Victorians on the Thames, R.R. Bolland, Parapress Limited, 1974

Waterlog, a swimmer's journey through Britain, Roger Deakin, Vintage, 2000

Westminster School: a history, John D. Carleton, Rupert Hart-Davis, 1965

The Wind in the Willows, Kenneth Grahame, 1908, Egmont UK Limited, 2012

The Works of the Rev. Jonathan Swift, 1801, Vol XV, J. Johnson; J. Nichols; R. Baldwin, London, 1801

Articles and other publications:

Bathing in the Thames, Hansard, 1 June 1815, http://hansard.millbanksystems.com

The 'Beckwith Frogs', Dave Day, *History Workshop Journal*, Issue 71, 25 February 2011

'Beckwith, Frederick Edward (1821-1898)', Dave Day, *Oxford Dictionary of National Biography*, Oxford University Press, May 2012; online edn, Jan 2013

Consumption, Professionalism and Amateurism in Sport and Entertainment, Keith Myerscough, University of Bolton, 2012

The Historic Crowstone, Essex Countryside Magazine, J Blundell, 1965

How clean is the Thames? Transcript of a lecture given by Martin J. Attrill, Professor of Marine Ecology, University of Plymouth, 2006, http://www.gresham.ac.uk/lectures-and-events/londons-ecology-how-clean-is-the-thames

How we first learnt to swim, Nicholas Orme, BBC History Extra Magazine, December 2011.

"A Modern Naiad". Nineteenth Century Female Professional Natationists, Dave Day, *Women and Leisure 1890-1939*, Women's History Network Conference – Midlands Region, 2008

'Nymphs, Naiads and Natation,' Keith Myerscough, *The International Journal of the History of Sport*, Taylor & Francis, 2012

Otter Swimming Club, Annual Report & Accounts, 2012

The Reflecting Pool of Society: Aquatic Sport, Leisure and Recreation in England, c. 1800-1918, Christopher Andrew Love, PhD thesis, University of York, 2003

'The rise of competitive swimming 1840 to 1878', Claire Parker, *The Sports Historian*, No. 21 (2)

'Water Defences: The Arts of Swimming in Nineteenth-Century Culture', Vybarr Cregan-Reid, *Critical Survey*, Vol 16, No. 3

"What Girl Will Now Remain Ignorant Of Swimming?" Agnes Beckwith, Aquatic Entertainer and Victorian Role Model', Dave Day, *Women's History Review* Vol 21, Issue 3, 2012

Websites and blogs

Where Thames Smooth Waters Glide http://thames.me.uk/, is an invaluable treasure trove when it comes to the river's history and was the starting point for many an investigation.

Other useful websites:

Boulter's to Bray Swim
http://www.maidenheadswim.co.uk/

Brian Gautier's Family History Data
http://www.gautier.me.uk/webtrees/index.php?ctype=gedcom

Chalkwell Redcaps Open Water Swimming Club http://chalkwellredcaps.co.uk/

The Channel Swimming Association http://www.channelswimmingassociation.com/

The Channel Swimming & Piloting Federation http://cspf.co.uk

City of London Archaeological Society
http://www.colas.org.uk/

http://edwardthesecond.blogspot.co.uk/

The Greenwich Phantom
http://www.thegreenwichphantom.co.uk/

Henley Open Water Swim Club http://www.henleyswim.com/how-swim-club/

Henley Swimming Club
http://www.henleyswimmingclub.org.uk/

H2Open Magazine
http://www.h2openmagazine.com/

International Marathon Swimming Hall of

Fame http://imshof.org/

International Swimming Hall of Fame http://www.ishof.org/

Kingston Ladies Swimming Club
http://www.klsc.org.uk/

Lost lidos http://www.lostlidos.co.uk/

Lost Olympics www.lostolympics.co.uk and https://www.facebook.com/LostOlympics

Museum of London Docklands
http://www.museumoflondon.org.uk/docklands/

Pathé News http://www.britishpathe.com/

Richmond Swimming Club http://www.richmondswimmingclub.org.uk/

River & Rowing Museum http://rrm.co.uk/

River Runs, Tracey Warr
http://traceywarrwriting.com/

Southend Museum
http://www.southendmuseums.co.uk/

Sporting Lives by Keith Myerscough http://sportinglives.blogspot.co.uk/2012/07/missannie-luker-it-was-possible-for.html and http://sportinglives.blogspot.co.uk/2012/07/missagnes-beckwith-agnes-beckwith.html,

Thames pilot http://www.thamespilot.org.uk

Thurrock Local History Society
http://www.thurrock-history.org.uk/

Tommy Burns Victorian diver
http://www.tommyburns.org.uk/

Victorian Web
http://www.victorianweb.org/

Visit Thames http://www.visitthames.co.uk/

Wargrave & Shiplake Regatta
http://wsregatta.co.uk/

Windsor Swimming Club
http://www.windsorswimmingclub.co.uk/

Acknowledgements

This has been the happiest non-fiction book I've ever written because swimmers love the Thames and they want others to as well. Around 150 people have given their time and help, dug through their archives, shared their memories and own research, and put me in touch with other swimmers.

But it's also been tricky to write because documentation can be frustratingly hard to find, reports can be conflicting and I've had to restrict myself to only a few places and individuals when there are so many more stories to tell.

I'm extremely grateful to Dr Ian Gordon, team doctor to the Great British swimming team, who has extensive knowledge of swimming history and an incredible archive of images that he generously allowed me to dip into and reproduce in this book.

Thanks also to:

Those whose enthusiasm, tips and advice started me off or kept me going, particularly Dave Day, Jean Perraton, Iain Keenan, Simon Inglis, Dorian Gerhold, Simon Griffiths, Keith Myerscough and Chris Romer-Lee.

The relatives of Thames champions who have shared their family history and archives: Brian Gautier, Doloranda Pember, Ian McAllister, Jill Morrison, Cathy Stroud and Barbara Allen.

All those who read the manuscript and made crucial comments and corrections, especially Andy Nation, Lewis Pugh, Gill Clark,

Dr Pieter van der Merwe, Rose Baillie, Charlie Wittmack, Mark Davies, Simon Wenham, June Sampson and Heather Armitage.

To the Chalkwell Redcaps and SwimTrek for organising two of my swims, Martin Garside from the PLA for taking me out on a patrol boat, and Brian Cox for donating an 1875 pocket watch won by Thames champion David Ainsworth.

All those from history societies, archives, museums and libraries, aside from those named in the text they are: Elizabeth Velluet from the Richmond Local History Society, Ruth MacLeod from the Wandsworth Heritage Service, Janet Smith from the Wandsworth History Society, Joyce Brown from the Oxfordshire History Centre, Helen Batten from the River Thames Society, Amy Graham from Kingston Museum and Heritage Service, and the British Library Reference Team.

Thank you to the Museum of London for permission to quote from the memories of Kathleen Ralphs, Piers Plowright for a copy of his radio programme *Thames Crossings*, BBC Radio 4, 2013, and his poem 'Thames Side Stomp', Peter Daniel for his father's Thames memories, Tracey Warr for permission to quote from Jenny Rogers' memories (http://www.vilma.cc/river/), Alan Hall for a copy of *The Diving Venus*, Falling Tree Productions, BBC Radio 4, 2011.

Everyone who provided images for the book including: Dad, Frank Chalmers, Brian Gautier, Jack Taylor, Gill Clark, Emma Craggs, Human Race, the Great Swim Series, Ella Foote, Katia Vastiau, Sue Newell, Iain Keenan, Keith Myerscough, Chris Romer-Lee, Peter Rae, Andy Nation, Ness Knight, the PLA, Southend Museum, Ian McAllister, Barbara Allen, Richard Walsh, Charlie Wittmack, Andy Stoll, Otter Swimming Club, Henley River and Rowing Museum.

And finally thanks to the team at Aurum, Robin Harvie, Lucy Warburton, Charlotte Coulthard and Richard Collins.